The uncollected
Michael Foot

The uncollected
Michael Foot

Essays old and new 1953–2003

Edited and introduced by
Brian Brivati

POLITICO'S

First published in Great Britain 2003 by
Politico's Publishing, an imprint of
Methuen Publishing Limited
215 Vauxhall Bridge Road
London SW1V 1EJ

www.politicos.co.uk/publishing

10 9 8 7 6 5 4 3 2 1

A CIP catalogue record for this book is available from the British Library

ISBN 1 902301 96 X

Printed and bound in Great Britain by Creative Print and Design, Ebbw Vale

Frontispiece:
Michael Foot, Jill Craigie and Vanessa during
the Ebbw Vale by-election campaign in 1960.

Contents

Part 6: Voices for freedom

Part 7: The poetry of places

Introduction:
Politics, poetry and passion
Brian Brivati

Politics

Weapons of mass destruction, especially the nuclear variety, their production, concealment, control and eventual abolition is the most important question facing mankind and womankind. If we don't destroy them, they will destroy us. In the final annihilation they will destroy us and, as the Iraq record shows, we may never know where the real guilt lies for unleashing the final horror.

Poetry

Almost from the very first day when I heard his name, Heinrich Heine became my hero. Some of his accomplishments strike me as being so exceptional that any counter-attack must be discounted in advance. I can tolerate no word of criticism from any quarter, or, at least, none which would diminish his greatness and his glory; almost any mention of him can stir all the old delights, exhilarations, and what he himself called 'seven league boots' ideas, the kind which can take continents in their revolutionary stride.

Passion

Jill Craigie was a raging beauty let loose on susceptible wartime London, but she had many other qualities she preferred her legion of suitors to remark upon. I discovered this reticence about her own physical perfection only somewhat later or I would have exploited the point much sooner ... She had the colouring of an English rose but everything else was a romantic, mysterious addition. She was half Scottish and half Russian, not a tincture of English reserve in her make-up. She had Celtic and Russian fires and passions intermingled with what seemed an inborn gift for appreciating painting and music and, as it seemed to me, every other art.

This volume brings together fifty years of essays to mark Michael Foot's ninetieth birthday on 23 July 2003. None of the pieces reproduced here has been anthologised before and about a third of the book is being published for the first time. The collection contains long essays on key figures from literature and politics, a large number of book reviews reflecting the immense range of Foot's reading, and a smaller number of pieces on places that he loves: Hampstead and Wales, of course, but also the two places to which he and his wife Jill Craigie returned most often on holiday, Venice and Dubrovnik. Finally, homage is paid to the virtues of his much-missed dog Dizzy, and to his friend the great typographer Stanley Morison.

Jill was, of course, much more than a holiday companion and life partner. She is another authorial voice in many of these pieces. Sometimes she is referred to in passing – a source of authority or a fellow witness. Sometimes she is the real subject of the essay. Foot credits Jill with bringing him certain key gifts – Rebecca West, feminism, the visual arts – and she shared, and to an extent inspired, his devotion to certain key causes, perhaps most notably the fate of

Yugoslavia. To understand the essence of Foot as a writer, reflect as you read these essays on the way in which Jill is deployed. His characteristic and unashamedly generous recognition of her influence is emblematic of Foot's originality. He enjoys, celebrates, adds to, and evangelises all the members of his own very public pantheon and at the same time encourages us to recognise the virtues of the scholars who write about his heroes (or at least the virtues of those with whom he agrees.)

Foot's originality is derived from the process of acknowledgement and enjoyment of others that threads through his work. He has none of what Harold Bloom has called an anxiety of influence. Indeed, he enjoys abundant confidence in recognition. By profession, Foot describes himself as a journalist. Given his long association with the *Evening Standard* we could accurately describe him as a tabloid journalist. But Foot has transcended the journalistic genre in his shorter writings. He has taken the review, the essay, the polemic and the column to new heights. In the process he has taken journalism towards poetry in both the subjects of the pieces and the style of the writing. In both writing and talking there is something profoundly creative in Foot's generosity to others. This is the core of his unmistakable voice and it amounts to a unique kind of art. Beyond the scope of this introduction is Foot's other major use of words, his oratory. He is one of the great parliamentary and platform – if not television – speakers of the last sixty years.

The very thing that makes Foot unique also inspires a seemingly telling criticism of him: his celebration of others, the championing of people like Nye Bevan, has led him to pursue the wrong life. Roy Hattersley once put it at its sharpest: why does a first-rate Michael Foot want to be a second-rate Nye Bevan? It has to be said that there is something in this. Foot has a particular kind of ambition. Part of him is intent on keeping the Bevanite flame alive. Part of him wants to transcend his hero. There was also a late flowering of vanity. The temptation to go one better than Bevan and that element of vanity, not a characteristic usually associated with Foot, was probably important but not defining in his decision to stand for the leadership of the Labour Party after James Callaghan's precipitate resignation.

In many ways Foot was the natural *deputy* leader for the 1983 general election campaign but he was persuaded and, more importantly, persuaded himself that he alone could keep the left in the party. The judgement looks better with the passage of time, especially as we watch the leadership travails of the Conservative Party since 1997, but it remains the defining controversy of his party political career. To argue that Foot stood for the leadership because of a need to outdo Bevan is to underestimate fundamentally the man. In particular, it does not do justice to his self-knowledge. It fails to recognise his own sense of fallibility and it ignores the fact that he blames himself for every Labour MP who lost a seat in 1983. Though he chose to be a man of literature in politics and not remain aloof, I do not think that vanity is a sufficient explanation for the drive that his career showed and for that fateful decision to lead the party in an election campaign in the television age.

To an extent we can account for his ambition by looking at his place in the extraordinary Foot brood – his need to assert himself against his brothers and sisters. To have grown up amongst such a talented group of siblings generated a sense of self which was indivisible and which everyone now recognises as authentically Michael Foot. Even if they despise, disagree and disparage what they see, they can see what they hate. In other words, self-belief propelled him to the leadership of the Labour Party. Duty and service played a part but he also had faith in his own ability to will the age to listen to the arguments and not just look at the pictures. It did not happen and hindsight is a powerful tool for saying that it was never going to happen, but it was not vanity or flattery or the need to do what Nye had never done which made Foot run. It was the belief that he could do it. This sense of himself contradicts the notion that Bevan made him or that, even more grotesquely, Beaverbrook did. It might be heresy, not least for Foot himself, but in the end, the acolyte and the middle brother became the high priest and father figure. While this is unquestionably the case in terms of writing, the question is was it also true in politics?

One reading of Foot's political stock at this moment is that virtually everything he has believed in a lifetime in politics has been abandoned. The idea of public ownership is discredited beyond redemption. The motion of history destroyed the policy of unilateral nuclear disarmament. Margaret Thatcher broke the link between trade unions and running the state. Foot's party is in power but it rules with an approach to means summed up as 'whatever works'. But for Foot the nature of the means deployed remains important. The embrace of the market, and market orientated solutions, to problems of public service delivery may be informed by values that Foot understands, but the means of achieving those ends is far removed from his perception of socialism. Only the National Health Service remains a beacon of his collectivist vision.

This way of seeing Foot reduces him to what Nye Bevan called the prose of politics. It leaves out the poetry and ignores the fact that Foot's personal example continues to set a political benchmark. When you want to attack something for being old left you call it a 'Michael Foot theme park'. In the insult is also a massive compliment: everyone knows exactly what you mean. If one is to take stock of a career like Foot's then the measurement of greatness cannot be in the number of lines of legislation passed. It must be in the number of lives changed. There are a number of ways to change somebody. Living your life as an example that stands for something is one way. The production and dissemination of meaningful words is another.

If generosity to his progenitors is the first source of his uniqueness, the integration of the different compartments of his life and mind is the second. In particular, in reading this collection, it is worth considering if Foot proves the futility of trying to separate literature and politics and demonstrates that a significant source of his greatness lies in the way he unifies them. Foot's greatness in this respect echoes the other British political figure whose most important political weapons were words: Winston Churchill.

Towards the end of his life Churchill had also seen almost everything that he had been in politics to defend questioned, undermined or destroyed. But what he had built was a wall of words, a rhetorical fortress that was immediately useful in the crisis of 1940 and thereafter available to his political descendants. It was a fortress because it was an essentially negative political message. It was based on ideas of defending race, empire, nation state independence and social deference to breeding. However, it was a legacy that has kept these kinds of ideas and feelings alive for much longer in mainstream British politics than in most other European countries.

Foot has not built a wall of words so much as a battering ram. It is a lexicon of positive politics; an overtly partisan rhetoric that has been forged from an intimate acquaintance with three centuries of radical writing. At times this rhetoric absurdly caricatures opponents' positions, but it is never dull. It is based on a belief in our shared humanity across races, peoples and to a lesser extent classes. At the heart of Foot's political credo is the articulation of a burning desire for equality of outcome. But perhaps even more pressing is the unrelenting demand for a peace that means more than simply an absence of war: a peace based on justice and international accountability. It is a credo concerned with how to live, how children should be taught to read, for example, which is infused with a love of language itself. Much of the writing in this collection is as much about literature for its own sake as about politics; as much about love as Labour; as much about passion as power. Indeed, Foot the great humanist has a credo based on a trinity: politics, poetry and passion.

The idea of separating literature and politics in Foot's life and work is to misunderstand fundamentally the man. Literature does not sit in a hinterland for Foot, as it does for people like Denis Healey or Tony

Crosland. It is part of the heartland. There is no centre and periphery here because for Foot politics is a vocation, not a mere career. The pursuit of office, and the ambition that fuelled that pursuit, are slaves to the ideas that launched and motivated the career, not the other way around.

As we watch the operation of our carefully packaged and choreographed governing class, the sheer chaos, the cacophony of competing enthusiasms in the messy, unkempt personae of Michael Foot presents a genuine puzzle. How does he keep it all together? It is like the miracle of one of his off-the-cuff sentences. He seems to have lost the thread entirely as he combines the bomb, a memory of Jill, Plymouth Argyle, and a new book on Swift into a set of clauses. In the end, by a few quick turns, the point emerges and he is home. His life is like one of these sentences. The image that I have of the inside of Foot's brain comes from a film by Powell and Pressburger: *A Matter of Life and Death*. Our hero is accused of cheating death and must face a trial. The courtroom is full and the banks of people rise into infinity. Foot carries just such a literary pantheon in his head and it lives together in his library – Rousseau, Montaigne, Wordsworth, Hazlitt, Heine and all the rest. Next to the writers Nye Bevan heads a political pantheon. Together they form a grand jury that determines the nature of the struggle to be fought at any one time, the book to be read and re-read, the polemic to hurled at some unsuspecting revisionist, and so on. However, as appealing as this image may be, Foot's mind also operates in Technicolor.

One need only have followed in passing Foot's engagement with the civil war in Yugoslavia to understand that the fate of the living matters more to him than arguments between the dead. The writing in this collection is ample testament to the fact that he is no mere antiquarian. For example, the essay on the work of Amartya Sen shows that the shape of the future is more important to him than the exact meaning of the past. This is another key to why writing was not, in the end, enough of a career for him. Nevertheless, one gets the impression that a concern with the present and the future must occasionally have trouble forcing its way to the surface through the piles of volumes from the last three hundred years of literature. In this sense, his life and his writing represent a bridge to the tradition of radicalism and romanticism that was born of the enlightenment project. His politics are a connection with that project and a proof that despite all claims to the contrary we do not live in a state of post-modernity or late capitalism. We do not know if this is late- or early-capitalism and we do not know if modernism has run its course or only just got started. We do know, because Michael Foot tells us, that 'all such questions' have been debated on the left (and as the inclusion of Edmund Burke in the pantheon testifies occasionally on the right) for the last three hundred years. They have been debated with the same passionate engagement that Foot brought to opposing the 2003 war of liberation in Iraq. Foot did not create the National Health Service. He did not win a general election as leader. But his writing, talking and the fact of his existence have already assured that he will be a unique presence in British history.

Brian Brivati

Kingston University, May 2003

Acknowledgements

Michael Foot and Brian Brivati would like to thank the following for their help with preparing this volume: Sheila Noble, Christian Bugge, Karen Heath, Alex Plaschinsky and the incomparable duo of Sean Magee and John Berry at Politico's.

In addition, Michael Foot sends his especial fraternal greetings to the printers of this book, Creative Print and Design – felicitously situated in his old constituency of Ebbw Vale and, he is assured, true disciples of Stanley Morison.

Books by Michael Foot

Armistice: 1918–1939
(1940)

Guilty Men
(with others, 1940)

The Trial of Mussolini
(1943)

Brendan and Beverley
(1944)

Who are the Patriots?
(with Donald Bruce, 1949)

The Pen and the Sword
(1958)

Guilty Men, 1957:
Suez and Cyprus
(with Mervyn Jones, 1957)

Aneurin Bevan: 1897–1945
(1962)

Aneurin Bevan: 1945–1960
(1973)

Debts of Honour
(1980)

Another Heart and Other Pulses
(1984)

Loyalists and Loners
(1986)

The Politics of Paradise:
a vindication of Byron
(1988)

HG: The History of Mr Wells
(1995)

Aneurin Bevan 1897–1960
(one-volume abridgement, 1996)

Dr Strangelove, I Presume
(1999)

Part 1

A better way

A better way to abolish the weapons

May 2003

Whoever may eventually take their place in the history books as the chief villains in the Iraq crisis of the new century, those of us who thought throughout that the most important aspect of the affair was the threat from weapons of mass destruction soon discovered our two incomparable indispensable heroes: Dr Hans Blix, the United Nations weapons inspector, and Mohamed El Baradei, the director general of the International Atomic Energy Agency. The two men worked together as true servants of the international community.

If our world is to be able to escape the infinite perils of nuclear destruction we shall need more than ever the expert, dedicated service of such men. No such awareness of their quality was shown by the American Secretary of Defense, Donald Rumsfeld in commenting on their past work and future prospects, but nobody can expect good manners from him. It is sad, however, that neither Geoffrey Hoon, our Defence Secretary, nor Tony Blair took the opportunity to repair the situation. It is not just a matter of good manners. As we can illustrate with a few latest examples, the whole future of our threatened planet may depend on the integrity of our international institutions and the re-establishment of the proper authority of the United Nations Security Council, so sorely impaired by the Iraq crisis. Each new crisis will further illustrate – and maybe quite speedily – that that is the supreme necessity.

Old-time CNDers like myself have continued to insist that weapons of mass destruction are still the greatest question. New-time multilateralists, such as the Labour Party leaders at the 1997 election, were no less committed. Robin Cook presented the whole international case and should be back in the Government to carry it out.

But consider now again some of the more immediate crises with an explosive nuclear content. Syria did not figure in President Bush's original 'axis of evil' when he first used the phrase, but the manner in which the American Defense Secretary made the reference may seem all the more threatening. Before any such perilous move against Syria was contemplated, all concerned, including the United Nations Security Council, if it was properly operating, should consider the evidence of Sir Andrew Green, who was the British representative in that part of the world and clearly a well-informed observer of the scene: 'The Americans allege that the Syrians have tested chemical weapons. Not a surprise. Several countries in the Middle East are believed to possess such a capability, including Algeria, Egypt, Iran and actually Israel. If Syria has chemical weapons it is for a good reason – as a second-strike capability against Israel. It is inconceivable that the Syrians would strike first, knowing the Israelis would immediately go for nuclear retaliation.'

Thus the tension between Syria and Israel is described by an expert. Both the Syrians and the Israelis have long lists of human rights offences against the other. Nothing could be worse than Mr Rumsfeld's remedy. It could be the stage for a terrible nuclear accident, worse than Chernobyl. The only final remedy is intervention by the international authority, with the inspectors at work in Damascus and Jerusalem. And if indeed this remedy could be applied, what a contrast it would offer to the fiasco of the weapons inspectors' searches in Iraq.

Even while the Iraqi crisis remained unresolved with its weapons of mass destruction still undiscovered – this should at least give some satisfaction to the nuclear disarmers – the third villain in President Bush's axis of evil insisted on its central role in any such controversy. North Korea did not deny that it once possessed some more proficient nuclear weapons than Saddam Hussein's, indeed that it might have the right to have them, as the only final deterrent, against other forms of aggression, including the final nuclear attack. At one stage in international arguments, Donald Rumsfeld had his idea of the remedy: a proposed regime change in Pyongyang to match that projected for Iraq, to be executed with the Chinese Government in Beijing assisting the process as Britain was doing in Iraq.

If diplomacy could not succeed, a real military strike would have to be considered. 'That would truly be insane,' said America's former ambassador in Seoul, Steven Bosworth. 'For us unilaterally to attack North Korea would in my judgement be one of the most immoral acts conceivable.' Indeed, in that part of the world they sometimes have a better comprehension of what nuclear war might do than we in the comfortable West. 'A strike might be an historic gamble that might work or might trigger a war that might incinerate hundreds of thousands of people in Korea and Japan.' Japan, of course, is the country which has had the sharpest real experience of the nuclear horror. Mostly her people have honourably used their experience to help ensure that it should never be repeated. They won some notable converts; campaigners for the cause that the paramount question facing mankind must be the control and abolition of the weapons of mass destruction.

Even more illegitimate – to use no harsher word – than the post-Iraq pressures on Syria or North Korea by the U.S. Defense Secretary were there renewed pressures on Iran. Since the pre-emptive strike has worked for the aggressors in Iraq the taste for such procedures has been enhanced.

Only a few months ago when the American experts seemed to be using the term so crudely, the British Foreign Office seemed to be using its influence in Tehran more wisely; Jack Straw even paid a visit there, presumably to emphasise that we had a more sophisticated approach to these matters than the Pentagon. But who knows, the Iranians may have made nearer approaches to the development of the real weapons than the Syrians, or indeed, the Iraqis of yesteryear. However, such disputes on such matters as weapons of mass destructions are much too dangerous to be settled by pre-emptive strikes from any quarter. As in other cases, the only safe solution must be sought in international action

Sometimes it was the scientists or the philosophers who led the war, the Bertrand Russells, the Albert Einsteins, the Professor Joseph Rotblats. Not immediately, but still not so long after, the politicians, or at least the greatest of them, joined the debate. The mid-1950s was a time when the argument rose to a new climax. Neither the United States nor the Soviet Union had yet tested their latest horrific hydrogen bombs, but they were just about to test their new monstrous mechanisms of destruction even more destructive than Hiroshima and Nagasaki.

Winston Churchill, still in possession of his imaginative political qualities if struck down in other ways, thought the moment might be right for discussions with new rulers in the Kremlin. He was deeply disappointed when his old fellow victor in Europe, now President Eisenhower, restrained maybe by his powerful military–industrial complex, refused to act with him. He found the best response from his old rival in the House of Commons, Aneurin Bevan, and he in turn was speaking the language with the same sense of urgency as Jawaharlal Nehru in India. If all these had had their way, in a negotiation at the highest level before each had developed their H-bombs, the whole monstrous agonies of Cuba, Vietnam and the rest could have been avoided. A full-scale Nuclear Non-Proliferation Treaty could have been achieved by 1960.

The world leader who worked most zealously in that cause was Jawaharlal Nehru. He took every opportunity to express his view that 'the terrible scourge and fear of warfare with atomic weapons would be banned and ended.' His India has never ceased to demand international action to tackle the question. His grandson, Rajiv Gandhi, when he had the chance, did his best to sustain that tradition. The Delhi Declaration signed by Rajiv Gandhi, as Prime Minister of India, and Mikhail Gorbachev for the Soviet Union was the most ambitious disarmament programme ever projected in the nuclear age. It proposed the total elimination of nuclear arsenals by the end of the twentieth century. It set out interim goals which could prepare the way for this final achievement. Two years later Rajiv presented his proposals to the United Nations General Assembly with the date for its implementation extended to the year 2010.

Tragically, before he could carry further India's historic policy on nuclear weapons he was murdered by terrorists on the eve of his re-election in May 1991. If he had lived, he would have faced the same pressures confronted by his successors. If Pakistan had taken the next step in producing nuclear weapons, his Government would have felt that it had to follow suit. I am convinced that he would have used all his ingenuity – his mother's guile and his grandfather's idealism – to emphasise how much he would have preferred to pursue the policy of the Delhi Declaration.

The deed was done in a manner which seemed to do great injury to India's international reputation. But the Government that did the deed had a case, especially in the light of the assistance both the United States and Britain had given to Pakistan, even their connivance with Pakistan's nuclear programme.

Whatever her other defects, India was a democracy. Pakistan could not say the same; the country would often lapse into military rule. The tensions had never ceased to be severe, but when each competed with the other in devising nuclear weapons, the insanity seemed to be of a special order. Sooner or later, the sooner the better, the international inspectors would be needed there.

India watched the development of the Iraq crisis with an especially acute eye. When I say India, I mean the Indian democracy which can speak with as many honourable voices as our own. India hates imperialism, both the American variety and our own. A wholesale condemnation of the American action was forthcoming from the best liberal voices. But official India, including even the Indian premier, Atal Behari Vajpayee, who can be most eloquent when he wants, seemed strangely tongue-tied. Since all matters of Indian policy are partly involved with Pakistan – and why not since the development of the nuclear rivalry? – the reticence is designed to secure a more intelligent, international response from Washington. No such reaction has been forthcoming from Donald Rumsfeld and Co.

The Indian observers of the scene are among the most sophisticated in the world. The most astute and far-seeing of them is M. J. Akbar, editor of the *Asian Age*. If his writings were properly read in the White House and 10 Downing Street, all our hopes for survival would surely be improved. He recalls the arguments in the sub-continent of a few months ago: 'A holocaust became part of the public discourse, and estimates of dead were placed at around 12 million. One might have added that the living would probably have envied the dead at the end of it all.'

Such are the infinite new perils which threaten our planet. The immediate crisis in the Indian sub-continent may be even more urgent than the Syrian–Israeli one. Meanwhile, there are deep suspicions about America's hidden agenda. 'Iraq was on the hidden agenda long before opinion was shepherded or bullied towards action, and then military success became the sole justification for that action.' Our Government, our Labour Government, committed to defend the highest ideals of the international community, found itself trapped on that same American agenda. No interference with the military timetable was to be allowed, no consideration of the injury done to the Security Council's reputation. Indeed, all the blame for any interruption was transferred elsewhere. Some American experts, most monstrously of all, blamed the inspectors.

Weapons of mass destruction, especially the nuclear variety, their production, concealment, control and eventual abolition is the most important question facing mankind and womankind. If we don't destroy them, they will destroy us. In the final annihilation they will destroy us and, as the Iraq record shows, we may never know where the real guilt lies for unleashing the final horror.

However, in the case of nuclear weapons some of our wisest advisers, some of those who actually helped their invention, have exerted themselves to the limit to ensure their final control and abolition. At the moment of the bomb's most dangerous development, scientists across the world formed what was called the Pugwash Group. Our own most eminent member of the group was Professor Joseph Rotblat, still alive and kicking. What the Pugwash scientists propose is to bring the Delhi Declaration up to date and demand that all the nuclear powers, either existing or aspiring, should sign their acceptance. This is indeed no more than the obligation that all the nuclear powers including Britain and the United States accepted under previous Non-Proliferation Treaties.

Almost always on previous occasions when the arguments about nuclear disarmament have reached this stage, the objection is raised that the inspectors will be unqualified or denied the chance to do their job. Hans Blix and Mohamed El Baradei and their skilled teams are there to ensure that on this greatest question the will of the international community shall prevail.

Gorbachev

Perestroika

Review of Mikhail Gorbachev, *Perestroika: new thinking for our country and the world*, in the *Times Educational Supplement*, 11 December 1987

On the same page of a Sunday newspaper which carried a subdued, slightly sour review by Norman Stone, Professor of History at Oxford, of Mikhail Gorbachev's book under the soporific invocation: 'Looking for a different sort of Russia', I caught a glimpse of a neighbouring headline over a book about John Dryden: 'A Daring Pilot in Extremity'. I wish some obstreperous sub-editor had managed to switch the titles.

Mikhail Gorbachev himself might complain. He quickly moves in these pages to dismiss the idea that his series of initiatives in international affairs are provoked by his extreme distress at home. Such a conclusion, acted upon by some maniacs among the Republican Right in the United States, could soon condemn us all to perdition. Gorbachev wants to persuade us about the real reasons for his actions, and he does so with real candour. But of course he cannot allow his Perestroika to be construed as cowardice. If that happened, he might soon be toppled, and we would all be heading back towards the abyss.

However, the daring, the statesmanship, the resilience, the imaginative grasp of the new leader of the Soviet Union, his awareness, above all else, of the nuclear peril, are qualities which should be expressed in the highest terms. (How did Ronald Reagan's 'evil empire' produce the phenomenon of Mikhail Gorbachev? That maybe is a topic for another day.) The great fact of the moment is that, against all the odds and prophecies and expectations, a new style of Soviet leader and leadership has emerged, and this book confirms how sensational, how world-historic, to use the old Marxist term, is the change.

Again and again, it must be stressed – and one of the virtues of this book is that it does so – that the domestic and the foreign implications of Perestroika are interlocked. If he was not seeking such mighty transformations at home, his foreign adventures would never be tolerated, and if he were to fail in his foreign initiatives ... the thought should be too horrific even to contemplate.

If he were to fail, the experiment would not be repeated, and the world would be destined to eventual nuclear extermination – with the Russian people themselves condemned to an even earlier crucifixion, a return to a new Stalin era.

These dire warnings are in place: what Gorbachev portends, what he would de-personalize under the term of his title Perestroika, will shape our world as well as his. So we should read with interest what he writes. No Soviet leader, at least since the days of Lenin and Trotsky, has written in such terms, with his own hand and from his own heart. We would be fools not to listen to every nuance.

One part of the story concerns his campaign in domestic affairs. 'Today', he says, 'it is as if we were going through a school of democracy again.' He gives some vivid examples of where the teaching is coming from – not least from his fellow citizens who bombard him with correspondence. Western readers would be unwise to dismiss these revelations as insignificant. What Gorbachev means by democracy is not what we mean; but nor is it the old, debased word which his predecessors employed. Gorbachev is fascinated by the thing, by its potency, by what it may do to shake the country he loves from its sloth. A second liberating Revolution is what he aspires to lead. If he could succeed, what a boon it would be for all mankind.

Yet he knows, as every sane man and woman the world over should know, that the condition for success is the one that concerns us all: the ending of the arms race. Sometimes he is content to set out the case coolly and persuasively. 'Let me just note once again', he writes at one point, 'that at all its stages the Soviet Union has been the party catching up.' The argument is not easily contestable, and this book would have its value as a direct, honest statement of the Soviet case.

But it is more and much more, for Mikhail Gorbachev is a man of passion. More perhaps than any other world leader in the nuclear age, he is stirred by the combined spectacle of the perversion of science and what could be its consequences for the whole human race. Some American Presidents have spoken in these terms, usually when they are leaving office, better late than never. Dwight Eisenhower did so in his farewell speech when he unmasked the industrial–military complex. Jimmy Carter did the same. Winston Churchill did so too in his very last speech in the House of Commons, after the death of Stalin, when he believed that the West, not the Kremlin, was blocking the path forward.

Mikhail Gorbachev has written this book in order to speak to the world on this greatest of all themes. Clausewitz's theories of war, he says, are now consigned to the dustbin or at least the libraries. We can make an end of 'the inflated role played by militarists in politics'. Then again and again: 'For the first time in history', he reiterates, such a responsibility has rested on the shoulders of the world's leaders and their peoples. He has no doubt about the supreme objective: 'a nuclear-free, non-violent world'. And again, 'We are all passengers aboard one ship, the Earth, and we must not allow it to be wrecked. There will be no second Noah's Ark.'

How pleasant it would be to record that our own Prime Minister, responding in proper terms at one of her lengthy meetings with him, had sought to keep the debate on this level. Alas, she showed no capacity to do so, made no such attempt. He must have tried again, patiently, as others have sought to do, in similar, if less momentous, confrontations. At last he was compelled, as the book records, to remind her that her policies – pursued in plain defiance of solemn undertakings given by successive British Governments – would block the path to sane negotiations and invite a host of other countries to accept her deadly logic. Perhaps this was just another reason which inspired him to write this book. I trust he handed her a signed, marked copy.

Alive and kicking

Review of Archie Brown, *The Gorbachev Factor*, in the *Evening Standard*, 28 March 1996

Mikhail Gorbachev is alive and kicking, as I can testify, having seen him in Moscow a few weeks ago. His mind and heart seem to be working as well as they ever did – when, for example, Western statesmen from Margaret Thatcher to Helmut Kohl recognised him as the man with whom they could do business. He put his stamp on the Eighties more than any other world figure and, when I saw him, he was brim-full of eagerness to do it again.

And yet at the recent Russian elections, which he did more than any other political figure to make possible, he was pitifully humiliated. He is denounced from different sides as the author, unwitting or not, of many of the trials and tribulations which now afflict the Russian people. How bitter and degrading these trials are, any visitor to Moscow can see for himself.

Russian political leaders, headed alas by President Yeltsin himself, have an interest in transferring some of the blame for these terrible conditions on to Gorbachev's shoulders. Scapegoats have played quite a

part in ancient Russian history but it's even worse now. I attended
election meetings in Moscow where Gorbachev was denounced both as
a traitor to Communism and to his own country. And sometimes these
cries are taken up in the strangest quarters. A school of American historians seeks to uphold the doctrine that the ending of the Cold War had
everything to do with American might and nothing whatever to do with
the Russian response, including Gorbachev's.

Such misunderstanding can be highly dangerous. If the part which
Gorbachev played is to be denied, the treaties he signed can be torn up
and no new ones might be negotiated. The world-wide nuclear threat is
not yet lifted as he wanted it to be. A new dictator might rise in Russia,
a new Peter the Great or a new Stalin. And to hold them in check we
should need a new Gorbachev – what about the existing one?

Archie Brown's book is not only a richly researched, easily readable
biography of Gorbachev himself. It should be studied at once in every
diplomatic service worthy of the name, starting with our own Foreign
Office. So don't be disturbed by the churlish comments which have
appeared in some learned journals about this volume. The problems
which Gorbachev faced with such vision and courage are still there,
clamouring for an answer. The method which he did more than any other
Russian to devise for solving them is there too – the right to dissent. The
Gorbachev factor is still present, even if Gorbachev himself is the victim
of such monstrous injustice.

Gorbachev in his own words

Review of Mikhail Gorbachev, *Memoirs*, in the *Evening Standard*,
7 October 1996

According to my book, Mikhail Gorbachev did more than any other
single individual engaged in the ugly trade of world politics to make

possible a peaceful ending of our war-ridden century, with the bonus of the final lifting of the shadow of the nuclear holocaust. Alas, his departure from the Kremlin may put these ideas in jeopardy, but without him even the hope of deliverance would never have been so well defined. Mikhail Gorbachev, in his own book, puts the case more modestly, if at greater length. But make no mistake: his 600 pages of memoirs is a wonder on its own, his own story recited in a manner worthy of the theme. He is passionately concerned to save both his beloved Russia and the world at large. He has the right to be heard, since it was his combination of political intelligence and courage that prepared the way for the decisive changes of the 1980s and the 1990s.

How he had to work for the chance to speak first on a national stage might have been enough for a volume on its own. He had to fight his way up through the suffocating Communist system. The bureaucrats could have beaten any sense of human decency out of him, as they did with so many others. But somehow he was always making deductions of his own: from his wartime experience when his village was occupied by the Germans, from a Russian literature which gloried in a special humanity, from a noble Indian visitor called Jawaharlal Nehru to his Moscow University who told them it was their duty to make a better world.

He had some special Russian words to describe what he meant by freedom and somehow he gained for them a world-wide currency. He was shaken and ashamed by the news of the Chernobyl nuclear power explosion. The scientists and the party specialists had sustained what he called 'a spirit of servility, fawning, clannish and a persecution of independent thinkers'. Across the planet as a whole there had been 151 significant radiation leaks at nuclear power stations, but in a sense the Chernobyl crime was the worst. It gave a driving impetus to his dream of a new nuclear policy for all mankind.

Like some of his predecessors in the post of General Secretary of the Communist Party, he faced unforeseen turmoil in neighbouring states which might have wrecked any programme of reforms, but he never believed military force could be the cure, and his restraint saved the day and changed the face of Eastern Europe. He did not foresee the pace of change in Germany and makes no pretence that he did, but this sudden crisis made his response to it all the more significant.

However, it was still in the broad field of world-wide disarmament that he showed the truest wisdom and originality. He knew that an end to the arms race was necessary if his country was not to be destroyed. He knew how his predecessors in office, even when they started to talk peace, might find it easier to yield to the demands of the military–industrial complex. Moscow had its version of that deadly machine to match the one that dictated policy in Washington.

Fortunately for us all, the Gorbachev who was seeking an escape from the Cold War, which overnight could lead to a hot one, found others in other countries who would respond to his overtures. He readily acknowledges that he could have done nothing without the response from President Reagan or Prime Minister Thatcher. They did discover that they could do business with him, and we were all the beneficiaries of that trade.

But it was Mikhail Gorbachev from Moscow who set the pace and maintained the momentum, and he naturally acclaims those political leaders who came with him most readily. He records the matter thus: 'When after the summit meeting with President Reagan in Reykjavik I flew to India to sign – together with Rajiv Gandhi – the Delhi Declaration on the principles of a nuclear weapon free and non-violent world, many people could not see any connection between these two events.' That declaration was signed on 27 November, 1986. It was designed to secure 'the total elimination of nuclear arsenals by the end of the century'.

Thus the Mikhail Gorbachev of those times, at the peak of his powers, looked forward to our present possibilities and dilemmas. It is a tragedy beyond measure that he no longer retains the political authority to help make his will effective. He was quite prepared for democratic reforms of the most far-reaching nature but he could not accept the destruction of any effective federal authority in the old Soviet Union. He prophesied that such a destruction might lead to several Chechen revolts, condemning patriotic Russian soldiers to 'fight for an unjust cause and become hostage to a shameful policy'.

He should have been there to deal with the challenge of the new century. The world would be much safer if he were. But since the job was so cruelly wrenched from his hands, he has done the next best thing. He has recited the whole truth and urged us all, with his own countrymen at the head, to face the task and follow the timetable he laid down: a worldwide disarmament plan, with all the nuclear arsenals suitably destroyed.

Churchill versus the H-bomb

Review of John Young, *Winston Churchill's Last Campaign: Britain and the Cold War 1951–1955*, in the *Evening Standard*, 13 May 1996

Some of us who heard Winston Churchill make his last major speech in the House of Commons – I was one of the lucky few on the Labour benches – were shaken by the actual words he used and the new tone in his voice. It was an unforgettable display of his greatness, touched by a lapse into a kind of combative humility.

He was stricken by illness; indeed he gave the House of Commons the first authentic information about his recent stroke, but he was even more, at the same moment, cast down by a political storm which seemed to overwhelm him – and still, in the last resort, matchlessly resilient in his resolve to face it. It was 3 March 1955, but here, also, was the Churchill of 1940.

What had taken possession of his whole imaginative genius – blocking out everything else as might happen with others on such occasions – was an awareness of the fresh portentous peril for the world at large involved in the invention of nuclear weapons; how the danger was not being faced by the leaders of the great nations; how they should be prepared to meet and confront one another, and seek the remedy still within their grasp but rapidly slipping from it.

One other speaker in the debate rose to the height of that great argument. He was Aneurin Bevan who, owing to some dispute with his own party leaders, was speaking from the back benches, but it was his intervention which enticed Churchill to say much more than he had originally intended.

Often they had been great parliamentary rivals who would give no quarter to each other. Like Disraeli and Gladstone, or William Pitt and Charles James Fox in earlier centuries. Suddenly their shared appreciation of the unprecedented nuclear menace gave them a common insight. Churchill even apologised to Bevan and the House for the length of his elaborate but unpremeditated intervention.

John Young's book describes Churchill's own approach to this last political crisis more exhaustively and sympathetically than ever before. Since his extraordinary combination of mental and physical energy was starting to weaken, a host of witnesses, headed by Churchill's own friends and apologists, were eager to protest that this last phase marked a sad aberration from the true cause of Churchillian greatness and glory – especially since the meeting Churchill demanded to deal with the H-bomb horror never took place.

How Churchill himself would have nailed any such insinuations! He would have resented the charge no less than the other revisionist tale that somehow he could have saved us much trouble by making a new Chamberlainite peace in 1940. He and his fellow Conservative ministers did make a terrible mess of several things after their return to office in 1951, but excluded from the crime sheet must always be Churchill's lone, valiant, intelligent struggle to seek an escape from the world nuclear peril.

Hitherto much the most colourful account giving Churchill's view of what he thought about this crisis was supplied by Lord Moran, his

doctor, in his famous and infamous diary. Eisenhower's clumsy administration in Washington, constantly assisted by the British Foreign
Office, had 'bitched things up'. He never used those unparliamentary
words in the Commons but he gave the impression he would have
wished to do so and, anyhow, he had confirmed the deadly accusation
from Aneurin Bevan that an American intervention had destroyed a full-
scale Churchillian initiative.

Within the confines of this Cold War history, as his title indicates,
John Young also supplies the most detailed report of Churchill's last
days and hours in Downing Street. It is one of the most pitiful and
disgraceful stories ever told, including the reason why Churchill was
provoked to feel 'a cold hatred' for his successor, Anthony Eden.
Despite all he had done for our country and the Conservative Party, even
the commonest courtesies were withheld from him. John Young places
on the cover of his book a cartoon by Vicky, showing an anguished
Churchill watching his hope of peace talks sinking down the hourglass.
The other great irony was that, at the height of one of their earlier great
parliamentary debates, Bevan had prophesied that, when it suited them,
the Conservative Party would cast him aside like a soiled glove.

Part 2

The women take over

Sally's broomstick

Preface to *Skoob's Directory of Secondhand Bookshops*, reprinted in
the *Hampstead and Highgate Express*, 17 January 1992

My father was the greatest reader who ever read, and, on the same strict
reckoning, spent a whole lifetime in secondhand bookshops. He had
several other diversionary occupations: politics, earning his own living
from the age of fourteen, rearing seven children. But, apart from our
mother, books were his real love. *Skoob's Directory* was not yet in
existence in his day. If it had been, I'm sure his copy would have been
marked with indelible entries on every page. He was a great marker of
books, and could always enhance the value of any volume which came
into his hands.

He introduced himself to these delights when, with his fourteen
shillings a week clutched closely in his fist, he visited the Charing Cross
Road. How much of that prodigious sum went on W. T. Stead's Penny
Poets? Thereafter, enough money could be earned, begged or borrowed
to keep the endless flow always moving onwards to fresh discoveries. As

far as I can recall, he never sold a book in his life, and at any rate not one of those real books which he had marked and digested. Often he would return to those especially treasured revelations of his youth or, no less excitedly, to the unread volumes which he had set aside somewhere on his shelves to await the inspired moment of temptation. Come to this question of rich reserves in a moment, in the proper order.

Way back in my own juvenile period – despite his example and instruction, I did not acquire the gift until the early twenties – I can now confess that I did not at first realise what was what: I had other extraordinary addictions such as playing chess, playing football, falling in love, walking across the Cornish moors, watching Plymouth Argyle and, oh yes, politics again: but there I needed a special introduction which my father could also give me. However, in those far-off times, as I can now vividly recall, it was my beloved sister Sally, twelve months older than myself, who broke the spell of ignorance even more than my father, who was quite properly too busy reading himself to waste time lecturing kids who ought to have had the sense to see the riches all around them for themselves.

Sally was a real born reader herself – how much she got it from him I don't know to this day and at the time I didn't bother to inquire. What I mean by a born reader is one who finds out for herself or himself what springs are needed to release the imagination. Decades later I discovered how some of the greatest writers who also claimed to have found their own imaginations constricted had found the liberation in the same way as Sally: that is, by engulfing themselves without restriction or restraint in the great novelists. William Hazlitt, whose name will appear in this piece in other connections, experienced this particular form of awakening. He read in his early teens Defoe, Fielding, Richardson and maybe even a little Swift, and could imagine no other pleasure in life to compare with such a boundless emancipation. And Hazlitt, by the way, some decades later, among his first claims to immortality, became the first great critic to treat the novel as an art.

But that's another side of the story. Maybe my beloved Sally, quite unwittingly, came near starting my own imaginative education. She could take me off on her broomstick so easily that she hardly stopped to explain which favourite authors had in their turn taught her. She had no difficulty in explaining that there were golden worlds of adventure and excitement waiting for us to explore. I was still stuck with *The Boys' Own Paper* or Talbot Baines Reed. She would first damn me with her scorn and then offer some new excursion in the company of one of those to whom she had already given an honoured place on her secret bookcase in the next room. She was reading Thomas Hardy and Joseph Conrad, two of my father's own favourites incidentally.

How boys and girls should be taught to read properly strikes me as one of the important questions facing the human race. Any hopes of good government in time to come, let alone survival, may depend upon it. And it so happens that despite my privileged education at the bidding of my book-mad father and sister, I did learn much from such mentors. Much the best of these still are the two little volumes by Arnold Bennett – *How to Live Twenty-Four Hours A Day* and *Literary Taste* – which I used to read on the bus in the city of Liverpool when I was on the way to work or back home. Together, they describe how Victorian or Edwardian readers like my father started to build their libraries. Every well-weighed word in these extraordinary productions still counts today.

Often since those distant times I have noted that no modern guide seemed to do the work half so well. Then, just to put all such lamentations to shame, came Fay Weldon's *Letters to Alice*, published by Michael Joseph in 1984 and now plentifully available in Coronet paperback. Fay Weldon purports to describe how she introduces her nieces or nephews to Jane Austen – who, of course, also figured on my sister Sally's exclusive list. By itself this would have been enough on any reckoning, but there is more and much more wrapped up in these wise and witty pages, the true, glorious, insatiable love of books described by a modern novelist of the first order.

But the subject is not only reading books but buying them; the two themes should never be kept apart. No true book lover should be content with the contribution of the libraries, indispensable to our civilisation though those institutions have been and still are. Even those who possess the extraordinary photographic gift to be able to remember almost everything they have ever read – the Macaulays and the Coleridges, the Byrons and the Karl Marxes – even they, or perhaps they most of all, are the people who transmitted from one country to another, from one generation to another, the priceless heritage of book learning, loved or lusted to have the books themselves in their hands, to see and feel the precious volume as the authors themselves first fondled them.

All the arts which go to the making of a book, including even or maybe headed by the printers, should be honoured. One of my father's latter-day crazes, and by no means a cheap one to indulge, was the printers of Italy, and more especially Venice, who anticipated some of the sensational printing discoveries which fashioned the new world of the European Renaissance. My father was a devotee of William Tyndale before some of the modern scholars had unearthed him; he knew how much the word of the Bible translated into English had unloosed all the other grand, revolutionary, world-wide commotions of which he so much approved. In the modern world, however defined, the right to read was the first right of all.

Here was the beginning of democracy in the very best sense of that debased word. Here was the way in which every man and woman, every boy and girl, could be given equal access, or something very near it, to the glories of the universe. Thus the book lovers should never be mistaken for some exclusive sect forever wishing to parade their superior tastes and secret vows. Here was a form of levelling which could never be dismissed or derided. It was no accident and no pose when Hazlitt used this same term as he heard the new kind of poetry from the lips of the young Coleridge. The same Hazlitt who discovered the novelists devised his own introduction to the poets, the painters, the dramatists, the musicians, even the politicians. Even they or the very best of them could be admitted to climb Parnassus.

William Hazlitt's selection of the political practitioners who could justly be claimed to be included among the greatest writers is an education in itself. Three of them were rivals who came to dominate the age just before his own and who, in Hazlitt's estimate although not that of many other observers, overthrew the eighteenth century establishment of Dr Johnson and his associates. They introduced a new kind of language into political debate as the poets also did, and soon they were followed by a new generation who carried forward the new accent and the new message into the new century: William Godwin, Thomas Paine, William Cobbett. For these, as for Edmund Burke, words were things, and had a revolutionary resonance of their own.

But Hazlitt could look back to the true tradition of human liberation, and in one sense it was a more remarkable feat than the prophecies of the future. He stripped away the overgrowths of superstition and religious mania and paraded before us a high and mighty procession of unacknowledged liberators. This was his own particular discovery in the secondhand bookshops, and once he had spoken or written the same mass burials of genius and political courage could never be repeated. He saw the tradition of those who fought for human rights in their different styles in Montaigne and Shakespeare, Francis Bacon and John Milton, Swift and Pope. These household names Hazlitt honoured in a manner previously unrecognised. Gradually his own century began to accept them at something much nearer his valuation, all, maybe, except Jonathan Swift, who had to wait yet another century for his full vindication. But enough of these diversions and distractions. Get to the books themselves. How many hundreds of thousands of proper introductions have *Skoob's Directory* already accomplished; how many millions lie ahead?

Our honeymoon

Evening Standard, 19 May 1993

It was strictly and scandalously and seductively illicit, but it worked. The truth has never been told before – for reasons divulged in the last paragraphs, but you will have to read the lot to make sense of it. Jill Craigie was a raging beauty let loose on susceptible, wartime London, but she had many other qualities she preferred her legion of suitors to remark upon. I discovered this reticence about her own physical perfection only somewhat later or I would have exploited the point much sooner. As it was, despite her qualifications as the first woman director to work in the British film industry, I could not take my eyes off this original apparition.

She had the colouring of an English rose but everything else was a romantic, mysterious addition. She was half Scottish and half Russian, not a tincture of English reserve in her make-up. She had Celtic and Russian fires and passions intermingled with what seemed an inborn gift for appreciating painting and music and, as it seemed to me, every other art.

This was no doubt the reason the aforementioned list of suitors included Paul Nash, who liked to see her as a pre-Raphaelite creation, Vaughan Williams, who gave and signed a page of music for her birthday, Sir Charles Reilly, the architect's architect who had first introduced us, and Henry Moore, one of whose wartime London Underground paintings still hangs on our wall.

Having made her first wartime film, with sensational novices in leading roles, she started work on a film about the bombing and rebuilding of my home town of Plymouth, where I was preparing to stand as the Labour candidate in what many considered a hopeless fight against the sitting member, Leslie Hore-Belisha, who had held the seat, the Devonport constituency, with huge majorities since the early 1920s.

So we met first in London and a few months later in Plymouth. No hint of a honeymoon or anything like it was conceivable to anyone then or for months thereafter.

But there was one momentous exception. My beloved mother wanted to see me safely and happily married. She was much more concerned about this than my departure from the family political tradition when I left the Liberals for the Labour Party. She caught sight of Jill directing some scene in the Plymouth film, and I could recall, ever afterwards, how excitedly she phoned to tell me: 'She'll do.'

It was a new variant on the old idea of love at first sight, but I had to explain to her, as my own investigations had discovered, that Jill was married already with a young daughter. My mother, it should be mentioned, was a strict Nonconformist, like the vast majority of my potential constituents in Devonport. Most of them would have disapproved most strongly of any departure from marital conventions, although several had been as captivated as my mother by the spectacle of the thirty-three-year-old Jill Craigie.

Several months later – as they used to say in the subtitles in the silent films, which both Jill and I still enjoyed – I had been elected Labour MP for Devonport, and Jill had completed her film.

She had introduced me, too, to Hampstead Heath, where she was something near a native, having protected the place from Hitler's bombs, and where we made good use of the excellent hedgerow shelters for loving couples. I said, 'Let's try a more luxurious honeymoon', or something like it.

Ever since I had seen the happy smile on the face of Bertrand Russell, the champion of companionate marriage, I had been in favour of it. And so was Jill. She was, if you like, the girl of my theories, but the girl of my dreams too.

So, on a few days' notice, in the new Parliament's summer recess in 1945, we set off with return tickets to Nice, where I had been just before the outbreak of war in 1939, in the company of my previous employer, Lord Beaverbrook. He had shown me around, and I would show her – not quite on the same scale, but a good imitation.

Which hotel did we mention at the airport? The Negresco. When we arrived at the place, in all its late-Victorian splendour, it seemed eerily empty. But we still thought we'd better order separate rooms, and found ourselves respectably barricaded in separate suites. The old wartime phrases were still ringing in our ears: never in the realm of marital experiment had such lavish facilities been made available for so few.

Diffidently, we made our excursions, first along the Negresco corridors and then along the beautiful French coast westward to Juan-les-Pins and Gulfe-Juan where Napoleon had landed from Elba, and where we were told Picasso was holding court.

Every resort was a desert; we were among the very first English post-war visitors, and the French waiters were shocked at our choice of dishes largely prompted by our steady diet of powdered eggs and the other delicacies of wartime rationing.

Had they any eggs – real eggs?, asked Jill, in her best French accent. And then she ordered *une omelette énorme*, and waved her arms to emphasise her instructions. Some while later the dish appeared – the largest omelette ever served on the French Riviera.

Even food could not overshadow other delights. The sea was as blue as we had ever been told; we had whole beaches to ourselves to choose from; Napoleon himself could not have been better received at the Gulfe-Juan. Mosquito nets were necessary in the best bedrooms, but all such impediments were overcome. We did not hear a single English voice or suffer a single investigative intrusion.

After ten delirious days and nights, we returned in secrecy and triumph to London. I made my way to my chaste top flat at 62 Park Street (restricted rent, thirty shillings a week), and she was soon back in her slightly more elaborate Hollyberry House, Hampstead.

But she was astounded to find a crowd of reporters outside the house, who greeted her with: 'We have reports that you've been away in the South of France with Michael Foot. What do you say?'

She replied, 'I'll ask him, if you like', and rang me at Park Street. A little while later, I devised this reply: 'Michael Foot offers his fraternal greetings to his fellow journalists – and the reminder that, if anything appears in the newspapers about his visit to France, he will be happy to reveal his latest information about the love affairs of Lord Beaverbrook, Lord Rothermere and a select list of other newspaper proprietors.'

The crowd of reporters, in Jill's own words, just melted away.

Janet Kidd

Review of Janet Kidd, *The Beaverbrook Girl*, in the *Evening Standard*, 7 May 1987

I cannot believe that even those who have never heard of Beaverbrook or the Beaverbrook girl will fail to find this book entrancing. It is stuffed with surprises and sensations, and written with an unfailing verve and narrative skill.

The art of autobiography is a much more difficult one than the large number of its practitioners might suggest. It calls for a peculiar combination of egotism and objectivity. To tell the whole truth about one's self or one's loved ones is a tremendous accomplishment. Yet Janet Kidd, I believe, has made a brave and brilliant attempt at it.

One part of the problem might be considered the chief asset: the nature of her monstrous father who dominates the book. Since she so loved her mother, whom the father so nearly destroyed, or her brother Peter, whose treatment at his hands was even more severe, the final portrait could have been drawn with strokes of indelible ferocity.

The miracle is that she can still summon to his aid – and hers – his redeeming charm: the habit of doing things his own way which some – political opponents like Stanley Baldwin, or personal opponents like Lord Louis Mountbatten – denounced as devilry, but which could turn out to be something quite different. Not for nothing did Beaverbrook himself explain to his long-suffering wife that their daughter had much more of him in her than either of her brothers, the handsome, amenable Max or persecuted Peter.

How would Beaverbrook, I wonder, have read these pages? He would have been shocked by the candour but reconciled to the craftsmanship. For we are given glimpses of the Beaverbrook who was fascinated by, and himself fascinated, a gallery of beautiful and intelligent women.

Women and wit, politics and laughter, and the kind of journalism which could mix all together constantly in the same magic potion – this was Beaverbrook's world. But Janet's world and her brother Max's and her mother's, presumably, was something different. They were natural athletes; they loved sports and fast cars, and horses, and even faster aeroplanes. They tried to teach their father who was not a willing pupil.

Round about the years between 1940 and 1945, all these curious mixed emotions and capacities in the Beaverbrook entourage were jumbled together, much to the benefit of our country.

The playboys of the 1930s became the fighter pilots of the battle of Britain. The playgirls could have done the same; at least Janet could. Without the expert tuition in modern ways which young Max and young Janet gave to their father, he would not have been the man who gave Churchill his finest support in Britain's finest hour. I had the good fortune to see the whole of that family at work and play during those years, and I confess I loved them, but that formidable father most of all.

Readers of this book are advised to read every word, to the last touch. They will find so many answers to unexpected problems: what the Mountbattens were up to, how other notables dealt with disobedient husbands, where mistresses intruded, what an uninvited Mr Hore-Belisha was doing in her bed. And Beaverbrook, I can assure you, would have shown much interest in these items, along with the mightiest themes of the 1940s.

Emmeline Pankhurst

Review of June Purvis, *Emmeline Pankhurst: a biography*, in the *Guardian*, 3 August 2002

Emmeline Pankhurst, along with other revolutionary figures such as Oliver Cromwell and Thomas Paine, endured vicious misrepresentation until some real historians appeared on the scene to do her justice. In the case of Emmeline, the scurrility of the attacks has continued right up to the present day: a whole male regiment can still be mobilised to deny her revolutionary stature. June Purvis's new biography is a full recognition of her greatness.

The fight for women's rights, like so many good causes, had its origin in the French revolution of the 1790s. It should have secured the vote for women in the British Parliament during the last decades of the nineteenth century. John Stuart Mill, the greatest liberal philosopher of the age, had given his blessing. His disciples, both men and women, could not imagine why so obvious a claim was thwarted. But the Liberal campaigners of those times found themselves facing the inscrutable objections of the Liberal leader William Gladstone, or the devious manoeuvres of one of his successors, Herbert Asquith, or, later still, extraordinary opposition from an up-and-coming Winston Churchill. The strange death of the liberal England of that epoch offered nothing stranger than the opposition to the women's cause right up to the outbreak of war in 1914.

Even while the Liberals were abandoning their principles on women's rights, the Labour party (we members may be eager to record) was showing a more imaginative, truly liberal approach. Just before 1914, the leaders of the women's organisations were noting these developments. Honesty also requires us to recognise that these liberal attitudes, not always shared by all sections of the Labour movement, owed much to the attitude of our leader, Keir Hardie, a supporter of the women's cause since his first election to Parliament in 1892.

The woman who best understood these varying historical pressures was Emmeline Pankhurst. She had learned her politics, like so many of that period, in the nascent Labour movement. Her husband, Richard Pankhurst, twenty years her senior, died when she was making her first appearances on the political scene. Yet he remained, as she was always eager to claim, the dominating influence in her life: the dedicated socialist who demanded that men and women take their place together on the stage.

Keir Hardie attended his funeral. Robert Blatchford, editor of *The Clarion* and a foremost supporter of the women's cause, attempted to secure financial assistance for the Pankhurst family. For the rest of her life, Emmeline was never to escape such anxieties. But she turned, ever more heroically, to face the challenges of public life.

The public platform was the place where she learned to wield her power more successfully than any rival before or since. Women in her day were not supposed to make public speeches: just before Emmeline, Annie Besant had dared to break this convention in the cause of birth control. Emmeline applauded her courage and example. For the whole of the pre-war epoch, Emmeline made herself the master – or the mistress – of the new instrument of public debate.

As Rebecca West wrote in a famous essay on her:

There has been no other woman like Emmeline Pankhurst. She was beautiful; her pale face, with its delicate square jaw and rounded temples, recalled the pansy by its shape and a kind of velvety bloom on the expression. She dressed her taut little body with a cross between the elegance of a Frenchwoman and the neatness of a nun. She was courageous; small and fragile and no longer young, she put herself in the way of horses' hooves, she stood up on platforms under a rain of missiles, she sat in the darkness of underground jails and hunger struck, and when they let her out because she had starved herself within touching distance of death, she rested only for a day or two and then clambered back on to the platforms, she staggered back under the horses' hooves.

What Purvis does for Emmeline Pankhurst in her new biography is to provide a detailed, scrupulous, excellently researched retelling of the story, and thus offer a vindication of the woman so finely observed by West.

When, in August 1914, every other issue was swamped by the outbreak of war in Europe, Pankhurst came to the quick conclusion that the defeat of republican France would not serve the women's cause or anybody else's. At times of such stress, she was accused of treachery to her own cause. But it was not so. Throughout the previous months and even weeks, the Asquith government's treatment of Emmeline had touched new levels of barbarity. So furious were the measures taken against the women's leaders that some of them decided that they must move to Paris to conduct their operations. Her daughter, Christabel, had been there for months. Emmeline would make the crossing whenever she could.

Both mother and daughter had good reason for claiming that the Paris they cherished treated them much more fairly than London. In Paris, too, they had a special vantage point for seeing that the attack from

Germany threatened their beloved France even more directly than England. Within a few days they took the momentous decision to call off all the militant operations in which the women's organisations had been engaged, and declared in support of the government.

It was one of the boldest decisions made in the history of women's emancipation. Emmeline made it, with Christabel at her side. Most of the other leaders accepted their judgement, but there was deep opposition from those who hated the idea of participation in such a conflict and could argue that greater efforts should have been made by Britain's leaders to avoid such a world catastrophe. Keir Hardie, the best friend of the women's cause, was one of these. A sizeable number of the Labour party shared his view, among them Emmeline's other daughter, Sylvia, who was horrified by Emmeline's decision.

1914 was unique in its challenge to the old world: so the participants and the historians might agree. But Emmeline knew what she was fighting for, and had the patience to wait for the new triumphs to match the audacity of the great suffragette campaigns.

Christabel was at her side throughout these defeats and victories. Together with Millicent Fawcett and the leaders of the other women's organisations, they successfully conducted the negotiations with the new prime minister, Lloyd George, which proved much more successful than their previous ones with the treacherous Asquith. But if the scene had changed so dramatically, no one had done more to achieve it than Emmeline.

Years later, Rebecca West summarised the matter thus: 'She was the last popular leader to act on the inspiration of the principle of the French Revolution; she put body and soul at the service of liberty, equality and fraternity and secured a triumph for them.'

Brigid Brophy

A woman of importance

Review of Brigid Brophy, *Baroque 'n' Roll and Other Essays*, in the *Independent*, 18 March 1989

Just at the moment when our memories are being jogged by the film on the Profumo–Stephen Ward–Christine Keeler affair, it is worth recalling that the very best comment at the time upon this, as on so many of the other of our national displays of hypocrisy, was made by Brigid Brophy.

She tried to give her verdict in a commissioned, paid-for BBC programme which was nonetheless stopped from being transmitted at the last moment even in the pre-Norman Tebbit age; but the piece was published in her 1966 book of essays and reviews, *Don't Never Forget*.

She called the Profumo affair 'the most dazzling piece of free entertainment laid before the British public since the Oscar Wilde trial'; and then she brilliantly quoted Wilde to scatter the new generation of hypocrites.

Algernon Moncrieff, it may be recalled, remarked to his manservant: 'Lane's views on marriage seem somewhat lax. Really, if the lower orders don't set us a good example, what is the use of them?' Always, Brigid Brophy can invoke Oscar Wilde to her aid better than anyone, and this collection of her essays contains one for which all true Wilde enthusiasts or Brophyites must have been eagerly waiting – her appreciation of the Richard Ellman biography.

The verdict is instructive, generous and favourable, but she feels justly entitled to comment on Ellmann's weakness in dealing with the relationship between her two heroes, Wilde and Bernard Shaw. The two were born within two years of each other in Dublin; their families were well acquainted; as critics in London they regarded themselves as fellow members of 'The Great Celtic–Hibernian School'.

Shaw, she acknowledges, made his 'sole gross critical blunder' in not recognising the greatness of *The Importance of Being Earnest*. But he more than made amends thereafter, as only Brigid Brophy has properly noted, and she concludes her essay with Shaw's adoption of at least part of the Wildean creed in *The Doctor's Dilemma*: 'I believe in Michael Angelo, Velázquez and Rembrandt: in the might of design, the mystery of colour, the redemption of all things by Beauty everlasting and the message of Art that has made these hands blessed. Amen. Amen.'

All the other proper Brophyite heroes and heroines are allowed their entries and exits in this excellent selection – Mozart, Jane Austen, Ronald Firbank. Old addicts will find fresh additions to some of their favourites, and new ones will be encouraged to go in search of the older, larger volumes, some of which are now out of print.

Every sentence here can be read and re-read with profit. Every theme takes an unexpected turn. Every particular entry must be drained to the last drop – such as this comment on the full-page advertisement which appeared on 1 February 1988 in what she called 'the British non-tabloid newspaper the *Independent*', expressing alarm about Clause 28 in the Local Government Bill then before Parliament:

The Clause forbade local authorities to promote homosexuality or to
teach its acceptability as 'pretended family relations'. It did not define
what it was ... The signatories of the advertisement, who were many
and of different political views and whose names were closely packed
on the printed page, included (in addition to Michael Levey and me)
the Marquess (thus spelt in 1988) of Queensberry.

Such vigilance and wit together will preserve, in 1989 and thereafter, the
true Shavian–Wildean cause of human decency.

Brophy and Mozart

Review of Brigid Brophy, *Mozart the Dramatist*, in the *Guardian*, 28
June 1990

The trouble with Brigid Brophy – or perhaps we should say the
awkward, irrepressible truth – is that when she decides to master a
subject (perhaps a new verb, to mistress, should be invented to suit her
case) she matches the best that has gone before, and then adds an
original line of delight or discovery all her own.

Thus she has dealt with her Irish-genius-heroes, Bernard Shaw and
Oscar Wilde, the genius being more important than the nationality. Thus
she extolled their eighteenth-century predecessors like, say, Alexander
Pope or Jane Austen (if you imagine in your conceit that Jane is not an
eighteenth century figure you haven't read Brigid – and she knows). Thus
she unleashes her great polemical pieces on animal rights or the essays
raising invective to the pitch of art: the one which comes constantly to
mind dealt finally with A. L. Rowse's Shakespearean pretensions.

But how would she fare with Mozart, an even more ambitious theme
along a track already well beaten? Incidentally, Michael Levey, her
husband, had written on this subject before her, and his volume *The Life*

and Death of Mozart has recently been reissued in paperback too. No
hint of rivalry is intended; the two volumes complement each other.
Indeed, as we approach the Mozart commemorations of 1791 in
liberated Prague and across the whole civilised world, no better joint
introduction to the revelries could be imagined.

Already it may be objected that this notice is too much stuffed with
superlatives, but the fault must rest entirely with the subject. Levey's
volume carries the epigraph from *The Public Advertiser*, printed in
London on 9 July 1765: 'The greatest Prodigy that Europe, or that even
Human Nature has to boast of, is, without contradiction, the little
German boy Wolfgang Mozart.'

That is the first part of the phenomenon, with the glowing capital
letters, which had to be explained, and the date was still some years
before the prodigy was able to fulfil his own ambition to turn his mind
to opera. As it happens, and as Michael Levey underlines, he had this
dream too at a prodigiously early age.

However, as Brigid Brophy's title indicates, it was this development
which she most wanted to explore. 'Mozart's unique excellence', she
says, 'lies in his double supremacy: as classical artist and as psychological artist.' It was the combination which made him the Shakespeare of
his century.

And to clinch the full claim what is required are the discoveries of our
new Freudian world. Brigid Brophy applies the whole range of this
knowledge without the slightest touch of pedantry or dogma or jargon.
Don Giovanni she says, 'is what Freud perceived *Hamlet* to be, an
unconscious autobiography.' But that is the merest glimpse of her
wisdom, compressed as often into an aphorism.

What she shows more elaborately and effectively than before is how
a new world for women was opening. Opera became 'the most uncon-
strained vehicle for personal emotions', and it was the women having
their first taste of liberation who profited most. As time moved on, two
other hitherto oppressed classes, the servants and the young, like the

women, were given their voice. To discern the first intimations of that
revolutionary spirit was part of Mozart's genius; to make the fact plain
is part of Brophy's insight.

One redeeming feature of our age, she insists, is the way Mozart's
reputation has been recognised. Somehow those Freudian discoveries of
our century were needed to enhance the glory of her beloved eighteenth
century. The combined Brophy perception and scorn were necessary for
the achievement, and she happily tells us in an aside how 'one of the
nineteenth century's strongest wishes was that some moralistic magic
would ordain that the eighteenth had never in fact taken place.'

Mozart was the expression of the spirit which could not be exorcised,
the heaven on earth which could be built by enlightened mortals, 'equal
to the gods'. She makes the case with such force that it becomes incon-
testable. 'The touchy problem of how to "place" Mozart admits of only
one solution. He stands on the very pinnacle of Parnassus.'

Brophy and Public Lending Right

Contribution to *Whose Loan Is It Anyway? – Public Lending Right
Twenty Years On*, 1999

Three women joined in holy or unholy alliance put the indispensable
finishing touches to the legislative act which produced the Public
Lending Right, not in all its proper glory but stamped with its first
primitive parliamentary approval.

Elsewhere in these pages the pioneers who started the fight for justice
or the high-powered experts who have protected and enlarged the
original achievement are most happily described. Such a volume as this
was certainly needed to recall how the writers themselves banded
together to achieve these beneficent results. But at one delicate moment
of crisis, when the whole odyssey was so nearly wrecked, it was the

three women who joined forces to save the day: Brigid Brophy, Maureen Duffy and Elizabeth Thomas. Brophy and Duffy had already established themselves as writers of the first rank, but somehow they were prepared to put their prospects and their earnings in jeopardy by the work they did for the Writers Action Group, the famous or infamous body which seemed so qualified to push itself into positions of influence at the moments of crisis. All the male members of that organisation readily concurred that they were little more than figureheads. It was the double-headed Brophy–Duffy machine which truly directed the whole operation.

Elizabeth Thomas had her own claims to literary achievement. She had formerly been the literary editor of *Tribune* and then the assistant literary editor of the *New Statesman*, thereby helping to launch on their careers a series of poets and young writers too lengthy to recite here. Throughout the whole of the Public Lending Right controversy, she was the political adviser to the Lord President of the Council, the so-called Leader of the House of Commons, whose offices looked outward from the most imposing part of Whitehall but which had access in the opposite direction not merely to Number 10 Downing Street or the Chancellor's Department next door but even more commodiously to the place where the Chief Whip presided in Number 12. Whatever the precise physical arrangements, both there and across the road in the House of commons, the communication between the so-called Leader of the House of Commons and the Whips was constant and instant. So narrow at first, and then non-existent in that House of Commons, was the majority of that Labour Government that we could never calculate before what measures we could surely pass.

The two men in charge in Number 12 were Michael Cocks, the Chief Whip, and Walter Harrison, his indefatigable deputy. Neither was noted for his broad intellectual mental sweep, but each had made himself an expert in the processes of that particular Parliament. Contrary to the outward appearance, each had a sneaking residual respect for the books which they knew had helped to produce their Labour movement. Each could offer expert assistance at the most exigent moments. Each could offer assistance at Number 11, the Treasury, where pressures were often most sorely required.

Elizabeth Thomas, in our lordly Lord President's apartments, held all these strings in her hand and could jerk them into action. And, presiding over the whole affair, in that exalted apartment, was a portrait of Jonathan Swift. He had been substituted, as our very first act on arrival in that office, for some nondescript Duke or Stuart royal who should have no place in any democratic pantheon. And of course Jonathan Swift had a special right to preside over our public lending rights festivities, now securely in the hands of our female hierarchy. Had he not written some two hundred years before women got the vote:

If women had the making of the laws
And why they should not I can see no cause.

Never had the women taken charge so perspicaciously as in the public lending right controversies. Never was the final feminine touch so delicate and secure.

The conjunction of events, with the women so fortunately in final control, was not always so evident. Honest reporting requires that we must mention another name whose association with the cause was sadly different. Jennie Lee was the best Minister of Arts this country ever had, and many of us had hoped that she would crown all her other achievements in that department with the introduction of the long promised, often postponed Public Lending Right. But the forces of darkness intervened. The campaign for simple justice which John Brophy and a few friends had launched with such high hopes in the early 1950s had to wait another ten years before another administration would show the will and capacity to frame the necessary legislation. Most members of that House of Commons backed the measure once it was properly presented to them, and most members of the House of Lords, since they had the expert guidance of Lord Ted Willis who had campaigned on the subject as long as John Brophy. Still, the whole enterprise almost foundered in the bogs and sands of parliamentary procedure. If the Public Lending Right Bill of 1979 had not been passed into law as the last or almost the very last act of that particular Government, with the Queen according to custom bestowing her royal assent the very next day, who can say whether the Brophyites would have been forced to wait another few decades to secure their elementary rights?

The Thatcher administration which succeeded the Callaghan one in that fateful year was by no means united on the subject. Norman St John Stevas, her recently appointed spokesman on the arts, was strongly in favour, but Nicholas Ridley, soon to take up an even more prestigious post, was no less passionately opposed. Who would have triumphed in that mighty contest? Moreover, a peculiar breed of parliamentary obstructionists known as the Sproats and the Moates was still in full cry. Since these particular specimens are now extinct, the mere mention of the matter may seem superfluous. But then a more substantial figure altogether sometimes emerged to back Ridley and Co: none other than the future Chancellor of the Exchequer, Nigel Lawson. Being, like St John Stevas, one of the few literate figures in the Thatcher crowd, he should have known better but didn't. No one could tell how this business would proceed and, moreover, the incoming administration would have the excuse that it must attend to some other matters first. It was fortunate indeed for the world of letters that the forces of light prevailed at the moment, especially since, as noted above, they had assumed the unaccustomed physiognomy of the Chief Whip and his Deputy.

Now that public lending right is in operation so successfully in so many countries, if still not as munificently funded as it might be from the point of the authors, it may be hard to recall how fierce and sustained was the opposition to the whole idea. The strongest opposition, if still the most hypocritical, was the claim that somehow the award of those rights to authors would eventually undermine the long-standing principle of free access to our public libraries. Nothing could be further from the thoughts of the authors and the institutions which they represented. Every scheme they ever proposed for establishing the authors' rights faced this problem head on and offered a solution. The vast majority of authors readily recognised that the free libraries were their best friends. So, far from wishing to undermine it, they had the most positive interest in sustaining the principle. But somehow an ironclad prejudice seemed to prevail against all such claims. It was, I suppose, an absolute allegiance to the principles of the free market, at that time being allowed a new lease of Thatcherite life. No such nonsense would have appealed to Jennie Lee at any stage of her political career. If she had known how dour and determined was the opposition of the Treasury, she would have been roused to new exertions, as she had been in the making of the Open University or Aneurin Bevan before her in the making of the National Health Service. As it was, in the arguments with the Treasury in those foetid confrontations of the 1970s, it was the Brophy–Duffy–Thomas combination which ensured that the good fight was fought with relentless application.

And to add a final word from which neither Maureen Duffy nor Elizabeth Thomas would dissent, Brigid Brophy brought to this task, as to everything else she wrote, her touch of genius. 'I am certain of nothing', she would quote, 'but of the holiness of the heart's affections and the truth of the imagination.' She was quoting Keats, but sometimes also she would be certain of something else. The good fight must be fought with a Miltonic fervour, and so John Milton too must be given his place among the campaigners who fought for the writers' rights. No one, second only to my own father and maybe Christopher Hill, the historian of the revolutionary Milton, had ever instructed me so authoritatively to return to John Milton if I wanted to know what heights epic poetry could scale or even how delicate and loving he could be in other moods.

Leaving her bedside one evening after she was stricken by her terrible illness, I saw at the secondhand shop a portable Milton which I naturally felt fate meant me to acquire. She had a few other competing favourites too whom I think she understood better than almost anyone else: Bernard Shaw, Oscar Wilde, Jane Austen and, of course, never to be omitted in any Brophy list, her beloved Mozart. It was that amazing combination of Mozart–Milton which truly scattered the forces of darkness at last.

Indira Gandhi

Her Governing Purpose

Contribution to G. Parthasarathi and H. Y. Sharada Prasad (eds), *Indira Gandhi: statesmen, scholars, scientists and friends remember*, 1985

It was hard to persuade Indira Gandhi to talk about herself. She was the least pretentious, the least egoistical of political leaders: almost a different breed. She wanted to discuss the way the world was going, to pursue an argument, to shun personalities.

After the portrayal of her as a ruthless natural autocrat, it was stunning to meet her: to see with what composure and courtesy she managed her entourage and her cabinet colleagues. She loved her family, of course, and suffered a mother's agony when she saw them pilloried or, as she believed, defamed. But she would still offer her encouragement or inflict chastisement in the same measured, beautiful, articulated accent.

And yet Dr Kissinger described her, on the day of her assassination, as 'self-centred,' and his President, Nixon, once dismissed her as 'that cold-blooded lady'. The scenes when these two notable impressions were implanted in these particular quarters must surely be recalled with some relish. When United States' power was at its zenith, and when it was being flaunted, as it quite often was, to injure India's interest or to insult India's pride, Mrs Gandhi could treat American emissaries with a scorn all her own. I doubt whether she even troubled to raise her voice at those memorable encounters.

It should not be forgotten, particularly at such a moment as this when international relations are smothered in platitudes from the White House and elsewhere, that Indira Gandhi's India, having to tackle problems of poverty and starvation of an awe-inspiring, near-Ethiopian scale, had to face huge additional burdens imposed by American policy: the arming of Pakistan in which capitalist America and Communist China competed with their favours.

She took the military measures necessary to defeat Pakistan, and then set about the more arduous task of seeking the kind of peace which the whole sub-continent cried out for. And she did it with precious little aid, and sometimes against direct obstruction from the West.

We might also remember, despite all the tributes which now flow from Downing Street and the Foreign Office, that it was not always so. India's role as the leader of the non-aligned states, the major independent power between the superpowers, sustained by Mrs Gandhi even more eagerly than by her father, Jawaharlal Nehru, often provoked sneers or real hostility. How helpful it would have been if some of the praise now lavished on her statesmanship had been forthcoming to back her initiatives at the United Nations or Commonwealth Conferences. Instead, almost every Indira Gandhi move was blocked or derided. British policy towards her was never quite so brash and insufferable as United States policy; but often we were content to trail along behind the Nixon–Kissinger example, and behave as if Indira Gandhi herself was the cause of the trouble.

And did she not perform dark and terrible deeds (apart even from the alleged appeasement of Moscow), in the suppression of civil liberties, the enforcement of the Emergency, the imposition of dynastic rule, the latest attack on the Golden Temple? Much more of modern Indian history will have to be unravelled before proper judgement can be passed on all these events. But having seen her in action on quite a number of occasions, I have no doubt about her motives and her skill and her courage in facing all these tests.

Her governing purpose, for which she was willing to risk everything, even her own life, was to preserve the unity of India. *The Unity of India* was the title of the book which Nehru published at the height of the war-time crisis with Britain. It was the unity of India, apart even more from the love of his own home, which made him risk defeats and humiliation for Kashmir.

The unity and the freedom of India could never be allowed to become separate causes. But that was the threat involved in the challenge of Sikh terrorism and she would not try to dodge it. What the Sikh extremists demanded would have achieved what neither Pakistan and insidious American policy nor Chinese pressure combined together had been able to achieve – the destruction of the inheritance her father had left her and her generation: a united India dedicated to the proposition that religious fanaticism was the most evil of all enemies.

Sometimes she would pursue the aim with a patience and fortitude which Nehru himself could not have matched. She had most of his qualities, including, when stirred, the same simple eloquence and dignity and political imagination. But she too had a power of decision in a crisis, a readiness to act alone. I recall going to see her in Delhi at the height of the Emergency: when liberal opinion in the West (liberal in the best sense of the word, more especially democratic socialist) was deeply and justly anxious about the forthcoming trial of the socialist leader, George Fernandes. I was warned by our all-wise Foreign Office officials how inadvisable it would be to raise a whole range of civil liberty issues with her. Even to mention them might cause a diplomatic-cum-auto-cratic explosion.

It was a curious introduction to a meeting in which, on her initiative, we discussed at length every forbidden topic on the list. I had been told she would not tolerate intrusion in India's domestic affairs; she enlarged upon them all. I was told she would never call another democratic election; I came away with the certainty that she would do exactly that.

Of course, she hoped she would win that election and fully expected to do so. Many observers agreed. But the moment when her own hope was confounded, and when she accepted the defeat with such grace and nobility and resilience, was probably the most important moment in the history of Indian democracy.

As it happens, I now recall, at that same interview we had discussed one personal question: political assassination. One political assassination had just occurred in Bangladesh, and some of the fanatical religious groups responsible for the murder of Mahatma Gandhi were at work afresh. Mrs Gandhi knew the peril: she had no wish to suffer the fate of Allende in Chile: some of those fears look more real today.

But she would still take few personal precautions. She would plunge into Indian crowds, to the dismay of her bodyguards.

She was closer to the Indian masses than any other leader, and she would allow nothing to sever the connection. She had a gentleness and coolness which were much more characteristic than the fury which was sometimes alleged to take possession of her whole being. She had an inner strength and a guiding star.

On the day when she was first elected leader of the Congress Party, she recalled some words which her father had written to her in a letter from prison, and which he had often repeated: 'Be brave and all the rest follows. If you are brave you will not fear and will not do anything of which you are ashamed.'

In serving the great cause of the unity of India, Indira Gandhi never acted in haste or in revenge or for personal interest. Sometimes, maybe, she acted with too much premeditation, as in this last crisis. But who will dare elevate that judgement into an indictment? The coolness and the calculation were not a pose. They derived from her deep, loving knowledge of the history of India.

When she was first elected to the party leadership, she recalled some lines from Robert Frost, which were also favourites with her father. He had interests other than politics but he, like she, was driven by the same devotion to his country:

The woods are lovely, dark and deep
But I have promises to keep
And miles to go before I sleep
And miles to go before I sleep.

That was in 1966. What other world leader has had to struggle, amid such tumult through such a time, to keep her promises with her people? She did so right to this terrible end.

The Gandhi–Nehru letters

Review of Sonia Gandhi (ed.), *Two Alone, Two Together: letters between Indira Gandhi and Jawaharlal Nehru, 1940–1964*, in the *Literary Review*, June 1992

'What do you do for books?' This is almost the first anguished cry from father to daughter recorded in these pages, and soon she was putting the same question to him. The persistence of the inquiry shows that there was no affectation between them on this supreme subject. How different from the home life of our own dear ex-Prime Minister where, it might reasonably be imagined, mother talks and money talks, and nobody and nothing else gets a word in.

The pre-eminence given to books within Jawaharlal Nehru's household may be partly attributed to the huge long periods he spent in prison. If reading and writing are permitted by the authorities, incarceration itself becomes a different matter entirely. It may be the making of the man, as with John Bunyan's *Pilgrim's Progress*. A substantial majority of the letters published here in this mammoth and magnificent volume were written in prison, either by Jawaharlal himself or by his daughter, Indira, even though other of their prison letters or writings have been published before and even though the last letters included here are those exchanged between them just before his death in 1964.

It is still the prison letters which can move us most deeply, as they were designed to shape the mind and heart of his beloved daughter. Some may recall how in a previous period of imprisonment – in the early 1930s – he had started to write, for the benefit of his twelve-year-old Indira, his thousand-page-long *Glimpses of World History*. For many of my generation, this was probably our first introduction to Nehru and certainly our first introduction to Indira.

Indira's reaction to the reception of that volume is recorded here, not exactly on her thirteenth birthday but not so long after. He was, of course, not only a loving father but an inspired teacher, and a master of English prose. He gives some hints here about how he achieved that feat, and the claim is made without any strain or boasting. He wanted Indira especially, but everyone else too, to understand what he was writing, and the requirement was all the greater when he saw how Indians had never been given the chance to tell the story of India. If he had not become India's first free Prime Minister he would happily have been India's first free historian.

However, he remained always, in the teeth of every temptation, a citizen of the world, and one who saw more persistently than any other leading statesman of the century that freedom must find expression in a universal language. He would often remark how, for his prison reading, he would be driven back to the classics. Often it was one of these in the famous Everyman edition which he would send on to Indira in what she disgustedly called her 'Female Ward'. She became as addicted as himself, adding to the dish her own taste for modern poets.

It is a delicious irony to be reminded what the Everyman edition of the English classics – now celebrating their rejuvenation – did for the British Empire. Just at the period when our old imperial masters such as Chamberlain, Baldwin, yes and Churchill too, were supposing they could keep the old world order by locking up Nehru and Gandhi and Co in prison, Everyman were quickly supplying the inmates with their revolutionary Bibles – Swift's *Gulliver's Travels*, Voltaire's *Charles XII*, Franklin's *Autobiography*, Milton's *Paradise Lost,* Plato's *Republic*. But don't be confused or confined by this list. The richness of Nehru's reading overflowed its banks like the Ganges.

Indira was born with a frail body, and this was one reason for her long separation from the father she adored. Keeping her in touch with India was one of his constant themes – 'Apart from Urdu and Hindi, it might be worthwhile for you to start on a voyage of discovery of India.' Indira needed little incitement. She longed to be at his side, and to translate her own ambitions and understandings into Indian realities. She turned that frail frame into an unbeatable will; indeed when she got the chance she broke more decisively with the old British connection than ever he was able to do, and he would not have complained. He longed to express his kinship with the Indian masses; she performed that role better.

Jawaharlal Nehru was supposed to be the foremost exponent of democratic statesmanship in this century, one who served his people with no thought of self and fulfilled his words in action, whereas Indira Gandhi is charged with faltering at the supreme moment of crisis, allowing personal emotion to sway her judgement.

In my estimate, it was not quite like that. The political temperaments of the two of them were not so dissimilar and, as we may learn afresh from these pages, they had both been taught in the same good school – with its excellent Everyman library around the corner. But Nehru never lost his streak of aristocratic scorn, sometimes a deficiency, sometimes an asset – for example, when forced to deal with English aristocratic nincompoops, and there were always plenty of them around.

Indira Gandhi was the least egotistical great statesman I ever met. She hardly ever talked about herself; she could reduce all personal questions to a proper perspective. She was much more interested in the great political questions: the way the world was going, how the unity of her beloved India could be preserved, how the poverty of her people could be broken, how nuclear annihilation could be averted. All these interests and allegiances she acquired when these letters, so admirably presented by Sonia Gandhi, were being written. Together they fashioned her unique character, and so I found this book the most faithful portrait of her ever painted.

Ruth Khama

Review of Michael Dutfield, *A Marriage of Inconvenience: the persecution of Seretse and Ruth Khama*, in the *Guardian*, 5 April 1990

Ruth and Seretse Khama had a love affair which could match anything in history or legend. Right at the start they made a vow of eternal fealty and kept it against odds far more overwhelming than any they could have foreseen. They were the modern Eloise and Abelard, and indeed there were so many sensational twentieth-century additions to the tale that another mystery is why we have had to wait so long for the unravelling.

Sometimes the romance of Edward VIII and Mrs Simpson is recited as the most spectacular of our century. I once heard – to my bitter shame, as I will explain – a British Prime Minister compare Edward's case with Seretse's, and that recollection on its own should help to remind us how sharply different are our thoughts today on racial inter-marriage from those still generally accepted fifty odd years ago.

When the twenty-four-year-old Ruth told her businessman, church-loving father that she intended to marry a young heir to an African

chieftainship, he threw her out of the house; she was given the tradi-
tional order never to darken those doors again. When the proposal was
broached to his doting uncle Tshekedi in faraway Bechuanaland, he was
no less outraged and determined to use every weapon at his command,
including incitements to the British Government to intervene, to stop the
whole scandalous business. His first step was to send an urgent
summons for help to the British High Commissioner in Cape Town, a
most eminent British proconsul with a famous name, Sir Evelyn Baring.

The little protectorate of Bechuanaland which enjoyed indirect rule
by the British High Commissioner in Cape Town or faraway London,
with occasional spasms of direct rule from the same quarters could
easily be overrun by forces from the neighbouring South African Union.
That much was obvious. What was not quite so clear was what was to be
the continent-wide consequence of the fiendish policy of apartheid on
which the freshly powerful Nationalist Party in South Africa was just
embarking or – to add an even more explosive secret ingredient to the
dish – what might follow from the discovery just at the same time of
precious supplies of uranium in nearby South-west Africa or the
Namibia of the future.

Ruth and Seretse could be pardoned for not being prepared to pay too
much attention to the South African connection. Indeed, they were
constantly assured by all concerned, British Ministers and civil servants
alike, that their banishment from Seretse's homeland had nothing to do
with South African pressure and everything to do with Seretse's unsuit-
ability for the role of chieftain of his tribe.

This was a lie, and it was the readiness of the British Government and
its agents to tell it which led to the sequence of injustice and tragedy and
infamy. The first sinner perhaps was Sir Evelyn Baring at the centre of
the South African web. At first hearing of the news he felt no sense of
hostility towards the Ruth–Seretse marriage; he was no friend of
apartheid; he hated the new mood of persecution which he saw rising in
the post-war South Africa. But he did think it must be appeased; he

thought any other route spelt bloodshed and conquest for beleaguered Bechuanaland.

Sir Evelyn's unpublishable view won approval, much of it grudging, some of it eager. Sir Percivale Liesching, Permanent Secretary at the Commonwealth Office – according to the present author's account – quickly became a positive enthusiast for the recommended course and was quite prepared to engage in acts of deceit against Seretse himself or large-scale deception of the British public. He got one reward a few years later when he was appointed High Commissioner to succeed Baring. He doubtless lived to appease another day.

However, many offered similar advice, without any of Sir Percivale's relish. They did fear a South African nationalist putsch with unforeseeable consequences for the whole continent. When Baring went to see the great, still widely honoured Field Marshal Smuts at the height of the crisis, he too came down solidly against Seretse. Trevor Huddleston, a justly trusted observer on the spot, gave similar advice which he later much regretted. And the two British Ministers primarily concerned, Philip Noel-Baker and Patrick Gordon Walker, found themselves torn by terrible emotions even though both came, as we would think now, to the wrong conclusion – the acceptance of the lie.

One man kept the same imperturbable demeanour throughout the whole affair, the Clem Attlee who made the mollifying comparison with Edward VIII, a rogue in his gallery. At the end he sent a special note of congratulation to Sir Evelyn Baring, but it is not recorded that any note of apology was offered to Seretse, even after he, with Ruth's assistance, had played such a notable part in making Bechuanaland one of the best democratically governed countries in Africa.

Michael Dutfield has written the best account of the wretched or glorious business. He clearly won the trust of Ruth Khama, the most essential element for his success, but he adds to it a wealth of knowledge gained from a variety of sources, Cabinet papers and the newspapers. I am sorry only to see that he does not include *Tribune* among his newspaper sources. *Tribune* unravelled the 'appeasement' aspects of the crime and the crisis at the time, and called upon both Attlee and Gordon Walker to offer an apology as 'a matter of principle'. It was claimed to be a matter of principle in 1950; Michael Dutfield proves the case in 1990.

Peggy Ashcroft

Review of Garry O'Connor, *The Secret Woman: a life of Peggy Ashcroft*, in the *Evening Standard*, 10 March 1997

She was as sweet as Juliet, as innocent as Desdemona, as faithful as Cordelia, as captivating as Rosalind, as merciful and magnificent as Portia, as playful and coquettish as Cleopatra, and this is only the short list. According to her latest biographer, she was, even more remarkably, the foremost woman Shakespearean actress who could hold her own in the age of Laurence Olivier, Ralph Richardson and John Gielgud, which means that she must be ranked among the greatest of all time.

Garry O'Connor loves the theatre and he loves Shakespeare; he has written lovingly about both. Whether he loves Peggy Ashcroft is another matter, and Peggy's friends may raise doubts. He has written about her private life in a manner which they will question and which she would have abhorred. He does so, quoting Dr Johnson as his shield: 'The business of a biography is often to pass slightly over those performances and incidents which produce vulgar greatness to lead the thoughts into domestic privacies, and display the minute details of daily life.'

Indeed. It can hardly be disputed that there is a case for the Dr Johnson form of biography and, coincidentally, Boswell clinched the case in his biography of Dr Johnson himself. However, this is an illustration of only one half of the argument. Intrusions into domestic privacies can be conducted on such a scale that everything else is elbowed out of the picture, including any kind of greatness, vulgar or classical. And this, alas, is what has happened to this biography. Long before its actual publication, sections of the press were screwing every kind of salacious details out of the story of Peggy's own love life. O'Connor cannot be held responsible for all these developments, although his own title, *The Secret Woman*, might be seen as an encouragement to it.

His book is much better than these pre-publication titillations might suggest. Peggy Ashcroft's legion of true admirers should have the patience to read every word of it, and they will be rewarded at last. Once he escapes from the gossip and returns to the theatre itself, the biographer seems to show a better judgement, or perhaps it is Peggy herself being allowed to take over. She could be secretive, never responding to the appeals to speak for herself. She would never do it.

What she could do and would do, with increasing confidence as she turned to play different roles, was to discuss her understanding of them, and how she would add brilliant new discoveries to the list in the works of, say, Ibsen, Beckett, Pinter and a few more.

But it was Shakespeare who retained his special hold on her and she on him. 'I think he must have loved women very much,' said Peggy herself. 'He felt that even when women were capable of acts of cruelty or violence, there was a compulsion of emotion or frustration which forced them on.' Her new biographer does understand the special affinity between the two.

He redeems his whole book with his conclusions. Nothing vulgar about her greatness; it was a new light shed on the infinite variety of Shakespearean womanhood.

Rebecca West

Review of Bonnie Kime Scott (ed.), *Selected Letters of Rebecca West*, in the *Guardian*, 15 April 2000

'I just love that woman,' Jill Craigie would say of Rebecca West, and Rebecca would eagerly repay the compliment. Their friendship blossomed only in the last dozen years of Rebecca's long life, but since it was chiefly on Jill's prompting that Rebecca returned to the journalism of her flaming youth, the two of them together took the century in their feminist strides. Like Jill, Rebecca was an artist in everything she touched and saw. Each had a specially sharpened visual sense, which Jill could translate into films and pictures, and Rebecca into words.

Again and again throughout our own quite lengthy lives, Jill and I found ourselves bumping afresh into some revelation of the H. G. Wells–Rebecca West saga. I first met him at a weekend party at Max Beaverbrook's country estate in the late 1930s. He was the hero of my early twenties, having completed my conversion to socialism with

Tono-Bungay and several other of his titles. At his side on that occasion was not Rebecca but his last and maybe truest love, Moura Budberg. She became for me a heroine, too, keeping alive my connection with HG until he died eight years later.

The H. G. Wells of the Second World War fought with all his might for the rights of man; Beaverbrook's *Evening Standard* played a notable part in that victory, proudly printing every one of his red-hot revolutionary words. Both Jill and I fell victims to Max Beaverbrook's charm. Outside observers could not understand the relationship, but he was a firm friend to both of us until the day of his death. No topic of conversation seemed to be banned between us – especially his interest in the worlds of H. G. Wells, Arnold Bennett and so forth – but in all our conversations, one name never cropped up: that of Rebecca West.

Not until years later, when HG and Max and Rebecca were all dead, did Rebecca's posthumously published novel *Sunflower* tell the story of how the slightly ageing HG was displaced in her affections by the magnificent young Max. It was a delicate, matchless love story, intelligently told. But no one could know about this at the time; Rebecca was presumably resolved to give offence to neither of her lovers.

What happened between Rebecca and Max in their original affair is not finally clarified either in the novel or in these letters, but every later development is honourable to them both. He helped her directly in her journalistic career, and would do his best to assist when her more outrageous friends, such as the anarchist leader Emma Goldman, were being pilloried in the newspapers.

If you have not yet read *Sunflower*, order your copy now. Don't be deterred by some of the jealous reviewers who dismissed the work as inferior when it did finally appear; Rebecca knew better. Her suppression of the novel must have been all the more galling when she saw that her literary opponents showed no such reticence. Enemy number one was her own son by HG, Anthony West, who wrote a damning autobiographical novel, *Heritage*, while Rebecca was still alive, and pursued his vendetta even after her death with an unrelenting fury that can still turn the stomach.

In these pages she can defend herself against all his accusations. 'Posterity will never forgive a bad mother,' she would sometimes say to Jill. Here she is vindicated; Anthony gets his due. He had, for example, a terrible quarrel with his father in HG's last days which he wretchedly tried to blame on Rebecca; in fact, it was much more the result of his own imperfect sympathies with his father.

Along with many writers of the century, headed by HG himself, Rebecca understood the importance of Anglo–American associations – she made her name in the US in the 1920s, and ever after kept a foot on both sides of the Atlantic – so the editing of this volume by the American Bonnie Kime Scott is all the more appropriate.

Some of the best liberal spirits of the age became her closest friends. A few of them at moments of stress might have questioned her allegiance, but, if need be, she could counter-attack with all her polemical might. Her insights take command at the most appropriate moments: 'The Statue of Liberty', she said at her first glance, 'is a washout – she gets her stays at the same place as Queen Mary's.'

A most prolific letter writer herself – she claimed sometimes to write several before breakfast – she had a special appreciation of how full volumes of letters could inform a proper judgement of the greatest writers. She had not always been as aware of Oscar Wilde's genius as might have been expected, for instance, but after his letters were published she sent his son Vyvyan Holland a glowing response, full of fresh understanding: 'I don't think anyone could read the volume without liking your father more than before.' These words were intended to bring comfort to Merlin, Oscar's grandson, as well as to his father. The Rebecca who wrote this letter and several more of the same quality truly knew what love was.

But what of her relationship with HG, the most significant of her life? They had their rows, but nothing to compare with the savagery of those with Anthony. For several years after their first meeting, HG drew on his own new knowledge of Rebecca to portray the new woman – from Fanny in *The Dream* to Helen in *The World of William Clissold* – and what a wonderful breed she was. The literary connection between the two was brilliantly unravelled by J. R. Hammond in his *H. G. Wells and Rebecca West*, published in 1991. He showed how each was indispensable to the other, and where each could claim to be innovators.

The last book I read to Jill was this collection of letters from the woman she so greatly honoured. No hardship, I can assure you: the wit pours forth on every page along with the lamentations. Jill sometimes suspected me of treating her Rebecca less kindly than I should – especially when HG was misbehaving in a big way. And yet, having read and re-read every word, the main conclusion is unchallengeable. The love between them triumphed over everything else: the reconciliations were always much more significant than the ruptures.

The last of these came in the 1940s, when they shared a vision that the England they both loved could rejoice in a victory over the forces of evil. Anthony failed to join that period of exhilaration: he even helped to spread the insinuation that his father's mind was failing. The reality was nothing of the kind: with Moura on one side and Rebecca on the other, he was celebrating the freedom which he had done as much as any of his countrymen to secure.

Part 3

The collaborators

Gore Vidal's Montaigne

Michel de Montaigne! The mere mention of the name has restorative effects, the kind of healing balm which our own Hampstead-reared John Keats claimed could be the quality of great poetry.

Keats himself, of course, was a Montaigneite, having been instructed in the habit either by William Hazlitt or Leigh Hunt, each of whom acquired the taste with their mother's milk or their mistress's liberations.

Hazlitt was, for my money, the very greatest Montaigneite of them all. He modelled himself on Montaigne, and provided in his own essays – the whole lot of them – the nearest equivalent to the mammoth autobiography, which is what Montaigne's own book of *Essayes*, published first in the year 1580, truly were. 'The great merit of Montaigne', wrote Hazlitt, 'was that he may be said to have been the first who had the courage to say as an author what he felt as a man. He was in the truest sense a man of original mind, that is he had the power of looking at things for himself or as they really were, instead of blindly trusting to, and finally repeating, what they told him they were.'

That was the beginning of his discoveries. Montaigne was the model for all the realist writers, all those who truly struggled to make words like things, from Jonathan Swift and Alexander Pope to Byron and Edmund Burke and Hazlitt himself, from Shakespeare to Joyce. But the names which must be properly dropped in this context are legion, as you shall all see – especially any pupils in the Hampstead Cockney School who might momentarily be enticed into foreign stratospheres of fancy and fantasy and sentiment off the leash. Montaigne can bring us all back to earth.

But first we must deal with the phenomenon of a new translation of Montaigne's *Essays*, and immediately the question is posed: Why not read him in the original French? I recall almost the first time when the name Montaigne was made to penetrate my thick skull. My father had just added Montaigne to his list of heroes, and he made up his mind – I should think he was in his early sixties – to learn French in order to appreciate the master properly.

Wonderful advice no doubt, but let me hasten to add that no one should be deterred by it from reading Montaigne in the currently available translations. Shakespeare did so, Ben Jonson did so, Swift, Pope and Hazlitt and a whole host of others – never forgetting the two Jewish Montaigneites, Disraeli, father and son, who upheld the cause of Jewish humanism derived from their great founder. And then again, Montaigne himself, for all his vast erudition, was quite ready to read some of his favourites in translation, if that was the only way he could get his hands on them.

So a few more necessary words about the translators. Montaigne published his various editions in the 1590s; each one following the first had his own scrawled additions in the margins. John Florio's translation, which was good enough for Shakespeare, was published in 1603. He held the field throughout most of the seventeenth century until Charles

Cotton published his in 1685–6. He was a real poet too, as successive members of the Hazlitt family recognised. Which edition provoked Bolingbroke to taunt his friend Alexander Pope about his 'old prating friend', and which one Jonathan Swift selected to assist the tuition of his Vanessa, is not quite clear. But the truth is that they were all good, and all had their special merits.

The same applies in modern times. Thirty years ago Hamish Hamilton published *The Complete Works of Montaigne – Essays/Travel Journal/Letters,* newly translated by Donald M. Frame. This was my introduction and it was hard to see how such an achievement could ever be excelled, and I was happy to read recently in the *Times Literary Supplement* that such a fine expert as Gore Vidal agreed with me.

But he was also commending another excursion: *Michel de Montaigne: The Complete Essays*, by Dr M. A. Screech, senior research fellow of All Souls, Oxford, following up with this splendid new edition his *Montaigne and Melancholy – The Wisdom of the Essays*, published in 1983. Gore Vidal concluded: 'Screech now replaces Frame at my bedside.'

I will not go so far. Indeed, since Colin Frame introduced me to Montaigne, I will never desert him, since also have I read and re-read essay after essay, among so many towns and villages which line the banks of Montaigne's Dordogne or in the municipal library of Bordeaux, where they will bring for your inspection their Bordeaux edition scrawled over by the author, who was never himself satisfied.

Moreover, on my estimate, Screech has slightly prejudiced himself in advance. He chose for the title of his earlier work *Montaigne and Melancholy*. Dr Screech later explained how Montaigne's melancholy was of a special sanguine nature. But the implication of that conjunction cannot so easily be removed.

One aspect of Montaigne's composure, I believe, was that he would never yield to these pressures. I opened Colin Frame's book almost at random and read an essay, 'Of Sadness':

I am one of those freest from this passion. I neither like it or respect it, although everyone has decided to honour it, as if at a fixed price, with particular favour. They clothe wisdom, virtue, conscience with it: a stupid and monstrous ornament. The Italians, more appropriately, have baptised malignancy with its name. For it is always a harmful quality, always insane, and, as being always cowardly and base, the stoics forbid their sages to feel it.

Gore Vidal's *TLS* article was called 'The Stoical Genius of Montaigne'. And the sub-titles read: 'Uncommon Sense: The Charitable Clarity of Montaigne's Perceptions'.* And on some of the greatest matters, such as man's relationships with animals, Montaigne was centuries ahead of his time. He taught that the deadliest sin was cruelty, although it was never scheduled by the Christians as such. He wrote (in the Florio translation): 'I cannot well endure a seelie dew-bedabbled hare to groan when she is seized upon by the hounds.'

The British House of Commons when it last debated the matter just before the last election had not caught up with Montaigne and while men and women could be guilty of such barbarous operations, he was not inclined to sympathise too readily with melancholic moods.

---

*   *Times Literary Supplement*, January 1984.

Edmund Wilson's Jean-Jacques

We serve philosophy worthily only with the same ardour that we feel for a mistress.

Jean-Jacques Rousseau, *La Nouvelle Heloise, Part II: Letters*

How to read history? The question may seem subordinate or trivial or, worse still, an unhappy memory of just another Philistine pursuit associated with the long forgotten, never-to-be-lamented Thatcherite era. But for democratic socialists, for those who still want to change the world and society to meet the tests of the twenty-first century, it is the most exciting and inescapable and persistent of all questions.

At least the historians, or the best of them, may be expected to concur. They seek to cover every branch of human knowledge and to raise the debate to the highest pitch – until at the supreme moments, the poets take over. Demarcation disputes at these lofty altitudes have their significance, but the different branches of attainment may merge much more readily than is sometimes supposed. Shelley may have stretched the claim when he called the poets the unacknowledged legislators of the world, but his defence of poetry was even more directly a defence of politics. The poets, or the greatest of them, devised a history of their own to match that of the historians; they expressed the spirit of their own age, and they sound the trumpets for the future.

Heinrich Heine, who will make several appearances in these pages – he had courage and imagination in the highest degree, and it is the combination of these two qualities which is the truest mark of greatness – expressed the same confidence in the writer's power with his customary readiness to challenge accepted opinions, even those of his own allies:

Mark this you proud men of action. You are nothing but the unwilling tools of the men of thought, who, often in the humblest silence have presented all your work, in the clearest fashion. Maximilian Robespierre was nothing but the hand of Jean-Jacques Rousseau – the bloody hand which drew from the womb of time the body, the soul of which had been created by Rousseau. That restless torment which embittered the life of Jean-Jacques – may it not have been due to a presentiment of the midwife of the thoughts required to come into the world?

Heinrich Heine, the poet–historian of his own people, still had a prophetic vision of something greater still, although his own people, particularly in their hours of death and persecution, would usually find it difficult to acknowledge that there could ever be anything greater, and would therefore turn in their fury to Heine himself, to brand him as Jean-Jacques was branded.

The men and women who have spoken most bravely in the interests of all humanity, prepared to shed at the hour of crisis their allegiance to any tribal god, exerting their intellectual power to the extreme limit to expose cant and fraud and intimidation in every form, are a very special company. How they have handed down the torch to us is the true prescription of the way history should be read.

When Edmund Wilson wrote his study on the writing and acting of history, *To the Finland Station*, – it was mostly written in the late 1930s and published in 1941 – he made only a few references to Jean-Jacques Rousseau. But this choice was not intended to express any disrespect or dishonour. It was rather his assumption that everyone could recognise, without the story being recited, how widely the revolutionary ideas of Rousseau had been accepted and how the world had moved on to consider the next stage in the Revolution. In humanity's advance, Rousseau's doctrine, Wilson assumed, 'had so permeated the air of the time that one did not need to imbibe it by reading: the doctrine that mankind is naturally good and that it is only institutions which have perverted it.'

As his title indicated, Wilson was chiefly concerned to trace modern Marxist interpretations of history, but he also introduced his new readers (including this one) to a range of writers, before and after Marx, who had produced a new kind of historical writing which initiated a new strand in humanist tradition: Vico, Jules Michelet, Leon Trotsky. All of these write about the driving determination to shape the future. Edmund Wilson himself in his *Finland Station* took and shared this intention, and the modern collapse of the Soviet system in the 1990s is sometimes invoked as a disproof of Wilson's theories or prophecies of the 1930s or the 1940s. Such misapprehensions may provoke a series of mistaken deductions. What the critics are eager to avoid is an appreciation of the democratic tradition which Rousseau enunciated.

It is a measure of the scale of the modern intellectual counter-revolution that the ideas themselves and the man who first enunciated them with such overwhelming force have now to be defended, are regarded even as one potent origin of mankind's (and womankind's) present afflictions. We shall return to Wilson's conclusion, but let us examine first how some others recognised the potency of Rousseau's doctrines and how many among the very best of man's modern achievements would be put in jeopardy if he himself is now to be exhibited as some kind of political scarecrow.

Fortunately for us all, Rousseau wrote in a beautiful French, a style of his own invention which was a revolution in itself – like Wordsworth's claim to have discovered a new, simple means of communication in his *Lyrical Ballads* preface – but Rousseau, be it not forgotten, did it first. Of course, something must be lost in translation. The safe rule therefore is to multiply tenfold, say, the burning heat which the sentences may still retain in English, and then their French or rather European effect may be gauged. By the way, it is worth recalling that the reading of Rousseau's writings vastly increased during the French Revolution itself. In one sense, the Revolution made him, as he had helped to make the Revolution. Moreover, in the four decades after 1789, all the truly effective, enduring defenders of the Revolution were disciples of Rousseau – Heine in Germany, Stendhal in France, Byron and Shelley and Hazlitt in England. Each was eager not merely to acknowledge his debt but to recapture the moment when they had first read his words of deliverance and exultation.

Jean-Paul Marat was a great admirer of Rousseau; and so was his assassin, Charlotte Corday. It was on Robespierre's recommendation that he was sent to the Pantheon; and he was the one author whose books could persuade Immanuel Kant, the philosopher of peace, to interrupt his daily walk around the streets of Königsberg. He wrote the first perceptive psychological study on the education of children, and, according to his own confession, allowed his own children to be taken off to the Foundling Hospital. He wrote bitter, ignorant invectives against the rights of women, and yet many of his women readers, including even Madame Roland or Mary Wollstonecraft, remained the willing, captivated devotees of the rest of his works. The seeming contradictions can be endlessly emphasised and multiplied. Frequently, even those who re-examine his writings with scruple and insight seem still to become lost amid the power and the passion of his full achievement.

Sometimes the conclusion offered is that his influence must be attributed almost entirely to his mastery of the French language. Certainly he was such a master, but could he also have been such a fool or such a monster, such a purveyor of poisonous, totalitarian doctrines as he is sometimes presented? It is hard to believe. Could *Mein Kampf* have been written in good German? Can a great work of literature also be a thing of inspissated evil? Possibly the writings of the Marquis de Sade may qualify under this heading, and yet not even he has been accused of such a comprehensive capacity for wickedness as Rousseau. Jonathan Swift's *Gulliver's Travels* certainly would fill this requirement, but this, in the truest sense of the term, is the exception which proves the rule. The charge against Swift can be turned against his accusers, as he himself did in his lifetime and as his real defenders have successfully proved in later times.

We must pause once again to remind ourselves how extensive and deadly is the modern charge-sheet against Rousseau. Writers in the age of Hitler and Stalin and Brezhnev and Gorbachev seek to brand him as one of the founders of twentieth-century totalitarianism. If responsibility for the Paris Terror of the 1790s can be successfully pinned upon him, these later extensions of guilt are made plausible and precise. If such assertions are dismissed as fanciful or far-fetched, we may cite the reception given to the most notable revisionist history of the French Revolution produced in the centennial year, *Citizens!* by Simon Schama, a brilliantly compiled new chronicle of events and yet at the same time one which offers a new interpretation. One of Schama's theses is that violence and bloodshed disfigured the revolutionary proceedings through the whole period and indeed started much earlier than the Terror of 1794 or even the September massacres of 1792. The cruelty and bloodlust were there for all to see when the Bastille was overthrown in July 1789. In Schama's handling of the whole affair, the achievements of the Revolution are reduced to nothing and the need for ever starting it is dismissed. His record of events is at least as deeply hostile to the men and women who made them as any of the great French conservative historians – Taine, for example. Indeed, Schama, it may be noted, to make sure we do him no injustice, is comparatively reticent in his treatment of Rousseau – a restraint which may be attributable to the fact that his own particular hero, Talleyrand, was also an admirer of Rousseau and, even after the Revolution, kept a statue of him on his mantelpiece at Valency opposite another of Voltaire.

Whatever the reason for his comparative restraint, Schama thereby drew a mild rebuke from his most enthusiastic reviewer. Mr Bernard Levin, writing in the *Sunday Times* of March 1988 asserted that he had only one reservation of any significance to make in his encomium. 'Schama makes almost nothing', he says, 'of the debt of the French Revolution, and of every tyranny since, to Rousseau's malign doctrine of the general will.' This doctrine, he continued, is 'in truth no more than the principle that some people know what is good for other people better than the others do themselves.' But in truth, to quote Mr Levin, Rousseau neither said nor implied anything of the kind, as a correspondent Mr N. J. H. Dent pointed out in a letter published the following week. Rousseau wrote, he said (*The Social Contract*, Book 2, Chapter 4): 'The general will, to be really such ... must come from all and apply to all.' Mr Dent's comment deserves full quotation: 'How a will which comes from all is the same as a principle that some people know what is good for other people eludes me. But the damage was done years ago; some people will always tell other people what they should think about Rousseau.'

Greater critics than Bernard Levin and greater historians than Simon Schama have found themselves baffled and entranced by the phenomenon of Jean-Jacques Rousseau. He was once the victim of a bitter dissertation from T. S. Eliot, but the deeply reactionary nature of his assault was partly corrected by the fact that it was accompanied by an attack from an exactly opposite point of view, from Bertrand Russell. Often Rousseau's intellectual contributions to the great debates of the eighteenth century were contrasted most unfavourably with Voltaire's, and this comparison came most easily to English readers, since Voltaire was always a strong Anglophile while Rousseau became at last a raging, impenitent Anglophobe. Wit normally survives better than rhetoric. Voltaire had a superabundance of the first gift and Rousseau none whatever. Voltaire looked across the Channel with the same cool, critical mocking eyes which he could apply to any problem, and his conclusion was all the more agreeable to his English readers. It was true that the post-1688 England had garnered a rich harvest from the Glorious Revolution, and the contrast with the suffocation in France was all the more grating and unbearable. Voltaire applied to the dilemmas of his age his combined wit and humanity. The first was the sharpest instrument used for the purpose of political demolition since the days of Tacitus, and the second also had its unique quality: *Ecrase l'Infame* was no dilettante slogan, and the chosen enemy was seemingly the most powerful institution in this world – or rather this world or the next. By contrast, the shapes or visions which appeared to Rousseau were ill-defined; he saw through a glass darkly; his chosen enemies had changing features; his special themes seemed to become constantly enlarged. The two men had to sift the same evidence, face the same challenges and forge conclusions which would envisage a new future. It was in this last sphere that Rousseau proved himself the great prophet.

Almost always, throughout their lifetime, they were rivals. Each could unloose against the other scandalous, unforgiving invectives; each could protest that to be mentioned in the same breath as the other was the deepest insult. Yet their fame and achievement were locked together for ever, comrades in arms, victors in the same cause. 'It is Voltaire's fault; It is the fault of Rousseau!' was the song of mockery sung by Victor Hugo's character in *Les Miserables*. The double accusation was just: no two men had contributed more to help produce the convulsions of the French Revolution, and yet, in one sense, an injustice is done by the comparison to Rousseau. Voltaire was the representative spokesman of the Encyclopedists who condemned the old society in terms which could never be refuted – until at last maybe the Schamas appeared on the scene to modify the indictment or to plead mitigation. But Rousseau, for the most part, thought and acted and above all wrote alone – even on occasion daring to take issue with some of the mighty leading Encyclopedists themselves. He himself thought he was engaged in original discoveries. He could pretentiously claim as much, or rather, the pretensions proved to be true, the resonance of his rhetoric was shown to be justified. What he forecast or encouraged or presented in the 1760s was translated into action in the revolutionary decade of the 1790s and whenever thereafter men and women in other lands or periods looked back to that epoch for inspiration. He was the prophet of democracy. He rarely used the word in its modern connotation; it had not been invented, or developed at the time when he was writing. But many of the essential elements in the modern democratic creed were elaborated by him and, what's more, given revolutionary potency at a time when the idea itself had not been deformed by the political philosophers. Why should the men of the people take orders from their self-appointed betters, who clearly had no claim to the title? What justification could there be for the cruel inequalities which men could see all round them? Why should they continue to suffer insult? What right had authority to exercise its powers and why should not something much better be put in its place? No one before Rousseau had put these questions in such blunt terms and given such blunt answers.

According to Rousseau himself, his *Social Contract*, published in 1762, was the most important of his political writings. But, looking back on his achievements, attention is naturally directed to *A Discourse on the Arts and Sciences*, published in 1749, which won him the prize at the Academy of Dijon, or the *Discourse on Inequality*, published in 1753. Each of these contained revolutionary stirrings more explicit than those he defined later, notably in his attack on the institution of property itself. One other irreverent document *Emile*, challenging the Church on its most intimate claim about the education of children, appeared in 1762. The year before, in 1761, had appeared *La Nouvelle Heloise,* which seemingly was of a quite different character altogether, and to which we shall return later. Each of these writings, and even more so perhaps the notorious *Confessions*, written later and only published after his death, had running through them a strand of originality. Each contained the glimpse of ideas and sometimes their definition which had never been treated before.

It is impossible to determine the exact effect of each new Rousseauite outpouring; each contained its original revelations combined with much else which could be dismissed as irrelevant or absurd. For the generation which came a little later, for those who, we shall see, understood his real worth, the liberating influences were the achievement of a kind of composite figure, the man and his work. It was as if a giant revolving searchlight was lighting up the tempestuous political waters all round; suddenly great stretches of sea were exposed by a blinding revelation, while surrounding areas were still left as black as ever. Neither his political philosophy nor his personal outlook was in any sense a consistent, elaborate whole – say, like Immanuel Kant's, although Kant, it may be noted, was a fervent admirer of Rousseau. Yet all his writings were imbued with a new spirit about man's rights, an appeal to the people against their rulers, against authority, an underlying democratic fervour. Although Rousseau himself so rarely used the word, it becomes necessary for the purpose of proper definition. Some of his special enemies did understand. When the French Minister, Choiseul, wanted to warn some of the men in charge of affairs at Geneva about the threat to the orders of the State involved in Rousseau's *Social Contract,* he advised them that, in the guise of accepting the will of the people, what he proposed was an absolute Democracy, with a capital D.

Each Rousseau book opens with a trumpet blast, *The Social Contract or Principles of Political Right*, to inscribe the full title, the most famous of all. Whatever the qualifications which might come later, he had a genius for declarations; memorable, forthright, resonant, forever fresh and challenging. Here was the opening paragraph of the first part of his 1749 *Discourse*:

It is a noble and beautiful spectacle to see man raising himself, so to speak, from nothing by his own exertions; dissipating, by the light of reason, all the thick clouds in which he was by nature enveloped; mounting above himself; soaring in thought even to the celestial regions; like the sun, encompassing with giant strides the vast extent of the universe; and, what is still grander and more wonderful, going back into himself, there to study man and get to know his own nature, his duties and his end. All these miracles we have seen renewed within the last few generations.

Or here were the first paragraphs in his *Dissertation on Inequality*:

It is of man that I have to speak; and the question I am investigating shows me that it is to men that I must address myself; for questions of this sort are not asked by those who are afraid to honour truth. I shall then confidently uphold the cause of humanity before the wise men who invite me to do so, and shall not be dissatisfied if I acquit myself in a manner worthy of my subject and of my judges.

I conceive that there are two kinds of inequality among the human species; one, which I call natural or physical, because it is established by nature, and consists in a difference of age, health, bodily strength, and the qualities of the mind or of the soul: and another, which may be called moral or political inequality, because it depends on a mind of convention, and is established, or at least authorised by the consent of men. This latter consists of the different privileges, which some men enjoy to the prejudice of others; such as that of being more rich, more honoured, more powerful or even in a position to exact obedience.

And here was the opening of the *Social Contract*, part familiar, part less so:

Man is born free; and everywhere he is in chains. One thinks himself the master of others and still remains a greater slave than they. How

*did this change come about: I do not know. What can make it legiti-
mate: That question I think I can answer.*

Others before Rousseau, in the quest to discover what could give an
effective or indeed the first authority to a government in a state, had
looked for it in some fanciful contract between the rulers and the ruled,
but both in the *Social Contract* and before in the *Discourse on
Inequality*, he described the process in terms at least as realistically
effective, as revolutionary or democratic, whichever term may be
preferred, as any of his predecessors. He could find no place to locate
this final authority except in the community itself. Those who obey must
in the last analysis command; the subject must be sovereign.

Later in his own writings, and even more so in the general debate
unloosed by his definition of the General Will, a whole range of sophisticated or even sophistical discussion turned on the question of what he
meant by the term, and often his own meaning was grossly distorted by
interested or even disinterested readers.* Such disputes derived not from
ambiguities in his writing; that was not his style. He thought he was
making himself clear. And present-day students of *The Social Contract*,
like those who first read it, must surely be struck, over and over again,
by the manner in which Rousseau returned to the essential democratic
doctrine that the rulers must be made to obey the ruled.

---

* A few good modern defences of Rousseau have been written to set beside the scandalous attacks.
One of the best, written by J. A. Doyle of the University of Virginia, called *Rousseau and Freedom*
tackles head on the supposed admission of his own guilt, as outlined in Book 1, Chapter VII, where
Rousseau wrote: 'In order then that the social pact may not be an empty formula, it tacitly includes
the agreement, which alone can give force to the others, that whoever should refuse to obey the
General Will shall be constrained to do so by the whole body; which means nothing other that that
he shall be forced to be free, for this is the condition which, giving each citizen to his own country,
guarantees him from all personal dependence.'
   The accusation is that this passage, and more especially the italicized words, express Rousseau's
potential totalitarian instinct. Mr Doyle's elaborate, brilliantly argued essay shows how this implication
of the words is at best quite unproven and at worst a travesty of what Rousseau sought to say elsewhere.
Whatever obscurities may be enfolded in Rousseau's doctrine of the General Will, the attempt to enlist
them in defence of the modern totalitarian hypocrisy whereby all forms of horror and cruelty are excused
is itself inexcusable. Anyone who doubts that counter-charge should read Mr. Doyle's treatise.

One chapter towards the end of Book 3, Chapter XVIII comes, under the aggressive title – 'How to Check the Usurpations of Government' in the following expression of the right of the people to revolt:

When therefore the people sets up an hereditary government, whether it be monarchical and confined to one family, or aristocratic and confined to class, what it enters into is not an undertaking; the administration is given a provisional form, until the people chooses to order it otherwise.

It is true that such changes are always dangerous, and that the established government should never be touched except when it comes to be incompatible with the pubic good; but the circumspection this involved is a maxim of policy and not a rule of right, and the State is no more bound to leave civil authority in the hands of its rulers than military authority in the hands of its generals.

Such a doctrine could read as a revolutionary declaration in many parts of our world today, let alone most of eighteenth-century Europe. If the complaint could be made against Rousseau that he would relapse from his normal clarity into mystical or religious obscurities of a truly inspissated darkness – many of his contemporaries, headed by Voltaire, did make the charge – then the absolute, repeated assurance of his statement of the rights of the ruled against their rulers becomes all the more startling and inescapable. Time and again, in the teeth of all discouragements, he did state the democratic case more boldly and plainly and passionately than ever before. And he did not just write a treatise on the subject; he set the whole theme to music in a new kind of prose.

Some other of his writings expose a quite different part of his mind, and one which seemingly had nothing to do with politics. Yet it was the combination of the two which was no small part of his originality – the bold programme of political emancipation and the liberation of the human heart. Voltaire called the success of *La Nouvelle Heloise* one of the infamies of the century. Between 1761 and 1800 seventy-two editions were published, and this infamous success was one reason why Rousseau could take his place alongside Voltaire as a creator of European thought. And compared with the political and philosophical works of either of the great creators of the Revolution, what was this extraordinary intrusion? It was the most sensational love story ever written. Never before had both the ecstasy and the torture of the love affair, of both the man and the woman, been told so faithfully and elegantly. 'Days of pleasure and glory, no they were not those of a mortal. They were too beautiful to have perished. A gentle ecstasy filled their whole duration and conveyed them like eternity into a point. There was neither past nor future for me, and I tested the delights of a thousand centuries at once.'

When St Preux and his Julie swear that their love will be eternal, no reader can doubt it. When the vow is broken, the curse must fall on neither of the lovers but upon the insufferable conventions of the age. When St Preux, after all his wanderings, returns through those same blessed places by the Geneva lakeside, we are still on tenterhooks to see whether the seduction is to be repeated. For the first time, a novel had been written in which the reader was invited to identify the hero with his creator. That might have been enough by itself to set the fashion which others soon followed, Goethe, Schlegel and Chateaubriand, but soon legions more. If that claim be true, it is enough by itself for his reputation. Was the baring of his heart and the invocation of sympathy as no one had done before, the reason why the age would call him infamous? That was part of the indictment: but surely also the shameless seducer added to the offence when he described a new political creed as no less uninhibited by custom and convention. And, anyhow, what was the meaning of these accusations? St Preux and Julie's love, sanctified by no religion, was presented as rapture, pure and undefinable. A few would even dare to imitate him, and not to disown their master. Byron's

Haidee might never have dared to steal the poem, if it had not been for Rousseau's example.

Both Voltaire and Rousseau were dead – they died within the same few months at the end the year 1776 – before the publication between the years 1782 and 1789 of the four volumes of what is often considered Rousseau's masterpiece: *Les Confessions, et Reveries du Promeneur Solitaire*, another innovation in literary history, an attempt by a man to tell the full truth about himself such as no one had attempted before, not even his model and master, Montaigne. Once again, at the very outset, came the unmistakable trumpet blast:

I have entered on a performance which is without example, whose accomplishment will have no imitator. I mean to present my fellow-mortals with a man in all the integrity of nature; and this man shall be myself.

I alone. I know my heart and have studied mankind; I am not made like any one I have been acquainted with, perhaps like no one in existence; if not better, I at least claim originality, and whether Nature did wisely in breaking the mould in which she formed me can only be determined after having read this work.

Whenever the last trumpet shall sound, I will present myself before the Sovereign Jude with this book in my hand, and say aloud, Thus have I acted; these were my thoughts; such was I.

This time, however, whatever had gone before, he was not telling the truth. Many of the details, whether incriminatory or not, may be exposed as misleading. If he had still been alive at the time of publication, he would have been forced into many fresh controversies, and many of the legion of anti-Rousseauites are able to plunder these pages for ammunition. Yet the true reader of the *Confessions* may escape these diversions and be left wondering all the more how such a new literary achievement on such a scale could be added to all the others. One way to capture this appreciation is to read what Saint-Beuve wrote about him, some seventy years later, in the midst of the nineteenth century when Rousseau was suffering one of his periodic demolitions at the hands of the French reactionaries, who were happily recruiting him as one author of what France had to suffer.

But Saint-Beuve had an extraordinary combined confidence and curiosity. For a start, he noted – quite contrary to the common supposition – how 'he [Rousseau] was the first who definitely brought women into the game.' Quite an introduction! Saint-Beuve remarked how gauche and nervous the real Rousseau could be in the presence of women. But he stirred up in his own interest that moiety of the human race, theretofore self-restrained and not indiscreet; the enthusiasm of the sex for him was unprecedented. How shall we describe that universal revolt which broke out after *La Nouvelle Heloise* and after *Emile* which anticipated the Revolution of '89, and at long distance prepared the way for it: Madame de Stael, Madame Roland – will not they soon appear in the front rank of those I call 'Jean-Jacques's women?' However, it is in the *Confessions* that the greatest of Rousseau's women makes her appearance and comes near to stealing the whole book. Jules Michelet wrote that Rousseau's genius was born of Madame de Warens. Havelock Ellis recorded that someone described her 'as a kind of superior Madame Bovary, with more vigour, and, one may add, better success.' Havelock Ellis himself gave an even better description of her and her achievement. 'She is the only person who can claim to be the teacher of the man who was himself the greatest teacher of the century. When he came to her he was a vagabond apprentice in whom none can see any good. She raised him, succoured him, cherished him, surrounded him with her conscious and unconscious influence; she was the only education he ever received. When he left her he was no longer the worthless apprentice of an engraver, but the supreme master of all those arts which most powerfully evoke the ideas and emotions of mankind.'

Saint-Beuve the critic might have found those words slightly exaggerated, but he too saw how, in so many fields, Rousseau had set the standards and the pace. Along with the women he brought another class into the national calculation. 'There is no writer', he quoted someone as saying, 'more apt to infuse the poor with arrogance.' Rousseau spoke for all those who, thanks to the gross inequalities of society, felt themselves insulted, despised, ostracised. Often he felt that these ignominies had been heaped upon himself. He himself had known hunger, scorn, outlawry. And yet he was not always bowed down by these misfortunes. When he escaped from his dejections, he could see at his feet a world of delights. There were whole days of perfect, limpid serenity.

Let us recall the night that he passed in the open air on the bank of the Rhone or the Saone, in a sunken road near Lyons:

I lay in voluptuous ease on the platform of a sort of recess or false gateway hollowed out of a terrace wall; the canopy of my bed was formed by the tops of the trees; a nightingale was directly over my head, and I fell asleep to his singing; my sleep was delicious, my awakening even more so. It was broad daylight; my eyes, when they opened, saw the water, the verdure, a beautiful landscape. I rose and shook myself; hunger assailed me; I walked gaily towards the town, resolved to spend on a good breakfast two fifteen-sou pieces which I still had left.

There we have the natural Rousseau complete, with his reverie, his idealism, his reality; and 'that fifteen-sou piece itself, coming after the nightingale, is not misplaced to bring us back to earth.'

Saint-Beuve prophesied in the 1850s that Rousseau's power as a great French writer would guarantee his conquests in the future, and one of our great English critics in the 1950s confirmed his judgement. Victor Pritchett offered three verdicts on the *Confessions* which showed that they had lost none of their magnetism. One concerned the telling of the whole story:

There is the self and there are the projections of the self, its sensations and opium dreams, the burden of its introspections, the half-world of its sentiments and morbid fancies which hang like a load upon the shoulders of the solitary walker. No one until Proust catches that dreamer and remembrancer in the act, as Rousseau does; no one so subtly catches the intermingling of the real and the dream; no one else, with a madman's detachment, treats the dream as if it were part of the dreamer. In this Rousseau is as exact and sly in hallucination as Don Quixote. He was generally regarded as mad when he wrote the Confessions *and one can see why: he was the only self in the world.*

Then the repudiations of the Bertrand Russell charge:

Russell has said that Rousseau is the father of Fascism and quotes Voltaire's sarcastic letter to Rousseau on the ineptitudes of the noble savage. No such impression can be gathered from the text. Our sensation is one of release. We see a personality set free by its own memory and the sense of completeness – even if Rousseau lied – is stimulating and lasting because it is imaginary.

But, most important of all, is the reassertion of the excitement of youth.

His pictorial eye, he says, confused his thought and so choked his mind, that he could not think or write until the calm of retrospect had settled on him; that eye was keener in youth and saw, as it were, with the genius of nature reflecting upon herself. That horseback picnic with the girls – in the early volume – is as exquisite as anything in the crystal pages of Tugenev; it glitters with the readiness for adventure.

Adventure dominates those first two hundred pages and to read them is to become young again. That is what the incurable adolescent, the suspicious parasite did for the mature, set, civilised and assured eighteenth century: he shook a whole hard-experienced society back to immaturity, recklessness, youth and dream.

When the Revolution came proper honour was paid to both its two great intellectual creators, both had their bodies transferred to the church of Sainte-Genevieve, henceforward to be known as the Pantheon. On a stormy day in July 1791, Voltaire's body was transferred there, with full honours offered among others by workmen who had demolished the Bastille, where he had twice been imprisoned. His bones were laid beside Rousseau's and they were left there in peace beneath the inscription – 'To great men, the fatherland in gratitude' – until the defeat of Waterloo. Shortly afterwards, on the instruction of the Archbishop of Paris and the newly-restored King's government, the two bodies were dug up and flung into a ditch. 'Victory in this contest', wrote H. N. Brailsford, the great English biographer of Voltaire, 'fell to the religion of love'.

The restoration of human decency came much more swiftly than anyone expected or recorded at the time, and the English poets played the leading role in its achievement. 1815 was supposed to be the year in which the memories of both Voltaire and Rousseau would be expunged from the public mind, and their ideas would be thrown into a pit, like their bodies. However, 1815 was the year in which Byron met Shelley for the first time; they had three momentous months together sailing on the lake at Geneva, and celebrating the sacred places where Rousseau had recalled his childhood or written of his Julie. If anyone supposed that the ideas of Rousseau had perished in the revolutionary terror or the Napoleonic defeat, Byron and Shelley gave the answer. They gladly paid tribute to the other 'gigantic minds' whose fame surrounded them – Voltaire himself, Madame de Stael, Edward Gibbon. But the one they honoured most was Rousseau, the one who had transformed their lives, the one who had changed history, and it was, as they saw more clearly than any of Rousseau's own contemporaries, the Rousseau of the *Social Contract* and *La Nouvelle Heloise* and *The Confessions*, the whole man.

Byron wrote his verses on the subject, and gave them to Shelley to carry back to London. Byron for sure had no difficulty in seeing that Rousseau the prophet of the Revolution and Rousseau the lover were the same. If the world had read his *Childe Harold* aright, they would never had been put asunder. 'The two key figures', wrote Jerome McGann, 'are of course Napoleon and Rousseau, and it is part of the brilliance of the poem that Byron treated both with such pitiless sympathy.' True indeed, and yet it may also be insisted that Rousseau displaces Napoleon. The famous, terrible war scenes in which 'rider and horse – friend, foe – in one red burial blent' make way, not as was sometimes over-emphasised to Wordsworthian scenes of mountain tops and loftiest peaks which Shelley had allegedly sought to instil, but rather to an ecstatic acceptance of the new doctrine which Rousseau had described first and foremost in a language which, however translated, had set the world alight.

Conquerors and Kings
Founders of sects and systems, to whom add
Sophists, Bards, Statesmen, all unquiet things
Which stir too strongly the soul's secret springs,
And are themselves the fools to those they fool;
Envied, yet how unenviable! what stings
Are theirs! One breast laid open were a school
Which would unteach mankind the lust to shine or rule ...

All too eagerly in the ensuing years – and even more so in this century – the greatness and originality of Rousseau were dismissed or denied. A highly select trio of near-contemporary critics, Hazlitt, Stendhal and Heine, all reared on *La Nouvelle Heloise* themselves, would repudiate any such slur. But the pre-eminence which Byron accords to Rousseau is in a sense all the more remarkable since he gave it first. A sly insinuation has sometimes been added that Byron had somehow been tempted to under-value him and his influence because of his lowly birth and plebeian manners and inept lovemaking. Instead, Byron understood the Rousseau of *La Nouvelle Heloise* – he recalled page after page to Shelley – and he also understood in every fibre of his being the other Rousseau, the herald of the Revolution. The verses in which he did it have never lost their brightness and their power. He taught his world – our world:

To look on One, whose dust was once all fire,
A native of the land where I respire
The clear air for a while – a passing guest,
Where he became a being – whose desire
Was to be glorious; It was a foolish quest,
The which to gain and keep, he sacrificed all rest.

Here the self-torturing sophist, wild Rousseau,
The apostle of affliction, he who threw
Enchantment over passion, and from woe
Wrung overwhelming eloquence, first drew
The breath which made him wretched; yet he knew
How to make madness beautiful, and cast
O'er erring deeds and thoughts a heavenly hue
Of words, like sunbeams, dazzling as they past
The eyes, which o'er them shed tears feelingly, and fast.

His love was passion's essence – as a tree
On fire by lightning with ethereal flame
Kindled he was, and blasted; for to be
Thus, and enamour'd, were in him the same.
But his was not the love of living dame,

Nor of the dead who rise upon our dreams
But of ideal beauty, which became
In him existence, and o'erflowing teems
Along his burning page, distemper'd though it seems

This *breathed itself to life in Julie,* this
Invested her with all that's wild and sweet;
This hallowed, too, the memorable kiss
Which every morn his fevered lip would greet,
From hers ...

It was, for the devotees of *La Nouvelle Heloise,* the most famous kiss in history; but with Byron, as with all others truly touched by the Romantic ardour, it marked the beginnings of a political faith too.

For then he was inspired, and from him came,
As from the Pythian's mystic cave of yore,
Those oracles which set the world in flame,
Nor ceased to burn till kingdoms were no more:
Did he not this for France? which lay before
Bow'd to the inborn tyranny of years?
Broken and trembling to the yoke she bore,
Till by the voice of him and his compeers,
Roused up to too much wrath, which follows o'ergrown fears?

And what if the result of the first turmoil was not what the revolutionaries had prophesied, not the unclouded dawn? But at once comes the true Byronic refusal ever to accept defeat:

They made themselves a fearful monument!
The wreck of old opinions – things which grew,
Breathed from the birth of time: the veil they rent.

And what behind it lay, all earth shall view.
But good with ill they also overthrew,
Leaving but ruins, wherewith to rebuild
Upon the same foundation, and renew
Dungeons and thrones, which the same hour refill'd,
As heretofore, because ambition was self-will'd.

But this will not endure, nor be endured!
Mankind have felt their strength, and made it felt.
They might have used it better, but, allured
By their new vigour, sternly have they dealt
On one another; pity ceased to melt
With her once natural charities. But they,
Who in oppression's darkness caved had dwelt,
What marvel then, at times, if they mistook their prey?

This was Byron, be it not forgotten, rejecting the doctrine that the misdeeds of the Revolution should condemn the Revolution itself.

Shelley wrote his verdict a few months later and included them in his *Triumph of Life.*

If I have been extinguished, yet there rise
A thousand beacons from the spark I bore.

Edmund Wilson, in his *To the Finland Station,* extolled – and introduced many of us in the process to – his own breed of philosopher–historians, the men who carried conviction notably by their respect for detail but also by their understanding of the sweep of history, Vico, Michelet, Taine, Marx, Trotsky. He included some references to Rousseau, but not the elaborate treatment of him which might have been thought to suit his thesis. However, no depreciation of Rousseau's greatness was intended, for in an earlier piece on the same subject – a new introduction to the

Confessions, written in 1924 – he had specified exactly the decision by the young Rousseau to enter for the Dijon prize when he felt how qualified he had become to reveal 'all the contradictions of the social system ... with what simplicity should I have demonstrated that man is naturally good and that it is through institutions alone that men have become wicked!'

The occasion had all the attributes which Edmund Wilson or his fellow philosopher–historians would require to describe the great axle-points on which history moved. Of course, he was not claiming that the whole Rousseau doctrine was comprised in this single discovery; as we have seen, Rousseau's achievement was how he interpreted this discovery in so many different artistic forms. Others might describe the defects of society; Rousseau denounced the guilt, and with flaming words was constantly summoning his generation to action at every critical moment of his own life or his country's. He never lost for long his belief in man's power to change the world. 'He did more towards the French Revolution than any other man.' wrote William Hazlitt. 'Voltaire, by his wit and penetration had rendered superstition contemptible and tyranny odious but it was Rousseau who brought the feeling of irreconcilable enmity to rank and privileges, above humanity, home to the bosom of every man – identified with all the pride of intellect and with the deepest yearning of the human heart.'

Hazlitt, like Rousseau himself, was not accustomed to using the word democracy in its precise modern sense; but he knew about action. This was the manner in which Edmund Wilson read Rousseau in the 1920s and this was how multitudes read him in the years before 1789, throughout the years of the Revolution itself (more copies were sold in the few years immediately after the fall of the Bastille than ever before and in the critical years after the Revolution's defeat when, in the interests of humanity, the message was more necessary to understand than ever before. William Hazlitt read him as a young boy in his teens when he was thrilled by the news from France, and thereafter. He had read the *Confessions* as one of the great books of the world and would gladly have approved the terms in which Edmund Wilson concluded his introduction.*

This moment was the real point of departure of the modern democratic movement. As it came almost precisely in the centre, so it was the turning point of the eighteenth century. All Rousseau's political works stemmed from this sudden inspiration; it never occurred to him to wonder how, if men were good, they had invented bad institutions; he had the blind force of religious faith. And all Europe was soon to be aroused by the conception of the natural man, of the man naturally good, of the good man oppressed by laws and debauched by civilisation, and to put to itself the question which Rousseau was soon to ask: do the inequalities of men in society correspond to their natural inequalities? That question and that conception were to be debated long and with much bloodshed; they are still being debated today on every hand; between the fascisti and the socialists in Italy, between the Communists and the Monarchists in Berlin, between the government of Soviet Russia and the governments of the Allies, and in America between the masters of the steel industry and Mr William Z. Foster's strikers. The train was already started on that hot day in 1749; already the fuse was lit which was to fire the phrases of the Declaration of Independence, which was to burn down the Bastille in the conflagrations of a whole society, and which was to warm the Red Armies of Russia as they fought for Communism in the snow – when it was suddenly revealed to Rousseau, the clock-maker's son of Geneva, the beaten apprentice, the thieving lackey, the vagabond of the roads, that all his shames and misfortunes had been due not to his own innate

---

* In 1988, a book in the Modern Critical Views series was published by the Chelsea Publishers on Jean-Jacques Rousseau, edited and with an introduction by Harold Bloom, Sterling Professor of Humanities at Yale. I was greatly comforted by Harold Bloom's first sentence of introduction to his excellent volume: 'William Hazlitt, in my judgement still Rousseau's best critic ... Praising the *Confessions* as a veritable Bible of revolution, Hazlitt saw in Rousseau the Romantic Prometheus, kindler of revolt against the sky-gods of Europe.'

perversity but to the corruption of the society which had bred him and that mankind, who seemed haunted by the memory of some inheritance of happiness and freedom which they had long ago enjoyed, might, if they could only reconstruct institutions, become happy and free again.

A passage like that no less than Byron's verses in *Childe Harold* should have made it impossible thereafter for any doubt to be held about his genius and his glory.

But of course it is the truth about him which made him hated and feared. Every few decades still the priests or the politicians (and usually the two in concert) find it necessary to dig up his body and throw it into a pit. It is fortunate that he has the poets, and some of our very greatest ones, among his defenders. He can never be finally traduced now; men and women will continue to read his double love story, his love of Julie and his love of humankind. If the proper place to trace the seeds of the Revolution itself is in the exultant egalitarian voice of Rousseau on the road from Annecy, the next most significant signposts were to be seen on the shores of Lake Leman, where Byron and Shelley together gave equal honour to him and designed their programme for the future.

Conor Cruise O'Brien's Edmund Burke

Review of Conor Cruise O'Brien, *The Great Melody: a thematic biography of Edmund Burke*, in the *Times Educational Supplement*, 23 October 1992

Somehow Edmund Burke retains his hold among discriminating followers across the political spectrum, Left, Right and Centre – more particularly in the last two categories than the first, maybe, but the whole phenomenon remains remarkable. He spent most of his political life immersed in the practical exigencies of party manoeuvre at a time when the British system was alleged to have fallen to the lowest depth of intrigue and corruption. A David Mellor foreign excursion would scarcely have been worth a footnote in those days, and even Lady Thatcher's Grand Tours or wholesale distribution of knighthoods would scarcely have raised an eyebrow.

Edmund Burke was supposed to have wallowed eagerly in that stye. So his full rehabilitation here is an achievement of the first order. Conor Cruise O'Brien brings to *The Great Melody* the combined understanding of politics and personality which he first displayed in his classic, *Parnell and his Party*. And, maybe, Burke is a greater man than Parnell, if not also a greater Irishman. But let us see.

First, it is necessary to dispose of the Namierite school of defamation, and O'Brien does the job with a devastating relish. Newcomers to the dispute today may find it impossible to imagine how for a while the Namierite thesis seemed to carry all before it. The old Whig interpretation of history and a host of Liberal historians along with it were scattered and in their place Professor Lewis Namier suffocated us with his statistics and his cynicism. Every man had his price, as the first Whig Prime Minister had testified. George III merely played the dirty game a little more skilfully than the Whig practitioners themselves. It was economic appetites in one guise or another which made the wheels go round, and the first business of historians was to expose these realities. This was deep down nothing more than a good old Tory doctrine, but it bore some outward marks of a kind of bastard Marxism.

I myself arrived at Oxford just after the publication of Namier's first and most effective study; so a word of personal testimony may be permitted. I can recall my fury on being torn away from such delights as Sir George Otto Trevelyan's *Early History of Charles James Fox* or J. L. Hammond's later history on that same titanic figure to pore over Sir Lewis's formidable lists of figures. Of course, it was soon evident that, to make the Namier claim stick, every political virtue, every kind of political ideal, would have to be stripped away from such a man as Charles James Fox, and to assist that process he would readily play off Burke against Fox and vice versa. 'Namier took the mind out of history', wrote Alan Taylor, one of Namier's pupils, as it happened. But his brilliant, conclusive retort was written only years later.

O'Brien's exposure of Namierism is the best I have ever read. Of course his main purpose and a most worthy one is to vindicate the character of Edmund Burke; the lengths Namier went to destroy him – a kind of *Sun* newspaper campaign transferred to the history books – can still take your breath away. But the process also unravels great epochs in our history in a way which has rarely been attempted before.

For example, here, to restore the real Edmund Burke, he must tell us, year-by-year, day-by-day almost, how George III and his fellow Tories played into the hands of the American revolutionaries and lost that first British Empire in what modern Americans might be taught was a kind of eighteenth-century Vietnam. The story on its own is exciting though. 1780 was one of the most dangerous moments in our history: the threat of invasion and defeat was as bad as, say, in 1688 or 1940. But at each twist and turn in the mounting crisis it is Burke, in his matchless, language who warns and advises and offers a better alternative course of action, and then delivers the terrible indictment on what the Tory patriots of that day did to our country. No wonder their successors want to tamper with the record.

How the great empire and the little minds came into collision in that American crisis is recreated so well that it is hard to see how the rest of the book should not come as an anti-climax. It was the most supreme occasion when a tiny, ostracised parliamentary group kept alive the idea and practice of English liberty in the face of fearful intimidation. But in one sense, even more creditable and potent in its long-term effects was his part in saving the reputation of our country in India. Not quite alone but almost and without even a party at his back, Burke brought Warren Hastings to trial. He believed that misdeeds and injustices committed against Indians were no less to be condemned than those perpetrated against the Americans. If anything, the test of his endurance and his selfless pursuit of the just cause was even greater in this instance; and the benefits for our country's reputation as one which would not deny the claims of magnanimity at the eleventh hour could be read by twentieth-century opponents of tyranny in India, headed by Mahatma Gandhi and Jawaharlal Nehru.

No one has ever recited that part of the Edmund Burke saga so well as O'Brien: maybe it takes, or took, two Irishmen to understand the real indignity of imperial rule and all its assembled, inescapable injuries and insults. Ireland leaves its imprint on this book from first page to last: but it would be most improper to spoil the biographer's last effect. However, before then readers must face for themselves the departure from liberal principle which appeared to be involved in Burke's attitude to the French Revolution, and the changes which that brought in his relations with his oldest enemies like George III and his oldest friends like Charles Fox. Readers may not be surprised to discover that O'Brien believes there was and could be no such departure. He has at least earned for his Edmund Burke the chance for a fresh hearing.

Where he does not face the full challenge – where he skirts round it for the benefit of his hero – is in what might be called the *democratic* argument. The word, much less the idea, was not in use at the time. But in one form or another the question whether the people as a whole – poor people and middle-class people as well as the rich – should have the right to choose their rulers in Parliament or elsewhere was becoming more and more the supreme question. Rousseau was the first to give expression to the idea ('He invented democracy', said the same historian Alan Taylor who put Namier in his place). And Thomas Paine was the Englishman who, partly provoked by Burke, turned the idea into his call to action in the great new cause on both sides of the Atlantic and both sides of the English Channel and both sides of the Irish Sea, for that matter, as Burke with all his incomparable powers of imagination should have understood.

O'Brien is not fair to that tradition. He dismisses at one stage the representatives of it as the 'Tom Paine people (or tags-of-Tom-people) and *ipso f*acto anti-Burke, usually without reading him.' The very name Tom Paine, by the way, was the Tory sneer against him which was why he preferred his full name. O'Brien is not guilty of the offence which the Namierites perpetuated against Burke: a monstrous perversion of every-thing he had said or done. But still the offence is not easily forgiveable. At one point he seeks to destroy Paine's famous phrase about 'pitying the plumage and forgetting the dying bird' by recalling that some two hundred years later it was invoked to excuse infamies perpetrated by Russian or Chinese Communists. On that same perverted reckoning, Burke could be cited to excuse crimes in Vietnam – a comparison which he had justly dismissed a few pages earlier.

Burke and Paine were combatants worthy of each other. Neither might have thought so at the time in the blazing heat of their controversy. But historians now can start to remedy the deficiency. The Paineites indeed often had the wit on their side – not something to match the glorious bursts of irony and satire with which Burke at his best could beat all comers, but still a sharp and serviceable weapon. When Burke sought to dismiss them as 'the swinish multitude' their riposte was to produce a journal called *Pigs Meat* in which the vulgar abuse was turned against their accuser but in which also they showed that they had an instructor in writing English and discussing politics who was a match even for Edmund Burke himself.

Many pages in the successive issues of *Pigs Meat* were devoted to the defence speech made by Thomas Erskine at the 1792 trial of Paine's *Rights of Man* – surely an issue on which, on the long-term reckoning of the interests of English freedom Paine had a better case than Burke. At least present-day defenders of Burke should be required to tell us where they stand. But the *Pigs Meat* journal was also interlarded with quotation after quotation from another master of language whom Burke should certainly have thought worthy of his steel and his invective.

Jonathan Swift was no democrat; he too had never heard the word in a modern context but – thanks to his experience in Burke's Ireland as it happened – he had learnt a hatred of tyranny no less violent than Burke's own but one which impelled him towards a quite different political conclusion. Burke believed that the business of governing man was a highly complicated affair, that changes should be undertaken only with the utmost care: the British constitution of 1688, after his Whig friends had devised some suitable modifications, was the most precious example. Swift, after an experience of politics no less extensive than Burke's, reached a quite different conclusion. He came to believe, and plainly stated, that politics was a matter suitable for many heads, and that most troubles were due to the wickedness and folly of self-appointed, self-perpetuating rulers. Presented with their handiwork, he advocated direct remedies.

Doubtless the Swiftian message could be crude; but it also had a beauty and a potency and a flaming sense of indignation about what was happening in the world all around them which appealed to men like Thomas Spence, editor of *Pigs Meat*, or William Cobbett, soon to become the foremost pamphleteer of the age and a match for Burke, or Thomas Paine himself. All of these writers, no mean controversialists, engaged in ferocious debate with Burke, especially when they saw him emerge as the leading apologist for the rulers and the system they hated, and they were angered all the more since they had seen him only a few years before as the enemy of their enemy.

William Hazlitt, another observer of that scene and thanks to the power of his pen a participant too, was a pupil of Swift, but even earlier he had been a worshipful admirer of Edmund Burke. He loved his style, his passion, his imagination. He said that Burke's words were most like things, and he meant it as the highest compliment. He saw some like-nesses even between Rousseau and Burke, and sought to devise a synthesis between the two. He was quite ready to call himself a Jacobin even when that term was the most odious in the English vocabulary of the day. Burke would usually use the word in that sense, but, not always, and the exception illustrates the nature of the different Edmund Burke whom O'Brien has understood better than any previous writer about him, better even possibly than Hazlitt.

Burke acknowledged that there was a form of Jacobinism which he respected – 'the Jacobinism which arises from penury and irritation, from scorned loyalty and rejected allegiance.' The roots of it 'take their nourishment from the bottom of human nature and the unalterable constitution of things, and not from humour and caprice or the opinions of the day about privileges and liberties.' Along with his hatred of all other tyrannies, Burke hated the tyranny which Protestant England exerted in his native Ireland. That could make him feel that what was required to meet the continuance of such proud infamies was a Jacobin insurgence. His head might warn against it, but his heart would yield. And, or course, as O'Brien has illustrated in chapter after chapter, the best passages of Burkean eloquence poured forth when his head and his heart spoke in unison.

This great biography mounts to its mighty climax not when he is thrust into his argument with Fox, although that is poignant enough; not when his prophecies about the horrific developments in France appear to be fulfilled; not even when his beloved son dies so tragically; but when the portent came from his native Ireland that he might find himself, if he was true to himself, on the Jacobin side of the barricades. 'I believe', writes O'Brien, 'that he was already experiencing, in imagination, a foretaste of those torments.' Only so great an Irish patriot as Edmund Burke would have felt those premonitions, and he like so many of his forebears or descendants, like the editors of *Pigs Meat*, would have turned for comfort to Jonathan Swift.

C. L. R. James's Michelet

Text of a lecture delivered at Bedford College, Boston, in May 1989 to mark the bicentennial of the French Revolution.

Anyone who ever heard C. L. R. James speak, either in private conversation or on the public platform, would be most impressed by his inexhaustible historical imagination. He did not merely make history live, although he could certainly do that; but for him, the past, the present, and the future were woven into a single tapestry, each strand as strong as the other.

Thanks to his natural modesty and his true respect for scholarship, he was always eager to acknowledge those who had taught him. He was a Marxist and proud of it. He was a Trotskyite and proud of it. He had the same respect for world literature that had helped shape the politics of both Marx and Trotsky. But he never worshipped at these two shrines or anywhere else as if they offered some exclusive, infallible doctrine. He drew sustenance from some other rich sources, some of them unexpected.

I went to see him at his house in Brixton, crowded with books and friends, in May 1989. A new edition of *The Black Jacobins* had just appeared, and of course that was part of the reason why our discussion turned to the subject of the French Revolution. Maybe his talk throughout this commemorative year would always turn back to that theme. He wrote me, a few days later, a letter which I naturally treasure (immodestly including the reference to my own book of Byron, which may seem to have more relevance later):

My dear Michael

   It was a great pleasure to meet Michael Foot in person.

   Conversation with you was not only profitable, but exciting. After fifty years the French Revolution means more to me than it did at the beginning of my serious studies. I was glad to have the opportunity to exchange thoughts with you on this great historical event. Thank you for sending me a copy of your book on Byron. I am having a rare old time with its title page. The Politics of Paradise, *to be written as a title, at once becomes the paradise of politics – with the prospect of many other such transformations, ins and outs, legitimate wasters of time. But Grafton Street restores me to the severity and dedication of near a century ago.*

   Yours etc. etc.

   C. L. R.

Thus I should underline that our talk turned almost as much on the historians as on history itself. He recalled again, as he does in the new edition of *The Black Jacobins,* how he learned his trade. The French Revolution, he insisted, was 'one of the greatest historical schools of Western civilization'. That school had the necessary respect for the Revolution itself without which the history of the period could not be written. What James, himself such a great and impenitent respecter of the historian's craft, would have made of the grotesque revisionist mockeries that appeared on both sides of the Atlantic to greet 1989, it is hard to estimate.

   Indeed, he might have brushed them all aside with his final encomium to the greatest historian of them all, Jules Michelet, who understood and proclaimed the role of the people in the Revolution better than anyone else. 'He has very little to say about the colonial question', James still asserts, 'but I believe that many pages in Michelet are the best preparation for understanding what actually happened in San Domingo.' Without Michelet's combined passion and insight, James could never have written as he did, but the rule applies to many others less willing to recognise his precedence.

English readers or students have a special need to mark this judgement. For generations, Jules Michelet was regarded as a French patriot too strong for English stomachs, not a historian in the proper sense at all, but a revolutionary propagandist soaked in the *Marseillaise*. A biography about him published in London in 1989 was greeted as if French scholarship was up to its old knavish tricks of mocking or deceiving John Bull. Nothing was allowed for what Michelet does to probe the moments when history is silent, to give voice to the people, very often women, who were denied any voice at all.

To read Michelet is to renew the spirit of those revolutionary times, and in particular the earliest years of the great promise. He tells of the fall of the Bastille as no one had told it before or since. A few sentences offer only a hint:

The attack on the Bastille was by no means reasonable. It was an act of faith. Nobody proposed; but all believed, and all acted ... Then let that grand day remain ever one of the eternal fêtes of the human race, not only as having been the first of deliverance, but as having been superlatively the day of concord. What happened during that short night on which nobody slept, for every difference of opinion to disappear with the shakes of darkness, and all to have the same thoughts in the morning? What took place at the Palais Royale and the Hotel de Ville is well known; but what would be far more important to know is, what took place on the domestic hearth of the people.

The people played the leading role in Michelet's beloved Paris, and as he described their achievements, the city assumed a mightier proportionate part in events than ever before – 'when I reflect on what Paris has done for the liberties of our human race, I feel impelled to kiss the stones of its monuments and the pavements of its streets.' How many travellers in Paris, how many readers of Michelet, have been swept along by his passionate reconstruction of the scene?

One more modern name to figure on James's list was George Lefebvre. He was even more closely associated with the rewriting of the history of the Revolution than Michelet himself. This example illustrates how the flaming torch of historical revision could be handed on from one master to another. Lefebvre died in 1959 at the age of eighty-six. In the art of exposition he had made himself at least the equal of two of his famous predecessors at the Sorbonne, Alphonse Aulard and Albert Mathiez. But he regarded himself rather as a direct pupil of Jean Jaurés, the socialist leader and historian who was martyred by an assassin in 1914. Like Jaurés, Lefebvre was a rationalist humanitarian in the tradition of the Enlightenment who believed that his own age, in allegiance to that same tradition, called for a great adventure in democratic socialism: 'I saw and heard Jaurés only two times, lost in the crowd, but if anyone cares to assign me a maître, I recognise only him.' And, of course, both Lefebvre and Jaurés had been powerfully influenced in their view of history by Karl Marx and had no wish to conceal the debt.

Thanks partly to Lefebvre's persisting influence, Marxist and near-Marxist interpretations became positively fashionable. The achievement was celebrated in the appropriate year, 1968, when an avowed fellow Marxist on this side of the Channel, Gwyn Williams, surveyed the latest developments in French Revolutionary scholarship in his *Artisans and Sans Culottes*. His new edition, published twenty years later, brought the survey up to date, and showed how substantial efforts had been made to fill some of the gaps. He noted how the words Britain or British were sometimes clumsily used to conceal the contribution which the Welsh, the Scots, or the Irish made to that of their English comrades, and he noted even more forcibly the change in role according to women.

With Gwyn Williams's safe hands to guide us, we may return more confidently to the question of women. 'My 1968 text', he wrote, 'could not fail to note the role of women in many of the *journées* in France and the quite spectacular leadership they exercised in the last revolts of Germinal and Prairial. Twenty years on, however, I cannot fail to note, in pain and shame, the barely concealed surprise which informs my writing at that point. It is certainly the advance of women's history which is beginning to transform our understanding of the popular movement in France.'

It may now be recalled in wonder that the historian whom James had hailed most notably had written almost in the same sense nearly 150 years before. Michelet saw 'the spirit of the Revolution' as his teacher. 'It knows; and the others do not. It possesses the secret of all the preceding ages.' The epic of the liberation of the French people, nay, the liberation of the human mind itself – that was what his history of the Revolution was to be. And maybe because he saw its comprehensive character, Michelet, before any other historian, always searched for the role that women – or their chosen champions – had played.

The house of Marquis de Condorcet had been the place in pre-revolutionary times when the rights and claims of women were first elaborated. His salon in Paris became, with his wife's association, 'the hearth of the republic'. Some other famous women, notably Olympe de Courges, joined with them in drafting a Declaration of the Rights of Women. The notorious Olympe – notorious for her seductions as well as her declarations – established the rights of women, according to Michelet, by one just and sublime saying: 'They have as good a right to mount the tribune as they have to ascending the scaffold.'

The English have usually liked to pretend that Jules Michelet wrote only for the French. His critics would have been wiser to note how he strove to make all causes, including the women's cause, part of the same liberation. Many of his writings are still unobtainable in any English translation. Now that he has been promoted to the head of the democratic corners by James, the great historian of Toussaint L'Ouverture, the deficiency in English culture should be remedied. Let us turn to *The Black Jacobins* itself. I first read it in the year of publication, 1938, and was swept along, like most other readers, by the excitement and the passion, the sheer narrative drive.

Re-reading the book today, with the modern additions, I believe it is greater still; a Marxist masterpiece, with constant, reverberating implications for the whole of our own turbulent century, let alone the one in which Toussaint L' Ouverture led his San Domingo revolution.

Let's glance first at those additions. James contributes a foreword and an appendix with specific references to modern times. He notes with pride and modesty how young Africans found copies of *The Black Jacobins* in their libraries and then recites, with even greater pride, how his West Indian intellectual forebears Marcus Garvey, George Padmore and Aime Cesaire – set the spacious pattern for the twentieth-century process of African liberation. His own name must surely be added to that list of honour.

But how can such large claims be considered admissible? How could such mighty consequences be traced to developments in one faraway, forgotten West Indian island, whose affairs today are much less significant than those, say, of Cuba or Jamaica or neighbouring American territories.

One part of the answer to those questions came to dominate James's original volume. San Domingo, he asserted, was 'the greatest colony in the world, the pride of France, and the envy of every other imperialist nation.' The huge profits beyond the calculations of any Marxist invective rested on the labour of half a million slaves, and how they got there was an essential part of the story. How the slave trade operated, how the rulers of England and France – even revolutionary France –

competed to keep their bloodstained hands upon it supplied the prologue. Nowhere else, I believe, has it been told with such pitiless, conclusive economy.

If this huge human and economic convulsion so often dismissed to the sidelines of history provides one background to the unique events in San Domingo, the revolutionary achievements in France provide the other. The intimate, day-by-day interaction of events and personalities on both sides of the Atlantic must be unravelled to make the record convincing and to display the role of the leading characters, most notably Toussaint himself. Three men in that age of great men, the author records, seemed to astonish their contemporaries by their combination of qualities – Napoleon, Nelson and Toussaint himself.

Not that these were the only great men of the period. There were others who had equal claims to pre-eminence. Even the statesmen in London who sent a great British army to its destruction in San Domingo's swamps were hailed, at the time, as their country's saviours. And the men who moved swiftly across the revolutionary stage in Paris have left their names and accomplishments imprinted forever on the records. Multitudes of people in revolutionary Europe believed what they said when they voted for liberty, equality, and fraternity. They meant the end of the race war too: 'Let us proclaim the liberty of the Negroes. Mr President, do not suffer the convention to dishonour itself by discussion.' How those highest hopes were betrayed, how Buonaparte who 'hated black people', prepared the revenge, how even Toussaint faltered, all this is faithfully recited too.

And the contrast may be properly made with two books that presumed to tell the story of the abolition of the slave trade from England's viewpoint R. P. Coupland's supposedly authoritative *Wilberforce: a narrative*, or his *The British Anti-Slavery Movement*, which held the field when James was starting upon his task. 'Both these books', he wrote, 'are typical for, among other vices, their smug sentimentality of the official approach of Oxford to abolition. As the official view, they can be recommended for their thorough misunderstanding of the question'. Let me reiterate my own judgement. *The Black Jacobins* is not only the best book about the San Domingo revolution; it is also the best book about the slave trade. It needed a new Jules Michelet to tell that story.

It may be thought that no other name could be mentioned in James's presence in the same breath as that of Jules Michelet. But there was one, and I can recall the radiance that spread across his face and the renewed vigour in his voice when I raised the name of William Hazlitt. It was Hazlitt who had introduced him to the England he most loved and honoured, and he never forgot to pay that debt to, as he defined it, 'the England of the early Dickens and of William Hazlitt.' His own words of tribute are so good that no one should tamper with them:

It was an England still unconquered by the Industrial Revolution. It travelled by saddle and carriage. Whenever it could it ate and drank prodigiously. It was not finicky in morals. It enjoyed life. It prized the virtues of frankness, independence, individuality, conviviality. There were rulers and the ruled, the educated and the uneducated. If the two groupings could be described as two nations they were neither of them conscious of the divisions as a state of things which ought not to be. You can see that clearly in the finest prose writer of the time. Hazlitt was an intellectual to his fingertips, and a militant, an extreme democrat who suffered martyrdom for his opinions. Yet he is not a divided man. He has an acute consciousness either of class or divided culture. He discusses with equal verve the virtues of a classical education and the ignorance of the learned. It is impossible to distinguish any change in his style whether he writes on William Cobbett, on his First Acquaintance with Poets, on John Cavanagh, the Fives Player, or on the Fight between Bill Neate and the Gasman. It would be comparatively simple to maintain that his essay on The Fight *is his finest piece. It is what he called 'a complete thing', giving such a*

picture of the England of his time as can nowhere else be found in
such a narrow compass. Wide as is his range, unlike the later Robert
Lynd, or A. G. Gardiner (to mention two at random), he does not fit his
subject into a practised pattern. He takes his whole self wherever he
goes; he is ready to go everywhere; every new experience renews and
expands him. He writes as freely and as publicly of a most degrading
love affair as of Elizabethan literature. The possibility of such
completeness of expression ended with his death and has not yet
returned.

Hazlitt's strength and comprehensiveness were the final culmination
of one age fertilized by the new. In prose, in poetry, in criticism, in
painting his age was more creative than the country had been for two
centuries before and would be for a century after. This was the age
that among its other creations produced the game of cricket.

To conclude such matters with the reference to cricket may seem dispro-
portionate, although Hazlitt certainly helped to introduce C. L. R. James
himself to these English mysteries and thereby opened up for him a
fresh vista of excitement and enjoyment where the people, black and
white, whom he truly honoured, could run their own affairs and yield to
no one who refused to accept their equal rights and common humanity.
These were some of the qualities he would recognise in Marx or Trotsky,
but he had learned them even better before from Michelet or Hazlitt.

Robert Woof's William Wordsworth

Review, written for the *Guardian* but unpublished, of Robert Woof (ed.), *William Wordsworth: the critical heritage*, Volume I, 1793–1820, published in 2001

When Wordsworth and Coleridge published their *Lyrical Ballads* in 1798 they both knew that they were doing something revolutionary, a response to the *democratic* mood of the age, a quite unfamiliar word and idea which promised even greater ferments in the years ahead. 1798 had not turned its back on 1789 or 1793, neither here nor across revolutionary Europe. At one stage the intention was that Coleridge should write the preface in which the claims for their originality in the use of the lyrical form was to be asserted. Two years later Wordsworth performed that role in the second edition. He was more confident than ever that he was speaking a new language to a new audience, a new world.

Whatever the diverse qualities of the two poets, each owed part of his inspiration to the ideas which the revolution in France had promised. Piece after piece among the new lyrics exposed the bitter hardship, the injustice which the men and, often more wretchedly still, the women of that age had to endure. Quite a number of the more orthodox defenders of church and state drew attention to these dangerous implications. One or two directly suggested that these wretched hardships, if they actually existed, must be due to the war against France on which the English had been forced to embark and that therefore the lyrical balladeers might be guilty of some form of treachery – an insult indeed with a modern tilt.

How inapposite such anachronistic insults can be was shown in the sonnet Wordsworth wrote just after the second edition of the *Ballads*:

I grieved for Buonaparte with a vain
And unthinking grief.

The young Buonaparte had indeed been one of Wordsworth's heroes. They had all shared the same blissful dawn, including too their admiration for Toussaint L'Ouverture, the great black leader on the other side of the Atlantic, and Thomas Clarkson, who led the fight against the slave trade nearer home. He could grieve for them too and then later lead the exultations.

Most of the venom with which Wordsworth's earliest productions, and especially the *Lyrical Ballads*, were greeted must be attributed to the ideas unloosed by the French Revolution and, more particularly, by Francis Jeffrey, who soon became his unrelenting critic, and more especially from the exposure of his alleged subservience to the great apostle of Geneva, Jean-Jacques Rousseau.

Every decent human instinct, every single code of civilised conduct would be at risk if the French example was followed. And the Jeffrey who expressed these views most determinedly was not just a Tory, high or low. He was the recently appointed editor of the most respected Whig journal, the *Edinburgh Review*. He might have been expected at least to share some of the principles of the greatest Whig of that age, Charles James Fox, who had sent a truly appreciative response to Wordsworth's gift to him of a copy of the *Ballads*. Jeffrey was left free to condemn the new school of poetry in ever more caustic and conclusive terms: 'The love or grief, or indignation of an enlightened and refined character is not only expressed in a different language but is in itself a different emotion from the love or grief or anger of a clown, a tradesman or a market wench.' Thus the pious Christians of that age, the defenders of church and state, defined a war between the classes such as Karl Marx himself had not yet defined.

The Wordsworth of those times was not to be shifted so easily from the poetic and political principles first adumbrated in the *Lyrical Ballads*. He had given the evidence there of how he expected to see his own experience woven into a larger philosophy. His 'Tintern Abbey' seemed to be the most polished and prophetic piece he had yet produced, the promise of even greater things to come, greater adventures in liberal ideas, the truly revolutionary word of the new century.

Another reviewer of Wordsworth's *Poems 1807* was the nineteen-year-old Lord Byron whose piece appeared not in the prestigious Edinburgh Review but in a journal called *Le Beau Monde or Literary and Fashionable Magazine*. Starting from a standpoint slightly more generous than Jeffrey – he had seen for himself, or been taught to recognise, real virtues in some of the *Lyrical Ballads* – he still feels compelled to dismiss the whole project, and yet with some first touches of the Byronic wit:

But this muse really seems to be in her dotage. We hoped that the childish effusions that were mixed among the poems in the former work, were the errors of a mind then in its poetical dawn, and that a more mature experience would wipe away the morning dew, and leave the flower untarnished and fair. But we now apprehend that this nurse, at the time she produced Lyrical Ballads, *was not the whining scholar but the lean and slippered eld, and that she has now shifted into that second childhood, in which, though sans eyes, and sans teeth, she unluckily is not sans tongue.*

The young Byron seemingly understood his Shakespeare better than his Wordsworth. He still achieved some intelligible comments on the 1807 volume. His most unforgivable error was his sweeping dismissal of almost all the twenty-six sonnets to liberty included in that same volume. "The lines to a Highland Girl', with a few errors, are very pretty; we think it but fair to extract them.'

Indeed the quoted lines, nearly 500 of them, may have captivated Byron's readers more than his criticisms. He returned to them in the end in a more severe mood:

A few beauties indeed are scattered abroad through their pages; but, like violets, they lie very low and are difficult of discovery. Mr Wordsworth has ruined himself by his affectation of simplicity. Most good authors have been content to form themselves on the models of published writers: Mr Scott in the present day has chosen to copy the language of barbarous ages; but it was reserved for Mr Wordsworth to imitate the lisp of children.

'Scorn not the sonnet,' Wordsworth himself wrote several years later. He might have replied more speedily and sharply if he had known that it was the young Byron who had sought to dismiss almost all his efforts with such a single contemptuous stroke.

A few of them were failures but the others helped to sustain the most noble causes at their moments of desperation: the salutes to Toussaint L'Ouverture and Thomas Clarkson, the eternal honour paid to Republican Venice, the hymns to English liberty which later disciples could honourably recite in 1914 and 1940; he had indeed recaptured the power of Milton's trumpet. And yet, in a sense, Wordsworth himself was heeding these admonitions. He had his own idea of how high a calling was the poet's; how he raised the great argument to the highest pitch.

Especially must this be so in the tumultuous times in which he lived. Nothing but an epic poem could fit such epic times: a poem to match the achievement of, say, Milton's *Paradise Lost* or Dante's *Inferno*, or Homer's *Iliad*. Some time soon after the publication of the *Lyrical Ballads*, and while he was still smarting from the rebukes, Wordsworth made the decision to write such a poem and not to be deterred by friends or foes from its execution. At first the poem was called *The Recluse*, then *The Prelude*, then *The Excursion*. Of course his friends, especially his sister Dorothy, must have heard those words recited by Wordsworth, but *The Prelude* was not published until nearly fifty years later. Soon after that the critical experts thought that the very best version of *The Prelude* had been written in 1803 and 1804 when he was still recovering from the attacks on the *Lyrical Ballads*.

A favourite phrase from Wordsworth of my father – he being the truest ever disciple of Wordsworth – and one which I heard later from J. B. Priestley, who was hardly less an admirer: 'We live by admiration, hope and love.'

Priestley's *Good Companions* seemed to live by those ideas too, and when the book was published at Christmas 1930, my mother, who was almost as good a reader as my father, seized it first and insisted thereafter on extolling all its delights, all maybe except the mysterious rites performed by the crowd returning from the football match on the first page.

For a while I hunted for the reference in vain in Robert Woof's brilliantly directed annotations. If truly we live by admiration, hope and love, the tale could be told only in epic terms. How much of his inspiration, how many years at the height of his powers did Wordsworth apply to the task. *The Excursion* was something incomparably more ambitious than anything he or his fellow poets had attempted. And yet when the monster of a book was finally published, Wordsworth's enemies thought the safest course was to strangle it at birth. Francis Jeffrey in the *Edinburgh Review* had already shown himself the most pitiless of Wordsworth's critics. The new assault, starting with the sentence he made famous – 'This will never do' – sought to wash away the whole new school of poetry, and Wordsworth in particular, in a torrent of ridicule. Every word of that indictment, of course, is reprinted in these pages. If modern poets feel they are sometimes abused by their prosaic colleagues, they should marvel at the brilliant daring of Jeffrey's attack and wonder how anyone could survive it.

Wordsworth himself seemed quite untouched by such assaults. His imperturbability was sometimes attributed to his egotism, but he knew better than anyone else that in the case of *The Excursion* he had sought to escape from egotistical limitations and present the world of the French Revolution and his own age in its proper epic context. Two of his younger readers read *The Excursion* in the manner and spirit Wordsworth invited: one was William Hazlitt and the other was the even younger John Keats, who had just become friends. Hazlitt wrote a three-part criticism of *The Excursion* in *The Examiner*. He recognised the whole of it as a fulfilment of the promise of the new school of poets whose *Lyrical Ballads* he had first heard from the lips of the poets themselves in 1798.

Wordsworth himself was singled out as the poet of the age: 'There is in his general sentiments and reflections on human life a depth, an originality, a truth, a beauty, and grandeur, both of conception and expression which place him decidedly at the head of the poets of the present day, or rather which place him in a totally distinct class of excellence.' He tackles the greatest themes, faces the most awkward crises.

William Hazlitt's immortal defence of Wordsworth's greatness – written at the very moment in the autumn of 1816 when it might have seemed even to his most dedicated admirers, including Hazlitt himself, that his genius was faltering – appears all the more just and significant when we recall again that *The Excursion* was still not so great a poem as the still unpublished *Prelude*. If Hazlitt had had the chance to read that text, his own first acquaintance with poets would have been an even greater event in our literary history: the full flowering of the new school of poetry to take its proper place in the ascent up Jacob's ladder – Hazlitt's own prophecy of how the revolutionaries would recover their path to victory.

Wordsworth's own publications seemed to display a sad deterioration. Francis Jeffrey renewed his assaults in the *Edinburgh Review*. Assaults from that quarter might be expected and discounted: Holland House, head-quarters of the Whigs, had never disowned their Napoleonic sympathies. But quite another anonymous critic in the *Monthly Review* of October 1820 greeted the publication of Wordsworth's 1820 poems with a sophisticated twist at the author's expense in almost every sentence, welcoming 'the dawn of a purer and nobler exertion of intellect in a writer of such acknowledged ability.' How would such patronage be read in Dove Cottage? The book, *The River Duddon*, a series of sonnets composed between 1806 and 1820, included also a poem called 'Vaudracour and Julia'. It was, wrote the critic, 'we presume, to record a love affair in all the less impassioned part of it.' A few sentences later the report continued:

We are by much too plain men to relish (or perhaps fully to compre-
hend) the poetical morality of the subjoined passage:

So passed the time, till, whether through effect
Of some unguarded moment that dissolved
Virtuous restraint – ah, speak it, think it, not!
Deem rather that the fervent Youth, who saw
So many bars between his present state
And the dear haven where he wished to be
In honourable wedlock with his Love,
Was in his judgement tempted to decline
To perilous weakness, and entrust his cause
To nature for a happy end of all;
Deem that by such fond hope the Youth was swayed,
And bear with their transgression, when I add
That Julia, wanting yet the name of wife,
Carried about her for a secret grief
The promise of a mother.

To our old English understandings, it seems less heinous for the lovers to be overcome by an unguarded moment, than for either of them to be 'inwardly prepared to turn aside from law and custom,' &c. We can fancy the indignant zeal of injured virtue, with which a poet, or perhaps a critic, of the Lake school (for such prodigies even as the last do actually exist!) would have censured the above sentiment in any of our classical effusions; in the Eloisa, *for instance, where indeed it is, unfortunately, to be found. It is rare that we have to reprove Mr Wordsworth for any such mistake as this.*

Every sentence in that essay has a special relevance even if the author did not know then that the young Wordsworth was indeed recalling his own love affair in France at the height of his excitement on his visit to France. How much Byron or Shelley would have enjoyed the tribute to exultant Eloisa as they sailed round Rousseau's lake. Had not Hazlitt hailed the kiss for Louisa as the most famous in history? What scorn he would have reserved for those who alleged that it was lacking in passion.

Poets especially but prose writers also who seek to speak a new language deserve a special understanding and protection. William Hazlitt understood that requirement maybe better than any of his contemporaries. He was himself engaged in designing a new prose style which would challenge Dr Johnson's rules and authority. Sometimes he could unloose invectives against some of his fellow writers which may shock the reader by their intemperance. But sometimes too they had been provoked by the failure, say, of some of the poets to support a fellow poet under attack, such as Robert Burns. A rich selection from Hazlitt's writing is printed in these pages. Sometimes he may seem to contradict his own assessments, but all such apparent contradictions may also be misleading.

Nothing disturbed his first judgement at the time of publication of the *Lyrical Ballads* that Wordsworth was the most original poet of the age, and the same claim was repeated in his lecture in London in 1818: 'They open a deeper vein of thought and feeling than any poet in modern times has done or attempted.'

A new generation was starting to read Wordsworth. This thousand-page volume takes the record up to 1820, every word of it read by my one remaining but still discerning eye for the benefit of *Guardian* readers, in the circumstances of extreme comfort in Butch Stewart's best hotel in Jamaica. A new critic actually born in Jamaica gets his place here, but that's another story.

It will be followed by a second magnificent Routledge production up to the late 1890s, when the most famous critic of the age, Matthew Arnold (second only to Hazlitt, of course) finally crowned Wordsworth and Byron as the two greatest poets of the century.

Wordsworth and Byron persisted in their quarrel until their dying days, indeed well beyond them, since the argument between them was inescapably a religious one. Wordsworth would call Byron perverted, Satanic, a spirit deeply evil once the disguises were stripped aside. From his Calvinistic upbringing, Byron had seen this religion itself as the enemy which must be exposed and destroyed.

'I know one may be damned for saying others never 'ere may be so.' But that was a mild rebuke directed at Southey who had also seen him as Satan. Against Wordsworth he could let loose torrents of abuse, either in the freshly discovered verse form which he had designed for his *Don Juan*, or more scurrilously in conversations with casual visitors. He would often express his contempt for Wordsworth's achievement which, as we have seen, may conflict with earlier judgements he had offered. In this sense, Robert Woof's volume is the first in which are presented the clashing verdicts on these mighty topics, however offensive the terms in which each may have formed their assaults.

Dove Cottage, Wordsworth's home, is the proper place for such mighty reconciliations. It is, first and foremost, the home of poets, what they wrote, the beautiful editions in which they first came into each other's hands, the manner in which they could be read by friends and enemies alike. But there also, hardly less memorable than the words, are the paintings and the portraits, the landscapes which they described but no less the portraits of the men and the women.

Some of these were more famous for what they did with the brush than the pen – William Hazlitt first and foremost. His John Thelwall looks looks down happily on the Wordsworth he encountered at Tintern. His Charles Lamb should be there also to show how this best of friends preserved his friendship in London and the Lakes. Thanks to Hazlitt also, Robert Haydon is rightly restored as a master of both arts. And where is Hazlitt's own portrait of Wordsworth – what a find that would be? No small part of the charm of Dove Cottage is the way in which the poets and the painters compete for our attention. Mostly that is the achievement of Robert Woof, the author of this wondrous volume.

However, a few years ago some even more remarkable events were staged at Dove Cottage or in nearby hostelries. Richard Wordsworth, a fine actor himself, recited some verses from Byron's *Don Juan*, and the heavens did not fall. Two years later, Jonathan Wordsworth, chief organiser of the whole affair, invited Jock Murray, direct descendant of Byron's publisher and himself a leading Byronic scholar of the first order, to officiate at the proceedings. One of Byron's portraits, now famous throughout the world, found its place among the Lakers. And did not Hazlitt also conclude his greatest essay with the best motto for Dove Cottage: *Esto perpetua*?

Postscript

Dove Cottage itself, as we have seen, holds its central place in the Wordsworth tradition. Dorothy Wordsworth made her distinctive contribution in her *Grasmere Journals*. In recent times these have been edited and presented by Pamela Woof in the Oxford World's Classics series as *The Grasmere and Alfoxden Journals*. Indeed, Pamela Woof now presents Dove Cottage with Dorothy's own touch and inspiration.

Our Heine

The age of gold of the human race is not behind us, it lies ahead of us; it consists in the perfection of the social order. Our fathers have not seen it; our children will arrive there one day; it is for us to mark the path.

Saint Simon, *On the Reorganisation of European Society*

There was a time when Heinrich Heine was accorded English honours of the highest order, when indeed his status as an international literary figure was established and unchallenged. He was hailed as the natural German successor to the great Goethe; such respected critics as George Eliot and Matthew Arnold paid tribute to his wit and originality, and many English publishers offered their recognition, as the secondhand bookshops can still testify, with an abundant flow of cheap editions both of his poetry and his prose. Somehow our Victorian grandfathers and grandmothers (the women writers were always among the most discerning of his readers) were undisturbed by his ribaldries, his indecencies, and his readiness to insult everything that was holy, headed by several expressions of English hypocrisy.

Today, it must be shamefully but truly recorded that his reputation is nothing like so well-assured and widely recognised. In the one-hundred-and-fifty-odd years since his death the variations in that reputation have been quite unexpected and incalculable. In modern times Hitler and Goebbels did their best to exterminate him altogether, and the restoration has been by no means complete. For a while, both the West Germany and the East Germany of the post-1945 epoch claimed him as their own, but neither could clinch the case with full moral authority. Even the university in his native Düsseldorf seems still to be infected by a touch of anti-semitism. Even some of the best of his apologists, Jewish or non-Jewish, have detected flaws in his character which supposedly inhibit the full defence. Even Matthew Arnold incorporated such an accusation in his final assessment, and left us with the portrait of a deformed Heine. He seemed to give some weight to the reproof he received from Thomas Carlyle, who was outraged that he should have placed 'the ignoble Jewish blasphemer in the same rank as Goethe.' Once heard, it is hard to get the Carlyle sneer out of one's mind: against whose God did he blaspheme and what was this *ignobility*, the most deadly accusation of all? After all, is it not true that he was a traitor, an infidel, an *apostate*, a socialist?

I wish to examine several of these items on the charge-sheet, especially the last, the most heinous, but I must declare my interest, as Members of Parliament are supposed to do. Almost from the very first day when I heard his name, Heinrich Heine became my hero. Some of his accomplishments strike me as being so exceptional that any counter-attack must be discounted in advance. I can tolerate no word of criticism from any quarter, or, at least, none which would diminish his greatness and his glory; almost any mention of him can stir all the old delights, exhilarations, and what he himself called 'seven league boots' ideas, the kind which can take continents in their revolutionary stride.

Possibly part of this enthusiasm may derive from the fact that I was once in love with a lovely Yugoslav-born Jewish girl who had brought

with her, on her escape from Hitler's Vienna, a naturally treasured volume of Heine's poems. It was from her that I first heard recited, as I am sure Heine would have wished, the words of *Der Lorelei*, and later came to picture her as the model for Heine's last love, Camille Selden, the lotus flower who restored him on his deathbed to his pagan faith. I had also just read an anthology of Heine's prose which arrived on my desk at the *Evening Standard* from across the Atlantic. The conjunction of events was exciting. I'd never read a word of Heine before; I never stopped for long reading him thereafter. And the excitement was naturally intensified when a few years later I met Heinrich Heine himself or his indisputable reincarnation, and he became my best friend. Little Vicky, the cartoonist, had every Heineite feature; he was the same diminutive size, of the same race, of the same faith or non-faith, the same iconoclastic temperament with a comparable artistic gift. He too, like my Jewish girlfriend, knew Heine by heart, and would summon his hero to his side whenever the political battle was most ruthless or pitiless.

The Heine who took Paris to his heart and who was in turn over-whelmed by a flow of reciprocal affection had already done enough for his fame. His poetry and his prose and his politics together had already marked him out as a man of the new age and the new Europe, one whose voice could not be confined to the German cities of his upbringing and education. Düsseldorf, Hamburg, Göttingen, Bonn, Berlin: he could extract what he wanted from each and then lash them with a satirical fury unknown in Germany before. His *Buch der Lieder* also struck a lyric note which seemed novel; his *Lorelei* was just one of them which would never cease to be sung afresh in every land and every language. He had started to produce his series of *Reisebilder*, his travel pictures in which every art was interwoven. He had been brought up in a Jewish home and then baptised as a Christian, chiefly for the purpose of being able to ease the earning of his livelihood. Such a bitter humiliation contributed to his understanding of politics. He recognised the unceasing battle between rich and poor and wrote, in one of his very first attempts at a larger theme of the two nations, savagely at grips, the 'satiated and the starvelings'. Almost everywhere he went, even in the Italy where a different sun seemed to shine, he would return to this theme.

'I know not', he said of himself (in Matthew Arnold's translation of the passage which he put at the head of his essay), 'if I deserve that a laurel wreath should one day be laid on my coffin. Poetry, dearly as I have loved it, has always been to me but a divine plaything. I have never attached any great value to poetical fame; and I trouble myself very little whether people praise my verses or blame them. But lay on my coffin a *sword*; for I was a brave soldier in the war of the liberation of humanity.' Naturally enough these words are often adopted or adapted, as Matthew Arnold did, as his final epitaph; no doubt that was part of his intention and he would not complain about the transmission. But it is worth noting that they were written before his thirtieth birthday, before he had reached Paris, when his poetry was indeed the chief cause of his rising reputation. How could he ask that such a judgement should be reached on the rest of his accomplishments? May not the claim, taken within its proper context, be dismissed as a piece of juvenile pretentiousness, a further revelation of the weakness in his character already detected? If this point in the debate were to be conceded, he would by this alone be reduced to a figure of much smaller stature, and this indeed was the conclusion of many of his contemporaries. He could never make up his mind whether he was a poet or a politician, an artist or a man of action. He would turn with frantic impatience from one role to another, and risk failing in them all.

The proper answer, in defence of the young Heine, I shall offer in a moment: how far he was prepared to carry his political doctrine in the 1820s is itself a startling revelation. But another approach may be to compare Heine's role with that of some of his greatest contemporaries. He was often called the German Byron, and he himself naturally welcomed the compliment. When the news of Byron's death at

Missolonghi reached him, he wrote most justly and eloquently of 'his cousin', of his 'comrade-in-arms', of who had been fighting in the same cause, indeed in the very spirit of his own premature epitaph. He had every right to do so, since he was surrounded, almost suffocated, by the pious persecutions of the Holy Alliance, against which Byron directed his great final invectives. The Europe of the 1820s was to be recreated in the old pre-Napoleonic, pre-revolutionary image. Byron and Heine were fellow partisans in that resistance movement.

Of course Byron first set the pattern, or sounded the tocsin, and Heine never wished to contest his leadership. He was much too eager to learn. He had often attempted to translate particular Byron poems into German, and one of his choices had been especially apposite. He was naturally attracted by Byron's *Hebrew Melodies*, and most especially by the one which

Shook Belshazzar in his Hall
And took his kingdom from him.

Those words were the Rights of Man and Heine gave them a force no less powerful than Byron's; indeed in his version Belshazzar met his fate at the hands of his rebellious people. But Heine's interest in, absorption with, Byronic themes cannot be indicated by individual comparisons. The association cuts much deeper. They found themselves ranged against the same enemies, the same miserable men and, even more, the same miserable gods. They devised the same brand of defiance; they each developed a heart for every fate. They both discovered that the true reaction to such a world – the politicians 'no less than the poets' – was to face the hideous reality all around, but to recognise too the folly, the absurdity, of human pretensions, especially as displayed by the mighty and the pious. The tone of so much that Heine wrote seems close to the final triumph, the combination of the tragedy and comedy which Byron developed in *Don Juan*. And since Byron came first, it might seem enough to treat Heine as his brilliant disciple. But there was more, as we shall see, and some signs appeared even in the barren 1820s, dominated by counter-revolution victories, when Byron's and Heine's common enemies appeared to have regained their absolute ascendancy.

A greater reputation even than Byron's seemed to dominate the intellectual world of the Napoleonic and post-Napoleonic epoch, and nowhere more so than in Heine's Germany. Byron himself recognised the pre-eminence of Wolfgang von Goethe and sought to dedicate to him one of his own books which contained the most explosively revolutionary of his own plays, the volume published in 1822 which included *Cain, The Two Foscari* and *Sardanapalus* and a preface which stated most boldly his own view of the Revolution. Poets were not expected to be strictly truthful in dedications to their elders and betters. But even so Byron's obeisance may be thought excessive: however, his choice of words do emphasise the position which the recipient held in Byron's world and Heine's world. 'To The Illustrious Goethe. A Stranger presumes to offer the homage of a literary vassal to his liege lord, the first of existing writers – who has collated the literature of his own country and illustrated that of Europe. The unworthy production which the author ventures to inscribe to him is entitled *Sardanapalus*.'* Alas, the gift never reached its destination during Byron's lifetime, but Goethe had already given what he may have considered fulsome evidence of his recognition of Byron's genius. The tribute had a touch of patronage; Byron, it was hinted, might serve his own splendid reputation better still if he left philosophy to others. But Heine of course had an even better reason than Byron for turning to the great prophet-poet-philosopher who presided over European letters from his throne in Weimar; he was striving to follow in Goethe's own footsteps, to adopt his lyric example in Goethe's own language. His own poems were already being recited, his songs were

---

*   The charming story of the unearthing of this little treasure is told in E. M. Butler's autobiography, *Paper Boats* (1959).

already being sung throughout Germany, and Goethe might have been expected to have heard them too. When, in the months just after Byron's death, the young man plucked up his courage to visit the Weimar already now more famous for Goethe's presence there than for any other reason, the young poet was twenty-six, the old poet seventy-seven but fully still in possession of his faculties, not yet quite having completed the master-piece of his old age, the matchless, inscrutable *Faust*.

What happened next is one of the saddest encounters in literary history. How many times had little Heine recited to himself what he was determined to say when he was finally admitted to the great man's presence? No question was possible about his resolve and his diffidence. Goethe was his God insofar as he would yield that title to anybody; along with Goethe's own fellow poet Schiller, were, for Heine's gener-ation, the mighty liberators. He had no other wish but to honour them; but suddenly he was tongue-tied or, rather, babbled meaningless plati-tudes. Goethe replied with some equal banalities about the excellence of the plums on the road from Jena and then paused to ask upon what new piece of writing Heine might be engaged, whereupon Heine in turn found himself blurting out, almost involuntarily, some words that he had never intended: 'A Faust'. The interview was brought to a sudden end; all Heine's carefully prepared compliments were swept aside by the utterance of this single insult. Heine was so shaken by the affair that he would not report it to his friends for several months; he would only assure them that 'the beer at Weimar was really first rate'. Goethe noted gruffly in his diary, '2nd October. Heine of Göttingen'.

A few months later Heine did record, for the benefit of one of his closest friends, what he truly felt about Goethe. Despite the soreness inflicted by his own dismissal, he discerned with much insight what was truly the political gulf, the clash of political temperament, which divided them. Goethe had been hailed as the first harbinger of a new age – 'This, the highest that can be said of written books, is to be said of these,' wrote Thomas Carlyle: 'There is in them a New Time, the prophecy and the beginning of a New Time. The corner-stone of a new edifice for mankind is laid there.' Momentous claims indeed. But Heine was himself daring to delineate a New Time, deserving even bolder capital letters than Carlyle had ascribed to Goethe, and one part of his nature he compared with Goethe's:

As a fact, I have caught at the enjoyments of life and found pleasure in them; whence the fierce struggle that goes on in me between my clear reason, which approves the enjoyments of life and rejects the devotion of self-sacrifice as a folly, and my enthusiasm, which is always rising up and laying violent hands on me, and trying to drag me down again to her ancient solitary realm; up I ought perhaps rather to say, for it is still a grave question whether the enthusiast who gives up his life for the idea does not, in a single moment, live more and feel more happiness than Herr von Goethe in his six-and-seventieth year of egotistic tranquillity.

However, to reduce the argument to a clash of egos and ambitions would be especially unjust to the Heine of this period, who was already striding ahead of most of his contemporaries. Provoked and embittered by some personal injuries – the detested Christian baptism, the breach with many of his German friends, the humiliation of the visit to Weimar – he was still able to publish the first of his far seeing political manifestoes. One further spur had been supplied, we must shamefully acknowledge, by his visit to England in 1827.

It was the England of the Lord Liverpool repression, of the Regency, of the Duke of Wellington, of the new industrial society which displayed all its callousness and cruelty and few of its redeeming prospects. The young Heine honestly searched for better signs – he found two, in the statesmanship of George Canning and the essays of William Hazlitt; an unlikely combination of events, and yet one which does credit to Heine's casual discernment. At the hour of defeat for most of the liberal causes which he served, he, like Byron before him, preached promise of a new liberating victory. Byron had chosen the metaphor of the sea, the eternal sea, to describe his final confidence in a great future for mankind. Heine did the same in a style which, in this field at least. outdid his mentor and master.

This Heine, we may remind ourselves again, had not yet visited his beloved revolutionary Paris, to see and feel for himself what the new stirrings there might offer. All the more to be noted and applauded was the spacious vision with which he asserted that the achievements of the revolutionary epoch must be defended from all assaults, from every quarter. He told the history of his time in the way all history should be told; it was at once a recital, a celebration, a prophecy and a call to arms. 'I suffer for the salvation of the whole human race. I atone for their sins – but I also enjoy them.' Was there ever an historian who carried his blasphemies more lightheartedly? And yet he could turn to face tragedy with equal equanimity. He stood on the battlefield of Marengo, and defended his own and his own generation's Napoleonic predilections – 'I loved him beyond all limit up to eighteenth Brumaire when he betrayed freedom.' And truly the captivation for him and for many others went on a little longer still. 'It was there at Marengo that General Buonaparte drank so mighty a draught from the goblet of renown that in his intoxication he became Consul, Emperor, World-conqueror, and first grew sober at St Helena.' But Heine and his comrades grew sober too, or, better still, discovered a new intoxication. He carried forward the challenge to a new era. 'What is the great question of the age? It is that of emancipation. Not simply the emancipation of the Irish Greeks, Frankfurt Jews, West Indian Negroes and other oppressed races, but the emancipation of the whole world, and especially that of Europe, which has attained its majority, and now tears itself loose from the iron leading-strings of a privileged aristocracy. A few philosophical renegades from freedom may forge, if they will, for us the most elaborate chains of conclusions, to prove that millions of men are born to be beasts of burden for a few thousand nobles, but they will never convince us until they make it clear, to borrow the expression of Voltaire, that the former are born with saddles on their backs, and the latter with spurs on their heels.'

More and more Heine turned his mind to the social question – what Carlyle was to call 'the Condition of England' question and what properly was the Condition of Europe question as the great question of the future. He had after all been the very first to speak of the two nations who were facing one another in the coming struggle But he always rejected the sophistry which would seek to divide the moral justification of the old revolution from the new one. What the French had done on the Paris stage in the sight of the whole world was necessary to be done, even the killing of the king. Monarchists, English or French, at least had no right to object; or did they claim that regicide was their privilege alone? Indeed, his Christian tutors in Catholic Germany had told him the story of the New Testament so well that he could see the events in Paris as a crucifixion. Who betrayed his saviour for the pieces of silver? The Bible, symbolically, by placing the banker among the apostles, revealed the unholy power which lay in the money bag and the faithlessness of business men – 'Every rich man is a Judas Iscariot.' This age sacrificed itself for the sins of the past and for the happiness of the future; it bore a bloody crown of thorns and a heavy cross; it was 'a Messiah among centuries'.

For Christians, this was the language of sacrilege. But for how long had his own people been forced to endure not merely the language but the murder and persecution which went with the incitement. On his last visit to Hamburg, he had heard news of a new pogrom, an event so common that it often passed without comment except among the victims. Heine ached for the establishment of a new religion in which all persecution, even the torture of animals, would be joyfully outlawed, and this was one more dream which beckoned him to Paris.

'Our Heine' was a term first applied to him not by his fellow Germans but by some Czech poet, victim of oppression, who translated him into his own tongue. Often oppressed peoples of other races and periods have had an urge to appropriate him for themselves. He knew how his own Jewish forbears had had to suffer insult and outrage, but he used that knowledge to declare a universal war against injustice. A new biography of him which appeared just after the 1939–45 war was written by an anti-Nazi Hungarian, Francois Fejto, and it was dedicated 'To my aged Father, departed in 1944 and disappeared. He loved Heine. And to my two Brothers also disappeared.' So much that Heine wrote was given a new poignancy by the Hitler terror and the Stalinite terror which followed. In a sense he foresaw them both and raised the standard of defiance which served so many stricken peoples across the whole European continent, and beyond. Yet our Heine also served another cause, and we are entitled to acclaim him too.

Heine himself said he was the first man of the century, and his joke, as usual, was a good one. What he meant to do, with his touch of insolence, was to note that he was born in the very first hours of the year 1800. In actual fact, he had got the date wrong, and the slight inaccuracy concealed his own illegitimacy. No matter: the reminder about the inexact date helps to illustrate many aspects of his life and relationships. He died in Paris at the age of fifty-eight, having seen the end of one Napoleon and the beginning of another. All his life, in the Germany of his birth or the France of his adoption, he lived in the world which had been shaped by the French Revolution and the Napoleonic conquests, and he would draw no sharp distinction between the two. For many people beyond the French frontiers, and especially for the Jews, both came as liberators. They, both the French revolutionary armies and their Napoleonic successors, preached a doctrine of fraternity; they opened the ghettoes; they would permit no blind restoration of the old order.

The Paris of the 1830s was alive with revolutionary ardour and expectation, and no observer and participant was better qualified to capture that spirit and set his own imprint upon it than Heine. Always elsewhere, he had found his free spirit suffocated by the legacies of the past – in the Jewish family of his upbringing, in the Christian Germany where he had been taught the rules of good conduct and bourgeois advancement, in the England of the previous decade where he had been appalled by his first sign of the horrors of industrialism. Across the whole of Western Europe swept the first wave of revulsion against this seemingly new threat to man's humanity. Soon the name socialist was to be applied to it. Heine, as we shall see, gave original expression to this word, although for a variety of reasons his declarations on the subject were often suppressed, as the vigilant censors in so many capital cities wished them to be. He himself celebrated his arrival in Paris with the words: 'When the fish in the sea ask each other how they feel, they answer: "Like Heine in Paris."' One element in the revolutionary Paris air was the prophecy of socialism, and Heine was one of the very first to sense it.

The Frenchman who introduced Heine to socialism had been dead for five years when he arrived in Paris; his first band of disciples were just coming into their own. Sometimes Count Henri Claude de Ronvroy de Saint-Simon, has been the butt of raillery or contempt, as the founder of any form of socialism worthy of the name: had he not been born in the very bosom of the French aristocracy? did he not bear the actual title of the most notorious of French gossip writers? and did he not himself boast that he was directly descended from Charlemagne? It was all true, but all such ungenerous comment from any quarter was quite misplaced. Maybe the ridicule derived from the tale of how, as a boy of fifteen, he had instructed his valet to call him in the morning with the summons: 'Get up, M. le Comte, you have great things to do.' I first read this delightful exchange in Ignazio Silone's book *The School for Dictators*; even he, the most magnanimous of men although an astringent socialist, could not suppress a faintly derogatory comment. But Henri did do great things, and he displayed a special brand of courage in doing them. More than once he risked his whole inherited future or livelihood to serve his freshly-devised political faith. He was one of the few French aristocrats who made an entirely novel and highly intelligent deduction from his understanding of the French Revolution itself. He saw that there could be no going back to the old infamies of the *ancien regime*, that a dramatically new compact, contract, call it what you will, between rulers and the ruled would have to be established, and not only in France, if such a monstrous horror as the renewal of the European war was to be averted. He saw that all other questions prominent in the post-revolutionary debate – for example, property ownership, money-making, the right to work, and clerical power – must be involved in the new Europe wide reappraisal.

Sometimes these great matters were discussed in language too remote from the world which Frenchmen saw around them to be understood, and sometimes they were not understood as well. On one celebrated occasion he illustrated what he meant by 'the useful members of society, the men and women who should rule'. 'We suppose', he began, 'that France suddenly loses her fifty leading physicists, her fifty leading chemists, her fifty leading physiologists, her fifty leading mathematicians, her fifty leading mechanics, her fifty leading engineers, civil and military, her fifty leading bankers and then several more to make up the total of three thousand leading servants, artistes and artisans of France'. The result of this loss? France would become a body without a soul; it would require a generation to repair the disaster. But pass, said Saint-Simon, to another supposition: 'Suppose that instead of all these France were to lose Monsieur, the Brother of the King, the Duc de Berry, and a few odd specified Duchesses, all the officers of the Crown and Ministers of State, all Cardinals, Archbishops, Bishops and the like, all judges and the ten thousand wealthiest proprietors who live nobly, 30,000 in all. The loss would be no more than a sentimental one, and plenty of judges, priests, etc. would step forward to fill the vacant shoes.'

This tale was given the name of the *Parabole de Saint-Simon*, and when published in the year 1819 he was immediately put on trial and was happily acquitted by a jury. He did not withdraw; indeed, all the evidence suggests that he spoke with an ever greater deliberation until the day of his death for *la classe la plus nombreuse et la plus pauvre*.

Saint-Simon did foresee some kind of ordered utopia in which those who did the real work would have the power, but he knew also that this desirable end could be reached best, not by some sudden *coup d'etat,* but by a steady understanding of the needs of the new world. He became more and more attracted by the idea of a general pattern of history which could explain the past and help to foretell the future for mankind – and indeed womankind, since the Saint-Simonians were among the very first to talk of women's rights. Even before Karl Marx, Saint-Simon helped to indicate what a comfort it could be for political leaders to sense that history might be on their side. And this, for sure, was one of Saint-Simon's special appeals for Heine. Heine's own historical imagination was a faculty of extraordinary range and individuality. He was constantly reshaping the world around him to fit some larger contour; his prophecies were sometimes of such earth-shattering accuracy that they can still leave us wanting to probe their strange origins. But, as he understood, they were also part of his equipment as a poet. Sometimes, he would say, the people, the multitude, understood better still: 'They seek their histories from the poet and not from the historian. They ask not for bare facts but those facts again dissolved in the original poetry from which they sprung. This the poets well know, and it is not without a certain mischievous pleasure that they mould at will popular memories, perhaps in mockery of pride-baked historians and parchment-minded keepers of State documents.'

Saint-Simonian influences may be detected in many of his subsequent writings, but the most direct and extensive of those appeared in the book to which he gave the general title *De Allernegre*. Madame de Stael had recently made this title famous, and Heine confessed or boasted that he always had this 'grandmother of the Doctrinaires' before his eyes when he wrote his comprehensive response. At any reckoning, it was a brave way to go about the business, since what he wrote was bound to give even more offence in his native Germany than in France. He would teach them a brand of German history they had never heard before.

Happier and more beautiful generations, who, begotten in free-choice embraces, will flourish a religion of joy and pleasure, will smile sadly at their poor ancestors, who, mournful and melancholy, abstained from all enjoyment of this beautiful world, and by mortifying and killing the warm, glowing, coloured sensuousness, almost wasted into cold spectres. Yes, I say it definitely, our descendants will be more beautiful and happier than we are. For I believe in progress, I believe that man was meant to be happy, and have a higher opinion of Divinity than those pious people who think it only created humanity to make it suffer. I would beforehand, by the blessings of free political and industrial institutions, establish that happiness, which according to the religious, will be first found in heaven on the day of judgement.

For emphasis too he made clear at the outset what hated instruments were to be used for the propagation of the new faith. The weapon which the German authorities used most readily was censorship, but Heine invoked against them the great German hero Martin Luther, who 'did not believe in the marvels of the church but he had a firm faith in devilry … On the Wurtburg while he was translating the New Testament, he was so disturbed by the devil that he threw his inkstand at his head. Ever since that time, the devil has had a great horror of ink, especially printer's ink.'

Luther also understood his opponent, but not so well as Heine.

Leo X, the refined Florentine, the pupil of Politian, the friend of Raphael, the Greek philosopher with the triple crown which the Council conferred on him, perhaps because he suffered from a malady which certainly was not caused by Christian abstinence, and which was in those days very dangerous – Leo de' Medicis, how he must have smiled at the poor, chaste, simple monk, who fancied that the Gospel was the chart of Christendom, and that this chart must be true! Perhaps he never really knew or cared to know what Luther wanted, so occupied was he with the building the Church of St Peter, the expense of which was to be defrayed by the sale of indulgences, so that it was really built by sin, and was a monument of lust – like that pyramid which an Egyptian harlot erected with the money which she had earned by prostitution. It might indeed be said much more truly of this church than of the Cathedral of Cologne, that it was built by the Devil. This triumph of Spiritualism, that sensuality itself should build for it its most beautiful temple, and that from confessions of fleshly sins the means were drawn to glorify the spirit, was not understood in the German North. For here, far sooner than under the glowing sky of Italy, was it possible to practise a Christianity which made the very least concession to sensuality. We of the North are of colder blood, and did not need so many indulgences for fleshly sins as the paternal Leo supplied us with. The climate aids us very much in practising Christian virtues, and on the 31st of October 1516, when Luther nailed his thesis on the door of the Augustine church, perhaps the moat of Wittenberg was frozen, and people could skate on it; which being a very cold pleasure, is consequently not a sin.

Martin Luther became in Heine's hands 'not only the greatest but the Germanest man in our history … His thoughts had hands as well as wings, he spoke and acted; he was not only the tongue but the sword of his time.' Yet he could be gentle and loving too, and from him too, although few but Heine cared to emphasise the point, came the old Saint Simonian rhyme:

Who loves not woman, wine and song
Remains a fool his whole life long.

Sometimes Luther was reproached for his passions but, for Heine, this was his saving grace. 'Pure souls cannot act.' And somehow this same

Luther gave language to thought and created the German language. He made the Reformation – and cut open the path for an even greater Revolution. Heine could never suppress the reverberations of his own time. Luther was 'a religious Danton, a preacher of the Mountain, who from its height hurls down varied blocks of words on the heads of his foes ... That song [of Luther's] which was the Marseilles Hymn of the Reformation, has preserved its power of inspiration to this day, and we perhaps shall use the old mail-clad words 'ere long for other battles ... He who will speak of modern German literature must begin with Luther.' So Heine himself launched his plan the new freedom from the strongest citadel. No free thinker had written of Martin Luther in such epic terms.

And soon this mighty ally found himself fighting the good fight, along with a few others such as Benedict Spinoza, against the darkest forces:

For there have always been men of imperfect capacities for enjoyment, of crippled senses and bruised flesh, who find all the grapes sour in his garden of God, who see the decoying serpent by every tree of Paradise, and seek their triumph in asceticism and their pleasure in pain. On the contrary, there are also and ever with us well-grown, bodily-proud natures, who like to hold their heads high; all the stars and roses smile sympathetically with them; they love to listen to the melodies of the nightingale and of Rossini; they love the beautiful Gluck and Titian's flesh, and to the dull fellow who hangs his head and to whom all such things are an abomination they reply in the words of Shakespeare's fool, 'Dost thou think, because thou art virtuous, there shall be no more cakes and ale?'

It was time to take the offensive:

The God of the Pantheists differs also from that of the Deists, because he is himself in the world while the latter is quite out of, or, what is the same, over it. The God of the Deists rules the world from above

downwards as if it were a separate establishment, but the Deists differ
among themselves as to the mode or manner of this rule. The Hebrews
conceive God as a thundering tyrant, the Christians as a loving father;
the pupils of Rousseau, or the whole Genevese school, imagine him as a
clever artist who made the world much as their papa made his watches,
and as connoisseurs they admire the work and praise the master on high.

The cakes and ale were all part of Heine's appropriation. Shakespeare
was on his side no less than Luther and Spinoza. The whole story was
brought right up to date. He even thought, in generous bursts of patriotism, that Germany might at last set the pace for France.

The political revolution which bases itself on the principles of French
Materialism will find no opponents in the Pantheists, but allies, allies
who have drawn their convictions from a deeper source or from a
religious synthesis. We promote the well-being of the material, the
material prosperity of the peoples, not because we, like the materialists,
despise the spirit, but because we know that the divinity of man
proclaims itself even in his bodily appearance, and misery destroys or
makes vile the body, the image of God, the spirit thereby utterly
perishing. The great word of the revolution which St Just pronounced,
'Le pain est le droit du peuple' (bread is the people's right), is according
to us, 'Le pain est le droit divin de l'homme' (bread is man's divine
right). We do not contend for the human, but for the divine rights of
man. In this and in many other things we differ from the men of the revo-
lution. We will not be sans culottes, *nor frugal citizens, nor economical*
small presidents. We found a democracy of equally lordly, equally holy,
and equally happy gods. You demand simple costumes, austere manners,
and cheap unseasoned pleasures; we, on the contrary, demand nectar
and ambrosia, purple garments, costly perfumes, luxury and splendour,
dances of laughing nymphs, music and comedies. Be not angered, O
virtuous republicans! To your censuring reproaches we reply what the

fool in Shakespeare has already said, 'Dost thou think, because thou art
virtuous, there shall be no more cakes and ale?'

The Saint-Simonians understood and wanted something of the kind,
but they stood on an unfavourable soil, and the Materialism which
surrounded them suppressed them. They were better understood in
Germany, for Germany is the most propitious soil for Pantheism; it is
the religion of our greatest thinkers and best artists, and Deism, as I
shall explain in another place, has there long perished in theory. It
maintains itself there, like many other things, only among the unthinking
masses, without reasonable warrant. It is not said, but everyone knows,
that Pantheism is the public secret in Germany. In fact, we have
outgrown Deism. We are free, and do not want a thundering tyrant; we
are grown-up, and require no fatherly care. Nor are we the bungled
work of a great mechanic. Deism is a religion for slaves, for children,
for Genevese, for watch-makers.

But, of course, the offensive could be carried much further still, into the
heart of the enemy's territory, and Heine could never resist the temptation, whatever the risk to himself. 'For religion,' he said, 'when it can no
longer burn us alive, comes to us begging'. This was the moment when
he called for the final resistance, with his own people, the Jews, taking
their place alongside the Germans and the French. 'Today matters are
changed in Germany', he insisted, and 'the party of flowers and nightingales is closely connected with the Revolution. The future is ours, and
the dayspring of victory is already dawning.'

This was the Saint-Simonian dawn which he saw and which, he
believed, would make all other gods bow before it, and he could write
of such events with reverence, since his historical sense in the final
analysis demanded no less.

A strange dread, a mysterious reverence, does not permit us to write
further to day. Our breast is filled with terrible compassion; it is the

ancient Jehovah himself preparing for death. We have known him so well from his cradle upwards, in Egypt, where he was brought up among sacred calves, crocodiles, holy onions, ibises and cats. We have seen him as he bid adieu *to these playmates of his childhood and obelisks and sphinxes, and became a small god-king in Palestine to a poor pastoral people, and dwelt in his own temple-palace. We saw him later when he came into contact with the Assyrian-Babylonian civilisation, and laid aside his all too human passions, and no longer belched wrath and vengeance, at least no longer thundered for every trumpery trash of sin. We saw him emigrate to Rome, the capital, where he renounced all national prejudices and proclaimed the heavenly equality of all races, and with such fair phrases formed an opposition to the ancient Jupiter, and intrigued so long that at last he rose to power, and from the Capitol governed the state and the world, urbem et orbem. We saw how he spiritualised himself more and more, how he sweet-saintly wailed when he became a loving father, a universal friend of humanity, a benefactor of the human race, a philanthropist. It all availed him naught.*

Hear ye the bell ring? Kneel down: they bring the sacrament to a dying God!

No such kindly reproof was allowed for some others, if the Saint-Simonian day should come – the English, for example, or at least the rulers of the English who had always figured most prominently on his list of the damnable and damned ever since he had paid his four-month visit to our shores in the late 1820s. His hatred for the moneymen who wrenched their livelihood from the new industrial horror, who would impose their values wherever they could, was well nigh uncontrollable. Since he also showed at the same time how he could honour English writers or politicians of varying political complexions – William Hazlitt and George Canning and Lord Byron and Sir Walter Scott all took their place on his catholic list –he could certainly prove that he was not actuated by some crude anti-English prejudice. He must have been among the first who protested against the menace of the machine on theoretical humanistic grounds – the motives which later inspired, say, John Ruskin or William Morris. Heine was struck by Mary Shelley's *Frankenstein,* published in 1817, but he was the first who embellished the whole story with the necessary socialist moral. He was struck by the sheer human horror of the Industrial Revolution, and his immediate response was that no compromise was possible with such an evil thing.

There is a story that an English mechanic, who had already invented the most artistically ingenious machines, hit upon the idea to make a man, and that it finally succeeded. This work of his hands could bear and behave itself perfectly like a man; it even had in its leathern breast a kind of human feeling, which did not differ greatly from the usual feelings of Englishmen. It could communicate its emotions in articulate tones, and the rustle and buzz of the inner wheels, rasps, and screws, when heard, had the very intonation of pure English pronunciation; in short, this automaton was a perfect gentleman, and all that he wanted, to be a real man, was a soul. But this the English mechanic could not give him, and the poor creature having come to the consciousness of his imperfection, tormented his creator night and day, begging him for a soul. This entreaty became so intolerable, that the artist at last fled in fear from his own work. But the automaton followed him at once by extra-post to the Continent, travelled constantly after him, caught him many times unexpectedly, and snarled and growled at him, 'Give me a soul!' We meet these two forms in every country, and those who know what their mutual relations are, understand their strange haste and anxious irritation. But when their peculiar conditions are known, one finds in it something common enough, and sees how a part of the English people, weary of its mechanical existence, demands a soul, while the other, agonised by this constant request, flies here and there, neither being able to remain at home.

Sometimes, Heine, the Saint-Simonian, would allow himself to be distracted from his more idyllic aspirations. He saw a good future for mankind, and was not prepared for long to accept an abatement of his hopes. But thanks to a whole combination of attributes – his flaming honesty, his poetic genius, his Jewish ancestry maybe – he would face the darkness and storms, and describe them as they had never been described before. One part of this prophecy derived from his under-standing of his Germany, and the most famous warning of all was given in indelible words, words, however, which the world did spurn in the wicked era of the 1930s:

The old stone gods will rise from long-forgotten ruin and rub the dust of a thousand years from their eyes, and Thor, leaping to life with his giant hammer, will crush the Gothic cathedrals! But when those days shall come, and ye hear the stamping and ring of arms, guard ye well, ye neighbours' children, ye French, and put not forth your hands into what we are doing in Germany, for verily evil will come upon you for that ... Thought goes before the deed as lightning precedes thunder. German thunder is indeed German, and not in a hurry, and it comes rolling slowly onward; but come it will, and when ye hear it crash as naught ever crashed before in the whole history of the world, then know that der Deutsche Donner, our German Thunder, has at last hit the mark. At that sound the eagles will fall dead from on high, the lions in remotest deserts in Africa will draw in their tails and creep into their royal caves. There will be played in Germany a drama compared to which the French Revolution will be only an innocent idyll. Just now all is tolerably quiet, and if here and there someone behaves in a lively manner, do not believe for that that the great actors have as yet appeared on the stage.

And the hour will come. As on the benches of an amphitheatre, the races will group round Germany to behold the great battle-play. I warn ye then, Frenchmen, keep very quiet, and for your lives do not

applaud. We might easily misunderstand it, and in our rude manner
teach you roughly to keep quiet.

So the mighty prophecy rolled on and of course it is impossible for us in this century to read it without the whole Nazi horror and the Russian response being unfolded again before our startled gaze. Occasionally Heine's critics in modern times, and he has had many from all sides of the political compass, have sought to dismiss these extraordinary outbursts as a freak, an inexplicable absurdity. It is much safer surely to seek to unravel the reasons why, when he made so many errors on trivial matters, he could be so splendidly and sombrely right on the greatest questions of all, why the long subsequent effort to destroy his credit, from the right and the left, by his own contemporaries and ours, is so wrong-headed, so perverse, so interested in the sense that so many people do wish to see Heine dismissed as a consistent thinker Christians, Protestants, Catholics, Jews, Germans, Frenchmen, Marxists all seem to feel that their worlds would be more secure, if Heine and more especially his ideas can be dismissed. Was he not subversive of them all, and was that his crime?

Sometimes the world was so deafened by these words and deeds and their thundering climax in our own century that the rest of his message was lost or buried or, more usually, grievously distorted. Throughout the nineteenth century Heine was widely honoured and acclaimed across the Continent and even here in the capitalist England which had often so bitterly assailed him. Many cheap editions of his poems and political writings were issued, despite all the protests that translations would prove incomprehensible.

Two such varied and authoritative critics as Matthew Arnold and George Eliot wrote of him in laudatory terms, as the true successor to the great Goethe, but neither they nor any other critics were inclined to attach the chief significance to his avowed political creed. Heinrich Heine, the Saint-Simonian, was treated as if he were no more than an aberrant, wayward figure. Neither his gentile nor his Jewish admirers wished to take to heart the magnificent invectives directed against them by his peculiar, original political faith. But Heine himself would always be ready to turn the tables on his accusers and taunt them with their lofty rectitudes: 'The stars of heaven seem so bright and pure because we see them from afar and know nothing of their private life. Doubtless there are among them many who lie and beg, deceive, are compelled to do all kinds of mean actions, kiss one another and betray, flatter their enemies, and, what is worse, their friends, just as we do here below. Those comets which we see sweeping wildly about with flowing hair, like Maenads of heaven, are perhaps libertines who in the end creep repentantly and piously into some obscure corner of heaven and hate the sun.'

Heine speaks for himself, as I hope I have freshly illustrated, but his best interpreter, Professor S. S. Prawer has produced the indispensable volume: *Heine's Jewish Comedy* (Oxford University Press, 1983).

Stanley Jones's Hazlitt

Review of Stanley Jones, *Hazlitt: a life from Winterslow to Frith Street*, in the *Independent*, 28 October 1989

Of all the great writers of the Romantic age, William Hazlitt was the one who found it most difficult to discover the nature of his own genius. He would never apply the word to himself, and nor would any of his contemporaries. Even at the time of his death, several of them who should have known better, such as Coleridge or Wordsworth, spoke of him with scorn or hatred or fear.

All would have been amazed at the modern critical judgement which seems to advance his fame afresh, from decade to decade, in so many fields: still the foremost of dramatic critics; still among the best of English art critics (according to Kenneth Clark); the first critic who treated the novel as an art; the serious literary critic, quite able to hold his place between Johnson and Arnold; the Shakespearean critic, a match for Coleridge; the essayist who could rival Charles Lamb or his own beloved master, Montaigne; the political polemicist, pupil of Junius and teacher of a whole tribe who would plagiarise or imitate him – the Macaulays, the Bagehots, and several more.

No one would be more amazed than Hazlitt himself at these developments, even though he would pride himself, at every personal crisis, on how determined he was 'to look abroad into universality', to see, in its full, exhilarating perspective, the scale of what he called 'the apocalyptical chapter in the history of human nature' unfolding all around him.

But before he could tackle these mighty themes, he had to endure a wretched, near fatal apprenticeship. Before he could write even the first halting sentences, the tears would wet the pages in front of him. He was in his mid-thirties before he wrote anything for which he was properly paid. He had to face defeat at every turn, including an absurd marriage which was doomed before it started.

Stanley Jones starts this new life 'From Winterslow ...', and the emphasis is stunningly vindicated. The whole hinterland of Hazlitt's mind and, more especially, the relationship with his father leave indelible marks on the portrait. But it is right to be reminded so sharply that almost all Hazlitt wrote which made him great was compressed into the following twenty-odd years.

One by one his new biographer recalls, with the aid of new scholarly discoveries and new insight, the moments famous or not so famous when Hazlitt expressed the spirit of the age, or put his own individual imprint upon it. Which was it when he pronounced Wordsworth – and the Wordsworth of *The Excursion*, not *The Prelude* – the most original poet of the age? Which was it when he saw Edmund Kean perform as Shylock? Stanley Jones places that winter's night at Drury Lane more precisely in our literary history than ever before, matching with graphic detail the critical discoveries which David Bromwich drew from the same scene a few years ago. It was the presence of Hazlitt there with all his boiling hatred of oppression which ever afterwards transformed the English debate about anti-semitism.

Hazlitt took his politics everywhere – like a giant mastiff, as someone said. Politics, of course, was the main reason why he had to fight against such fearful odds to get into print at all. Once he had made something of a name for himself, he might have been excused if, for a moment, he had relaxed, especially since there was no pose at all in the passion with which he loved all the good things in life: the open road, the fives court, the music, the art galleries, the theatre, the poetry.

But then followed the harrowing years when the words flooded from him – words which were things, in the phrase which he would adapt from Burke, words which were shaped in sharp epigrams or tumultuous bursts of eloquence, words of a rich colloquial combination such as no master had employed for these purposes before – and when he discovered what penalties established power would exact to suppress him, if they could. If the truth is to be unearthed, all the gruelling detail of his persecution at the hands of the Tory England of that day must be recited, and here it is offered with a knowledge and sensitivity possessed by no previous Hazlitt biographer.

Twenty years ago, I made the acquaintance of Stanley Jones when a letter appeared in the *Times Literary Supplement* from some academic ignoramus alleging, as an item of common knowledge, that Hazlitt had raped a country girl on one of his visits to Wordsworth and Coleridge, and that this was a primary cause of their longstanding hostility to him. Both Stanley Jones and myself jumped to protect our libelled hero. No such evidence against Hazlitt existed. The so-called Keswick affair was something very different, and both Coleridge and Wordsworth had shown themselves to be on good terms with him long after that date. But the behaviour of the rest of the scurrilous Tory pack had a political derivation.

However, Hazlitt's love life, in all its strange manifestations, was one reason why some of his nineteenth- or twentieth-century admirers were deterred from writing his life. His *Liber Amoris* was long regarded as a lewd and loathsome production. The old Coleridgean slanders were always liable to be revived and given fresh credence.

Stanley Jones knows better; he approaches this aspect of his subject with the relish and understanding of a Stendhal. And, truly, Hazlitt and Stendhal were kindred spirits, even if their methods of lovemaking may have been very different. The writings of each of them on these tender themes are as essential for the proper appreciation of those times as their devotion to the ideals of the French Revolution. The best way to understand Hazlitt is to read Stendhal, and *vice versa*. Each had some inkling of the genius of the other. Each felt in their own experience the conquests and the defeats of the Revolution and Napoleonic age. This new biography weaves the common English and French inspiration together as never before to make it, on its own, an outstanding contribution to Romantic literature.

Jonathan Bate's Hazlitt

Review of Jonathan Bate, *Shakespearian Constitutions: politics, theatre, criticism, 1730–1830*, in the *Guardian*, 24 May 1990

At first sight the title of this book may seem something of a puzzle, and all questionings are not removed by the epigraph from Jane Austen: 'But Shakespeare one gets acquainted with without knowing how. It is part of an Englishman's constitution.'

A pity if any doubts persist, for what follows is a little masterpiece – original, erudite, a splendid essay in scholarship, presentation of a series of eminent figures in a new light – actors, artists, satirists – but with one real hero making an entry worthy of Edmund Kean, and stealing the show.

What the early pages describe is how, in the middle of the eighteenth century and thereafter, Shakespeare became accepted as the national poet: and how his plays and his language and his characters were inter-mingled with the way the English peopled talked and thought about each other. The author explains how the unknown process defined by Jane Austen had worked in practice when such minds as Dr Johnson and

David Garrick, Edmund Burke and John Kemble were applying their capacities and learning to the task.

No doubt this story has been often told but the author has his own individual emphasis. He shows how the caricaturists of the time, like David Low or Vicky of our own century, made themselves the Shakespearean experts. They knew that this was the way they could speak most swiftly and surely to their audiences. James Gillray was the greatest practitioner: a German magazine in 1806 called him 'the foremost living artist in the whole of Europe'. But there were others, the Cruickshanks and the Rowlandsons, who were hardly less proficient.

But then suddenly, although a few premonitions have been allowed, the whole scene is transformed. William Hazlitt appears at the London theatres to write his notices, and the consequence was that the national argument about the national poet was raised to a much loftier level. Of course it did not happen at once, sensational and seminal as Hazlitt's first theatrical writings were. But thanks to Hazlitt and a few others Shakespeare did become an even greater influence in our national literature and our national life than ever before, and the momentum persists.

It was most curious, first of all, that Hazlitt should have become such a Shakespearian expert. He had soaked himself in several other writers long before – Fielding, Cervantes, Defoe, Swift, Rousseau, Burke. He longed to paint before he ever thought of writing, and took his ideas of composition into the theatre. He was for a while more interested in politics than literature. He saw the battles between right and wrong, between rich and poor.

Once the late-developer realised what he had missed, he changed not merely his judgement about Shakespeare but his whole way of writing. Everything else he wrote thereafter became, as one observant pupil at one of his lectures called him, 'the Shakespeare prose writer of our glorious century'.

Several of Hazlitt's particular verdicts about individual plays changed the way the world thought about them as the real force of his ideas overcame prejudice and ostracism. He was the first to insist that Lear was the greatest of the plays, the first to make Henry V step down from his patriotic pedestal. He rescued *Cymbeline* from near oblivion. He saw Edmund Kean perform as Shylock, and together, actor and critic, they made *The Merchant of Venice* an instrument to fight oppression of all varieties.

But all of these variations in tone or accent, were they not political in origin? Whatever Hazlitt's merits as a critic, was it not a debasement to give politics such pre-eminence? And was he not aware that Shakespeare, the politician, could be recruited as the defender of the established order, and not merely by interested Tories like Dr Johnson but by a much wider company?

The chief virtue of Jonathan Bate's book – indeed the chief virtue of Hazlitt himself – is that he takes these accusations head on and hurls them back on the accusers. Hazlitt expounded the full case in his review of *Coriolanus* and the subsequent exchange of invectives with William Gifford. 'The capacious soul of Shakespeare', wrote Hazlitt, 'had an intuitive and mighty sympathy with whatever could enter into the heart of man in all circumstances.'

Hazlitt had something of that capacious soul too; at least it was why Shakespeare came to displace all his other heroes. As Hazlitt seeks to describe him, he unconsciously delineates some of his own features, not in any pretentious manner but as part of his growing discernment. Tragedy, he said, 'gives us a high and permanent interest, beyond ourselves in humanity as such. It makes man a partaker with his kind. It saddens and softens the stubbornness of the human heart. It is the refiner of the species: a discipline of humanity.'

Some 270 years after he died in poverty and neglect, Hazlitt's reputation continues to grow. Stanley Jones's biography of a few months ago added a series of fresh insights and revelations, and now Jonathan Bate gives the Shakespearean connection a new dimension. Such a volume, like some of Hazlitt's own, may not be immediately read but it can help to reshape the theatre of the 1990s. No one should dare to produce *Lear* or *Coriolanus* or Shylock, for a start, without Hazlitt's imprint.

Richard Holmes's Coleridge

Review of Richard Holmes, *Coleridge: early visions,* in the
Independent, 4 November 1989

At the age of twenty-five, just at the moment when he was riding the
crest of his first wave of popular fame, Coleridge had his portrait
painted in the fashionable 'French Directory' style of the period, and it
is not surprising that such a commanding, colourful countenance, with
the black curling hair, the parted lips, the radiant eyes, all hoisted high
by the white silk stock, could captivate any audience, large or small,
sacred or profane, male or female.

Or rather, it is not surprising for readers of Richard Holmes. For it
must be insisted at the outset that our sense of the manner in which
Coleridge could exercise his charm is a product of Richard Holmes's art
as a biographer. Several good lives of Coleridge have been written; vast
repositories of critical studies are available. But no one before has
described so well how he could subdue at will each new friend or
admirer; or multitudes of them assembled together. He could exert from

the pulpit or the platform the same immediate, magical powers. How easily, amid these temptations, the poet could have been lost forever.

Time and again, it was touch and go. Coleridge's natural capacities were so catholic and comprehensive that he might have succeeded in so many other professions: he might have been an orator to equal Edmund Burke or a preacher to succeed John Wesley, a scholar and prophet to match Dr Johnson, a reformer to anticipate Robert Owen. Yet always, at the moments of passion and crisis, some development would steer him off the beaten path. The world's loss and his own agony were our gain. He would return to his poetry with his extraordinary powers refreshed.

The means whereby Coleridge changed his mind or developed his art can be stated in philosophical or religious terms. But they need also to be described with all the humility and humour and wit which Coleridge himself can offer. These qualities are not always so readily accorded to him, but Richard Holmes rectifies the injustice. No previous biographer has made such good use of the boisterous wit which fills the innumerable notebooks.

He had just failed to sell a single copy of one of his books of poems to the benighted householders of Birmingham. He might have been out of spirits, but he still found time to record: 'I enquired my road at a Cottage – and on lifting up the latch beheld a tall old Hag, whose soul-gelding Ugliness would chill to eternal chastity a cantharidized Satyr – However an Angel of Light could not have been more civil.'

Coleridge was one of the great talkers of all time. No one with ears to hear ever disputed that, least of all William Hazlitt, who had an especial gift for recording how his great contemporaries could argue or monopolise the debate. Richard Holmes makes more discerning use than ever before of the wonderful moment in the history of our literature, in the last summer months of the sacred year of 1798, when Hazlitt overheard Coleridge and Wordsworth discussing the preparation of the *Lyrical Ballads*. Hazlitt, he acknowledges, understood what was happening better than anyone else except the poets themselves: 'He saw their poetry as almost physically embodied in their figures – the animated quicksilver darting and drifting of Coleridge; the grave, the steady, striding watchfulness of Wordsworth.' And he notices especially Hazlitt's observation of their contrasting physical exertion and its effect: 'how Coleridge's poetry of these months brings the entire Quantocks landscape alive.'

Never was a new spirit in our poetry received by so sensitive and generous a critic. All the more melancholy, therefore, was the aftermath, the treatment Hazlitt later received at Colerige's hands. Coleridge was one of the very first who recognised Hazlitt's capacities, and he in turn, even when he was upbraiding Hazlitt afresh, knew how intimate was their intellectual understanding – 'the only one who knows me', he once said in a phrase which Holmes does not quote now, but should in his next volume.

Yet Coleridge, in Hazlitt's case, would make no move towards forgiveness or reconciliation, and pursued his vendetta even beyond the grave. Hazlitt, the old dissenter's son, whatever his own misdemeanours or aberrations, could always give the pious Anglicans a lesson in magnanimity.

But Richard Holmes cannot, even for this passing moment, be arraigned with his new hero. He is utterly absorbed by the way the creature-spirit works to produce great poetry, by the birth pangs of genius. He unravels these moments of creation with unfailing zest and skill, and the Romantic age naturally offers him the best opportunities. After Shelley and after Mary Wollstonecraft, another of his matchless creations, maybe he thought he must in common fairness offer these same dazzling facilities to figures on the Right.

And how it does work: Coleridge lives, and talks and loves, and breaks the hearts of his readers, as he did those of his friends and lovers, in these pages as never before. But it is still, thank heaven, the young Coleridge – not quite solely the gallant, charismatic near-revolutionary of that famous portrait, but almost.

Part 4

An Irish interlude

Celtic nationalism

Review of Owen Dudley Edwards et al., *Celtic Nationalism*, in the
Evening Standard, 12 November 1968

Are the Celts on the march? Will Wales and Scotland, not to mention
Cornwall, soon emulate Ireland? Could they survive without England?
And could England survive without them?

Being myself one quarter Cornish and one quarter Scotch and
therefore only half English; representing as an honorary Welshman an
indisputably Welsh constituency; and having been named after an Irish
patriot sent to Dartmoor prison for a crime he never committed, I
approach these tremendous topics with tenderness and fascination.
Could it be that the intransigent Celts will dominate English politics in
the 1970s and 1980s as they did in the 1870s and the 1880s?

Many may turn for enlightenment to *Celtic Nationalism,* a
symposium by Owen Dudley Edwards, Gwynfor Evans, Ieuan Rhys and
Hugh MacDiarmid, and only the most incorrigible of anti-Celts – of
which, of course, there are multitudes in this still United Kingdom – will

be able to read the opening pages without a quickening of the pulse. For the first section of the book presents as splendid an outburst of modern Irish eloquence as one could hope to hear. Mr Owen Dudley Edwards, whose name suggests he might have been born in Ebbw Vale, but who in fact is as Irish as they come, purports to offer an historian's reflective conversation piece on his country's history. But the breathless monologue continues, unchecked and uncheckable, for two hundred pages. It is more like a speech from the dock in the best national tradition; glowing, astringent, witty, original; turning the tables on all accusers, if any still exist, by the device of acknowledging the national vices but thereby making the whole story the more glorious.

'What, then', he asks at the end, 'is Irish nationalism? It is St Colman preaching the gospel according to his ancestors. It is the reproach of a Gaelic bard. It is the ghost of the Great Kildare ... it is Wolfe Tone, laughing as he dies. It is Emmett, alone, encircled by his enemies, throwing everything into a final, immortal appeal to the future. It is O'Connell refusing to shake the hand of a slaveholder. It is ...' But there is more and much more; this is just the approach to the peroration.

And do not imagine that Mr Edwards is content to worship conventional heroes. On the contrary. 'Irish nationalism is distinguished from other forms by a readiness to canonise the adroit compromiser. Indeed, Irish nationalism owed much to European, American and even English inspiration.' Surrounded by his suspicious countrymen, that takes some saying. But truly Mr Edwards' brand of history is no dusty antiquarian chronicle; his perspective is international, and he can look back upon the exploits of Swift, Wolfe Tone, Parnell and the rest from the age of Vietnam and Black Power. It is a superb performance, and one that should do much to fortify Mr Edwards' reputation as a brilliant young historian. But what unwitting injury has he inflicted on his fellow contributors. How can they be expected to compete?

Wisely, maybe, Mr Gwynfor Evans, MP for Carmarthen, and Ieuan Rhys, do not attempt to do so. Their chapter on Wales reads more like a textbook; as sober and sedate as a Congregational chapel and without the Welsh choir that at last takes the roof off. Here, reasonably argued, are the matter-of-fact arguments which Welsh nationalism invokes to persuade the sceptical English. Only occasionally are there flashes of the stronger temper which has, in the words of the authors, brought 'the Welsh people nearer to self-government than at any time since the early fifteenth century.'

And as for Mr Hugh MacDiarmid, alas, his essay on Scotland is little more than a rag bag of undigested statistics, unproven accusations, and third-rate rhodomontade. It does not clinch his case when he insists that the present rulers of Scotland are as eager to inflict genocide on the Scots as their ancestors were at Glencoe. It is sad to see the great Communist poet quoting the Earl of Dalkeith as an authority on Development Areas. Only when the shoemaker returns to his last and he squeezes in a few paragraphs on Scottish poetry does he begin to persuade us that we may be witnessing the 'regeneration of the Celtic spirit'. Maybe. But the regeneration will not be assisted by confining ourselves in narrow nationalist blinkers. Ireland was a special case, in the sense that English crime and folly dug a gulf so deep that only full separation could satisfy Irish dignity. It is not necessary to repeat or multiply the error.

England needs the Celts! That is the real case against present-day Scottish and Welsh nationalism. How impoverished our literature, our politics, our national life would be without them. Time and again, long before the present regeneration, they have travelled back and forth from Dublin, Edinburgh or Ebbw Vale renewing the vitality of those whom Aneurin Bevan called 'the bovine Anglo-Saxons'. From Jonathan Swift to James Joyce, they have even been responsible for taking in hand that most precious of English possessions, the English language. Often, it has been the Celts who alone have enabled England to speak to the world.

Why retreat from glory? Irish nationalism, as Mr Edwards so dazzlingly shows, was, at its best, an international creed, drawing its strength not only from the Celtic mists, but from the France of the Revolution, from American democracy, from the England of the Chartists.

The year of liberty

Review of Thomas Pakenham, *The Year of Liberty,* in the *Evening Standard*, 17 March 1969

Since Ireland is now restored to its rightful place on the agenda of English politics, we may expect to hear the peoples of the two countries talking to one another afresh with their old intimacy and fury. A sign of the times surely is Thomas Pakenham's *The Year of Liberty*, in which the author revives what became little more than a footnote in the supercilious English textbooks and suffuses it with an uncanny topicality.

The year of liberty was 1798, and for English historians, with their eyes fixed on swashbuckling victories in the Mediterranean and the Channel, the intrusion of a few French soldiers on to Irish soil could be reduced to a trifle. But it was not so at the time. The Irish Rebellion-cum-French invasion was truly one of the tremendous might-have-beens of all time, as Napoleon himself lamented at St Helena.

If he had only listened more carefully to the young Irish leader, Wolfe Tone, who came to plead the Irish cause in Paris; if the French invasion fleet had sailed from Brest a few weeks earlier; if the nature of the Irish explosion had been properly gauged; there could have been re-enacted a French Revolution in Dublin with incalculable reverberations on the other side of the Irish Sea. It was touch and go: 1798 could have been the English 1789. But there were serious faults in the conduct of the Irish leadership, even occasional lapses into farce. Lord Edward Fitzgerald, the amiable and feckless leader who found himself momentarily in charge of the Dublin conspiracy, discovered a convenient hiding place but left his boots with his name in them outside to be cleaned.

A plan, and not a bad one, was devised to capture half the Ministers in the Irish Government at one swoop while they were attending a famous trial in the Parliament buildings; alas, it was turned down by the one vote of the Government spy on the conspirators' pretentiously-named National Directory.

Time and again inexperience or folly or the work of informers brought disaster, and when the French officers in charge of the invasion were captured and escorted out of Dublin, they vowed never to return to a country where there was neither 'wine nor discipline' and the people lived on 'roots, whiskey and lying'.

At moments, the affair was an absurd shambles. But it was much more. The year of liberty was also ferocious, extreme, cruel, incredibly heroic, staggering in its scale and momentum. Great peoples' armies traversed the land, like country fairs on the march, led sometimes by priests, with pikes, pitchforks and crucifixes mingling among the banners; led more often by devoted readers of Thomas Paine's *Rights of Man* who believed that Protestant and Catholic, red Belfast and green Wexford, could unite in the same revolutionary struggle of the United Irishmen and repeat the triumphs, inspired by the same Thomas Paine, on the other side of the Atlantic.

For the Ireland of the 1790s had links and associations which accepted no frontiers – like, say, the Civil Rights demonstrators in the Derry of 1969. Bernadette Devlin would have been much at home among the Leinster Maenads who helped set up their own little Irish republics and held them for weeks on end against all comers. It is perhaps the truth that only a writer who has witnessed the neo-revolutionary years of the late 1960s could interpret properly the Great Irish Rebellion which the English so easily blotted from their memories.

However, to weave all these strands – the savagery and the humanity, the ridiculous and the sublime, the atrocities and the golden dreams – into a single coherent narrative; to substantiate every paragraph with scholarly references; to avoid the pitfalls of anachronism and melodrama and to achieve suspense and excitement: all this calls for a rich historical imagination. Clearly, in tackling this subject, Thomas Pakenham owes much to his Irish blood and his knowledge of the holy ground over which all those forgotten battles were fought. But it may be also that the book marks the appearance of an historian of the first order, one even to out-Pakenham all the legion of Pakenhams.

The Fenian chief

Review of Desmond Ryan, *The Fenian Chief,* in the *Evening Standard,*
6 February 1968

Secret societies have not figured much on the modern English scene,
and we may like to think this is due to our open, democratic ways. The
Irish would beg to differ. Barely 100 years ago a conspiratorial organisation born in the back streets of Dublin grew so strong that it threatened
a full-blooded revolution.

The Irish Republican Brotherhood, or the Fenians as they were
nicknamed after the primitive Irish militia of pre-Norman times, were
dedicated to two propositions: that Ireland must become an independent
Republic and that the aim could be achieved only by armed rebellion.

Those who joined swore a solemn oath of secrecy and obedience,
thereby outraging the Catholic hierarchy and frightening many devout
patriots. At the society's head, in its greatest days, was a chief
organiser, in effect a dictator and a man who did not boggle at the
word, James Stephens. Considering the national craving for hero-

worship, he might be expected to occupy a secure place in the crowded Irish Valhalla.

However, secret societies can outwit historians, no less than the police. Conspirators run the risk of being lied about without remedy ever afterwards – witness the unfortunate Catiline. Only recently has it been shown – in Mr. E. P. Thompson's classic volume *The Making of the English Working Class* – that the Luddites were serious and intelligent people who never deserved the unspeakable fate of adorning a Ray Gunter peroration. So with James Stephens. Too often his hard arrogance, his rasping egotism, a touch of the charlatan, have robbed him of his glory.

But now comes a splendid biography which circumvents all these obstacles and pitfalls. Desmond Ryan in *The Fenian Chief* presents a portrait which bears the stamp of profound truth. It will be seized greedily by all interested in Irish history but it might be profitably studied too, by anyone tempted to doubt the resilience of the human spirit.

All readers, for example, of Cecil Woodham Smith's bestseller *The Great Hunger*, might turn to this as a worthy sequel. It shows how men and women can pick themselves up from the dirt and fight back. James Stephens sensed, if he did not inspire, that rebirth of a nation. After his first long exile in Paris (learning sixteen languages, as he boasted, and translating *Martin Chuzzlewit* into French) he tramped 3,000 miles all over Ireland, testing the mood of the people, discovering trusted confederates, arguing into the night.

Then, incited partly by American exiles, he founded and shaped the Fenian organisation. Back and forth across the Atlantic, he collected money, guns, disciples and enemies. Bruised followers invented titles for him – the Wandering Hawk, the Old Imposition, the Great Sir Hocus Pocus. Often there was more fear than affection in their mesmerised tributes. Most damaging of all was the accusation that when the Fenians did eventually strike and were miserably scattered, Stephens was once again in exile. He had refused to give the order for the revolutionary *putsch* two years earlier when most thought the moment more propitious, when indeed the Fenian power was at its peak.

One of the many virtues of this book is that it allocates intelligent sympathy between Stephens and his critics in that most fateful decision. 'The Fenians made only one mistake. They never should have fought.' That was the verdict of the greatest Irishman of the century, Charles Stewart Parnell, and it is the vindication of Stephens.

Desmond Ryan had a unique qualification for writing this biography. He himself took part in the Easter Rising of 1916, the historic sequel of the Fenian struggle, and his careful scholarship and restrained language are still somehow hot with the fire of revolutionary Dublin. He died with the book near completion and the final product is lovingly and expertly edited by Owen Dudley Edwards, who adds a most tantalising postscript.

Stephens and Parnell returned to Ireland on the same mail packet: Stephens after twenty-five years of exile and Parnell broken by the O'Shea divorce and soon to die. The two men, one the so-called terrorist and the other the so-called constitutionalist, honoured one another, and, if Parnell had lived, might have formed a most explosive political compact. Perhaps it was the special brand of Parnell–Stephens dynamite which won Irish freedom thirty years later.

Daniel O'Connell

Review of Angus Macintyre, *The Liberator*, in the *Evening Standard*, 12 August 1965

Daniel O'Connell rolled round his Irish tongue language which, alas, few politicians would dare whisper today. He dismissed a member of the House of Lords as 'a bloated buffoon', called Disraeli 'a disgrace to his species and heir-at-law of the blasphemous thief who died upon the cross', and finally branded *The Times* newspaper, in words which one feels Mr Randolph Churchill has been searching for, as 'the venal lady of the Strand',

He had a magnificent presence and voice, and, although arriving in the House of Commons at the late age of fifty-five, managed to win domination over that assembly with what one observer called 'that huge massive figure staggering with rage – the face darkened with all the feelings of scorn and rancour.'

He was also a physical prodigy, enduring a routine severe even for those arduous times. For something like a quarter of a century, he would rise at 4 a.m., work for three and a half hours before breakfast, and then put in more than eleven hours legal and political work. His professional income rose steadily from £60 in 1799, £420 in 1800, to the spectacular sum of £6,000–£7,000 by the late 1820s. During this same period he founded and inspired the most powerful political machine of the age, exploiting with boundless energy and acumen the press, the platform and the back stairs.

A giant of a man for sure, and one about whom it should be impossible to produce an unexciting book. Yet Mr Angus Macintyre, in the *Liberator* almost achieves the feat. The burly swaggering O'Connell in his green frock-coat and black hat does not find it easy to elbow his way through masses of statistics and electoral registers. Only the faintest echoes of his eloquence ever reach us.

Mr Macintyre allows himself to be hobbled by the absurd Oxford theory, prescribed by the late Professor Lewis Namier, that what politicians say and the ideas they propagate matter little compared with the manner in which political machines are operated and oiled. It is sad to see this treatment accorded to one described by Gladstone as 'the greatest popular leader whom the world had ever seen'. High praise: too high, of course. Yet Gladstone knew more about popular leaders in his little finger than all the Namiers and his disciples will ever comprehend.

Sad, too, because Mr Macintyre with his immense scholarship and scruple has much to tell which does add to the story. He shows how the O'Connell Party was indeed a novelty – a party of rebellious landlords; how he built its independence and then destroyed it in compromise with the Whigs; how he was one of the very few third-party leaders in British history, fewer than people think, who held the balance between the two great ones. Mr Jo Grimond might find here some enticing holiday reading.

And all of us, especially privilege-threatened journalists, can rejoice to hear O'Connell declaiming with comparative impunity against 'the six-hundred scoundrels' who in his judgement infested the Commons or, more particularly, referring to the 'foul perjury in the Tory Committees of the House of Commons who took oaths according to Justice, and voted for Party.'

O'Connell, one feels, had a firm grip on reality. He knew what to say and how to say it. He was an orator in a race of orators. In the words of a fine Irish patriot, John Mitchell he was a 'wonderful, mighty, jovial and mean old man'. A good man to meet and meet again, but sad to see him muzzled and uncomfortably sedate.

Isaac Butt

Review of David Thornley, *Isaac Butt and Home Rule*, in the *Evening Standard*, 2 June 1964

All other Irish leaders look like Lilliputians beside the giant, Charles Stewart Parnell. His brief life (he died at the age of forty-five) ended in failure, but no contemporary worth heeding questioned his preeminence, and the force of his personality lingered on beyond the grave.

Ungifted for debate and contemptuous of parliamentary institutions, he still became the master of the House of Commons. 'A marvellous man, a terrible fall,' said Gladstone. His towering stature made that fall the most piteous tale in British political history.

Among the others dwarfed by him is Isaac Butt, Parnell's predecessor as leader of the Irish party and the subject of this fresh and scholarly study. The contrast between the two men illumines much more than Ireland's struggle for independence; politically speaking it exposes to the harshest glare every neo-Gothic nook and cranny in the House of Commons itself.

For Isaac Butt, a forgotten name today, was once a great figure. He devised the words 'Home Rule' which were to terrorise or mesmerise English politicians for the next half-century, and built a new party around his explosive slogan. He was, moreover, a born and carefully bred politician, possessing in boundless profusion the splendid qualities to which MPs in all ages have chosen to ascribe the rise to success and power in their discriminating company.

He was generous, direct, warm-hearted, without a single taint of malice. He could be genial, radiant, grave or gay, according to the occasion. He appealed to reason, justice and common sense with the assurance of a supreme advocate. And he said it all in musical accents, with eyes sparkling, subduing his audience beneath a handsome leonine mane and countenance.

He never mistook 'the feeling of the House'; prided himself on his 'moral influence'; warned how a tight party discipline dictated from Dublin or the obstreperous tactics advocated by a few of his wilder followers must impair his subtle negotiations with Gladstone or Disraeli. When he moved his first 'Home Rule' resolution his speech was acclaimed on all sides as a model of persuasive eloquence. Yet the motion was defeated by 458 to 61, both Tories and Liberals rejecting the proposition out of hand.

That same week another Irish member, Joseph Biggar, tried his luck at obstruction. Disraeli deplored 'a new style'. Butt backed Disraeli, and Disraeli replied: 'The honourable member has spoken like one who is proud and justly proud of being a member of this House.'

One can almost hear across the century the purr of pious approval for Butt's sense of decorum: the unceasing anthem to parliamentary propriety which complacent parties in power and reverential parties in opposition so often contrive to sing in unison. Parnell despised that tradition: his allegiance lay elsewhere. Butt was a lion without teeth or claws. How convenient for England that Ireland's champions should be kept performing in their parliamentary cage.

Parnell, instead, taught his followers to behave like Irishmen, not Englishmen, like patriots, not gentlemen. He made parliamentary obstruction a science, and broke the hold of Butt in the process. He based his strategy on one bitter precept: 'England respects nothing but power.'

One observer of the Westminster scene gave his verdict in language so much less flattering than that with which MPs delude themselves. 'The House of Commons', he said, 'is like the Kingdom of Heaven in one respect, though unlike it in others; it suffereth violence and the violent take it by force.'

Parnell understood and his enemies understood too. That was why they bounded together to destroy him so ruthlessly when the chance came. Oddly, if private morals were to be the test of a man's fitness to lead, Isaac Butt could have been a victim much earlier. He was notorious for his dissipation, was perpetually in debt, and had at least two illegitimate children. But who cared? Somehow the English political world knew in its bones that he threatened nobody and nothing. Neither puritans nor priests on either side of the Irish Sea tried to invoke against him the cries of outrage with which Parnell, the passionate lover, was hounded to his death. Only real revolutionaries or rebels are also required to be saints.

And thus the political moral is reinforced. Parnell never forgot what Butt never knew, the two laws of parliamentary opposition, often neglected, but never yet annulled. One: always play to win, never just for the fun of the game. Two: always keep an eye fixed on the agitations *outside* the House of Commons, never be captivated by the civilities *inside*.

Observance of these laws draws the distinction between the politicians who count and those who do not; between those who make speeches and those who make history.

James Larkin

Review of Emmet Larkin, *James Larkin*, in the *Evening Standard*, 2 March 1965

The age of agitators is gone; that of bureaucrats, political technicians and public relations officers has succeeded. And one accompaniment of the melancholy change is that the great agitators begin to look like creatures not merely from another period, but another planet. One such, one of the very greatest, forms the subject of a magnificent new biography, *James Larkin* by Emmet Larkin.

Jim Larkin was born in the Liverpool slums, saw his Irish father die of tuberculosis, and was thereafter bred, almost from the age of eleven when he left school, as a dockside politician and union organiser. Having learned his mission to preach the 'divine gospel of discontent' in this militant university, he crossed to Belfast and shook the place to its depths as it had not known for a hundred years and has never known since.

In the Orangemen's City, Larkin, a Catholic, led the workers, Catholic and Protestant alike, in swift and successful struggles against the bosses. One was Thomas Gallaher of the Belfast Steamship Company, whom Larkin denounced as 'an obscene scoundrel' adding, for good measure: 'Although St Patrick was credited with banishing the snakes, there was one he forgot, and that was Gallaher – a man who valued neither country, God nor creed.'

Then he turned his attentions to Dublin, founded a newspaper, *The Irish Worker* (and had seven writs in the first year), fashioned the Transport Workers' Union in his own turbulent image and lavished his scorn on all who would not rally to the sacred cause of the working class.

He was an international figure, and the record of his journeyings in the United States disinters another buried epoch in modern history when many foretold that New York and Chicago would follow Dublin in the revolutionary path. 'We socialists', Larkin told 15,000 people in Madison Square Garden, 'want more than a dollar increase for the workers. We want the earth.' He had come to the States for a few months on a speaking tour; he stayed for several years, including a stretch in Sing-Sing for sedition, before he returned in the Twenties to his civil war-stricken homeland.

Such, in bare outline, is the story of a man who, fifty years ago, appeared on both sides of the Irish Sea, on both sides of the Atlantic, as a mighty black-haired Samson, capable of tearing down the pillars of society, but whose personality and exploits now are submerged in unpardonable oblivion.

For this passionate giant is part of our century. He knew what poverty was in his heart and every fibre and was resolved that he and his people should not submit to it. He would never believe that such an infamous thing as he saw in the back streets of Liverpool, Belfast and Dublin should be fought politely and circumspectly. He had an iron integrity which no one dared question, a red-hot courage equal to anything displayed on other battlefields.

Mr Emmet Larkin (no relation) has documented this account of his unfamiliar theme with immense care and skill. He is an American

University professor and he has done for a neglected part of British history what more of our own historians should be doing. For these are deeds which must not pass away and names that must not wither.

Tim Healy

Review of Frank Callanan, *T. M. Healy*, in the *Observer*, 22 December 1996

Great curses, however justified at the time of their original delivery, may leave a trail of pain and bewilderment. This is why Jeremiah is justly given a bad name. Occasionally, the historians must be ready to put even the prophets in their place.

Frank Callanan prompts me to start with a review of his book thus, since he is constantly quoting, with deadly intent and effect, what James Joyce said about the man whom he considered one of the two greatest Irishmen of modern times: Charles Stewart Parnell. The other was Jonathan Swift. Not only did Joyce honour Parnell, he turned his fury on the men who destroyed him, starting with his own lost poem, 'Et tu, Healy', and unleashing later shafts of glorious invective.

Callanan is fully equipped for the task. Along with the Joycean rage, he has a lawyer's training, a rare strain of historical insight, and access to some extraordinary material, headed by a near lifelong correspondence between Tim Healy and his brother, validated all the more by their mastery of Pitman's shorthand. He could not claim impartiality between his leading figures, having already produced a brilliant, original work on the theme in which Parnell's last stand is presented more heroically than ever before. Healy pursued Parnell with a venom which can still turn the stomach, but Callanan cuts his back to ribbons with a relentless Parnellite lash.

Yet there is plenty left for a 600-page biography of the victim. The man whom the biographer seeks to mask still peeps out from these pages. He is another Tim Healy, the one who could assert his Irish guile at will, especially on the susceptible English, but who also showed, at the moments of crisis, a true devotion to the Irish cause.

The great Parnell dominated the British Parliament throughout the 1880s. He put the Irish cause squarely on the English map as had never been done before. It was an astonishing feat, especially for a man who scorned the most obvious parliamentary arts. The young Tim Healy, who followed all the tempestuous events of that period, applied an opposite method of subduing his audience.

Against all convention, his maiden speech within hours of his arrival in the place was a furious personal attack on a leading Minister, the Marquis of Hartington: 'If the Noble Marquis thinks he is going to bully us with his high and mighty Cavendish ways ...' Parnell learnt the standing orders of the House of Commons by breaking them. Healy was his most enthusiastic pupil in the obstructionist campaign, and yet he added an ingredient of his own. When he wanted, he could charm the place. According to Yeats, his combined humour and wit revived the genius of Swift.

One of the first who appreciated his manner was none other than the Old Man himself, the Prime Minister. Gladstone stopped him in the lobby and hinted that he could not fail to applaud his demand that the 'pension of the Old Man should be cut'.

Thereafter, the relationship between the two was a matter of some significance for both men and their countries. An observer of these exchanges, the public philippics and the private reconciliations, was the young Lloyd George, who was sitting in his first Parliament. Gladstone was his political hero, never to be shifted from the pedestal, but he was thought also to have modelled his style partly on the scintillating, dare-devil Tim Healy.

The two Celts had a common understanding of these nationality problems which Gladstone in his own magnificent way understood too. They both saw Gladstone at his greatest, which was a sight worth seeing. Together, 100 years ago, those three showed the way for a peaceful, honourable settlement of the Irish problem, if it had not been for the Parnell crisis, if it had not been (some might viciously insist) for Parnell himself, his arrogance, his pride, his severance from those who could serve the cause best.

Healy sometimes made those charges against Parnell himself, most notoriously when he asked at the Irish Party meeting who was the mistress of the party. But a gibe was blurted out when one of Parnell's lieutenants asserted that Gladstone was seeking to make himself the master of the party. In the circumstances, that was an unconscionable and mortally dangerous lie. But thereafter, the chief tactic of the Parnellites became one of turning the whole debate against Gladstone, against the Liberals, against the only English friends of Irish Home Rule.

Healy saw how fatefully stupid such a policy must be, not because he was wooed by flatterers in the parliamentary lobbies, but because he had learned better than Parnell how Parliament worked and how essential it was for the victory of the Irish cause that the last triumph must be won there.

He already had a flying start in that first sensational decade, but he soon turned himself into a brilliantly effective, all-round parliamentary fighter. In the Commons or the courts, he devoted his talents to many good causes. His speeches in defence of the suffragette leaders happened to suit his desire to attack another English leader, Asquith, but it was inspired by his sense of justice.

But, of course, it was the developments in Ireland which were closest to his heart and understanding. How to reconcile the resort to force in Ireland with successful parliamentary pressure was always part of the problem. It was there in pre-Parnell times; it was intensified by the Parnell split; it often looked insoluble, the clash between those who insisted that the English rulers of Ireland respected nothing but force and those who retained the distant faith that they might bow to a vote in their precious Parliament.

Tim Healy clung to that last hope with all the considerable agility necessary for the purpose right from the Parnellite crisis of 1890 to his strange departure from the scene in 1918. It was the Irish resort to force in 1916 which transformed the whole scene, and set in train the sweeping victories of Sinn Fein.

Healy did not favour such action, but he understood the fury of its perpetrators against both the English and the Irish parties in Parliament, and was truly horrified by the English reaction. He denounced the executions, sought to defend the remaining prisoners, and offered good advice to one of the leading prisoners, Eamon de Valera.

Throughout the most critical years between 1916 and 1922 when Ireland's fate was decided, he was always striving to guide the force of Irish nationalism into parliamentary channels, sometimes with little hope of success, thanks to English procrastination or even English barbarism. That was what 1916 was, and there were some ugly repetitions soon afterwards. But Irish patriots could also commit crimes against themselves, most notably in the murder of Michael Collins, which was a ghastlier folly than the imprisonment of de Valera. Our biographer traces all these twists and turns without a single moment of relaxation in his Parnellite fury and yet, in the years afterwards, the Parnellites and the anti-Parnellites had to join together to secure the three-quarters of a loaf which was better than none.

So take your pick: an Irish Iago with the devil's wit, a monkish taste of hypocrisy and a mastery of Pitman's shorthand to add to the original armoury, or one of the great Irishmen of the century who can still offer good advice to his countrymen who wish to see their country united. These are the two sides of Tim Healy. Anyhow, don't miss this book: a splendidly rich production from the Cork University Press, itself a worthy representative of the forward-looking, modern Ireland which both Parnellites and Healyites have helped to establish under the Jonathan Swift-inspired presidency of Mary Robinson.

Oscar Wilde

Review of Rupert Hart-Davis (ed.), *The Letters of Oscar Wilde*, in *Tribune*, 29 June 1962

A good claim can be made for Oscar Wilde as the wittiest man who ever lived. He wrote the best English comedy since Congreve and a few other plays which still retain their shimmering brilliance. Some of his essays are among the finest in the language. One of his poems is never likely to be forgotten.

Altogether, there is much to be said for his own boast, written at the time of his humiliation: 'I was a man who stood in symbolic relations to the art and culture of my age ... I made art a philosophy, and philosophy an art: I altered the minds of men and the colour of things: there was nothing I said or did that did not make people wonder ... I awoke the imagination of my century so that it created myth and legend around me: I summed up all systems in a phrase, and all existence in an epigram.'

All this was accomplished by one who died at the age of forty-six. What might he not have achieved, what would have been his place in

English literature, if the tragedy which well nigh killed his powers had not overwhelmed him? And the tragedy itself, such a mixture of drama, horror, poignancy, pathos, and sordidness as never was, now bulks so large that even the achievements become dwarfed.

Unhappily, the publication of his letters, done with monumental care, sympathy and scruple, may merely distort the portrait still further. Here, we are told by some commentators, is the real Oscar Wilde, delineated or unmasked by his own hand: but here, in fact, is nothing of the kind.

Owing to the accident of the particular letters left behind and the extra weight unavoidably given to those written in the last pitiable years, the picture is grotesquely out of proportion. Insufficient glimpses are offered of the gaiety, wit, and prophetic power which poured forth in such superabundant measure before.

'The gibbet on which I swing in history now is high enough,' wrote Wilde in prison. These letters, so often whining and wretched, may almost make it higher still.

Only on a few occasions in them is he exerting his genius. Then, suddenly, new worlds open before us, and we are reminded afresh of the wonderful light, beauty, and exhilaration with which the name of Oscar Wilde should be associated.

Much the longest and the most valuable letter printed here (in accurate completeness for the first time) is the famous one he wrote to Lord Alfred Douglas from Reading Gaol. It was, as he said, 'a terrible letter'. 'You were my enemy: such an enemy as no man ever had.' Then, within a few months of his release, the enemies were lovers once more, and the story peters out in a mass of personal intrigue, financial squabbles, lies, and wretchedness.

'The supreme vice is shallowness,' was his conclusion in prison, and it is easy to convict him with his own accusation. Yet anyone who supposes that Oscar Wilde in his great moments was shallow must be a stubborn, oblivious fool. In his first play, *Vera, or The Nihilists* (1880), a failure, he sought to express 'that Titan cry of the peoples for liberty, which in the Europe of our day is threatening thrones and making Governments unstable from Spain to Russia'. And, time and again, his poetic insight gleams from his pages.

'He is the Philistine,' he wrote in the same letter from prison, 'who upholds and aids the heavy, cumbrous, blind mechanical forces of Society, and who does not recognise the dynamic force when he meets it either in a man or a movement.' Modern applications of the indictment may be made without much strain.

He was a true originator. 'Most people', he wrote, 'are other people. Their thoughts are someone else's thoughts, their life a mimicry, their passions a quotation.' But he himself was not prepared to borrow his chief opinions, which is no doubt one reason why his essay on socialism sounds more modern today than most of those produced by his contemporaries. And the wit, much more often than the citing of his best known witticisms might lead one to suppose, was not derived from verbal trickery. Compressed wisdom was his real talent.

'It is not the prisoners who need reformation. It is the prisons,' said Wilde, one of the greatest of prison reformers. 'A modern city is the exact opposite of what everyone wants,' said Wilde, the socialist, who had learnt from William Morris when multitudes of others had not the intelligence to decipher what he was saying. But once start quoting Oscar Wilde, and there is no stopping. And what he wrote, according to those who knew him best, was only one small part of what he talked.

Read his letters; the tragedy still absorbs. But, better, read his life story, beautifully told by Hesketh Pearson. Best of all, read Wilde himself, his plays, his essays, his poems. In our England, 'land of intellectual fogs', land of 'cold philanthropies', he is still a revolutionary. 'Disobedience, in the eyes of anyone who has read history, is man's original virtue ... The only thing that one knows about human nature is that it changes. Change is the one quality we can predicate of it. The systems that fail are those that rely on the permanency of human nature, and not on its growth and development.'

Must his imaginative understanding be neglected because he said it all so wittily, and suffered such an agony? If he had been happily married and had set it all down in vast volumes, he would now be regarded as one of the major prophets of our century and not merely his own – honoured, if unread.

Irish guns against Irishmen

Review of Carlton Younger, *Ireland's Civil War*,
in the *Evening Standard*, 10 December 1968

When the so-called fifty-year rule forbidding access during that period
to Cabinet secrets was recently reduced by our intermittently beneficent
Government to thirty years, an exception was made about 'certain Irish
affairs,' and a few suspicious MPs vainly attempted to discover the
reason for this curious limitation.

Whatever was it that our rulers wanted to hide? Why did Ireland
remain so sensitive a topic? Could it be that revelations about those
distant times might be considered discourteous to the President of the
Irish Republic who was then first becoming internationally famous and
who is still alive and able to kick?

Alas, the precise answer to these questions stays buried in the bureau-
cratic mind. But an indication of the dynamite which can be disinterred
from the archives of half a century ago is given in *Ireland's Civil War*. It
is a book which starts awkwardly for those unfamiliar with the period.

But let no one be deterred. The author's zest and insight soon take command to produce a document worthy of the tragic theme.

Those were the days when the words which struck terror into English nurseries and English society – worse even than Hun or Bolshevik or Soviet spy – were Sinn Fein. Just across the Irish Sea, or sometimes, even more shockingly, on the English side of it, gangs of cut-throats were engaged in perpetrating outrages in the name of an impossible Irish republic.

If the Irish won their independence, would not the Indians soon be making the same demand? If unthinkable concessions were granted to the Sinn Feiners, would not this strike the first blow in the break-up of the British Empire?

The challenge tested to the limit the cunning and nerve of the man who had to meet it – Lloyd George.

What Mr Younger is able to extract from the Cabinet papers about Britain's response to the Irish cataclysm would alone make his researches worthwhile and topical. For many of the post-1945 convulsions which have shaken great empires – in India, Africa, Vietnam – find an exact reflection in that old-fashioned post-1918 Irish mirror.

But this is only one implicit strand in Mr Younger's book. His main aim is to unravel the record of raids, murders, ambushes, reprisal killings, burnings, arrests, executions which formed the prelude to Ireland's civil war and then mounted to something more horrific still in the civil war itself, 'death answering to death like the clerks answering one another at Mass', as someone wrote.

The bloody shambles became so seemingly senseless that Sean O'Casey could put into the mouth of one of his characters an immortal verdict on civil wars, in Nigeria or Vietnam no less than Ireland: 'I believe in the freedom of Ireland, an' that England has no right to be here, but I draw the line when I hear the gunmen blowin' about dyin' for the people, when it's the people that are dyin' for the gunmen!'

Yes, that could be the verdict, but alongside it Mr Younger offers something finer. By his meticulous assembly of the facts, through his imaginative effort to comprehend the inspiration of the warring factions, out of the mouths of the survivors of those terrible days, he presents a picture of dedicated heroism, even when Irish guns were directed only against Irishmen, which comes near to ... the horror of the remorseless, endless killing.

In particular, he shows us Michael Collins, once, in English eyes, 'the leader of the murder gangs', the man who signed the treaty with Lloyd George, making his last journey through County Cork, the countryside of his upbringing. Probably he was on a mission to end the civil war, to seek peace with his old comrade and rival, Eamon de Valera. Probably his ambushers did not know who their victim was.

The waste and wantonness of that death, and the daring and nobility of the life that led to it, are memorably enshrined in Mr Younger's pages, and Michael Collins is only one in his crowded gallery of heroes. Only a hair's breadth of principle divided them, but they turned it into a river of blood. To tell that story, one of the most heart-rending in human history, without melodrama, distortion or moralising hindsight, is an accomplishment indeed.

James Joyce

Women in full Bloom

Review of Suzette A. Henke, *James Joyce and the Politics of Desire*,
in the *Observer*, 22 July 1990

One of the best scenes in the whole Joycean saga – uninventable and
unforgettable – is the one in which the hero braves every kind of insult
and outrage at the hands of his young religious persecutors to proclaim
Byron the greatest poet. Byron, he is warned, was a charlatan, a heretic,
an expert in lasciviousness, a poet for uneducated people. Little Joyce is
sent home to his mother, bleeding but impenitent; he will not have one
streak of his Byronism beaten out of him.

Joyce put this story into the mouth of Stephen in *A Portrait of the Artist
as a Young Man*, which is not claimed by the feminists as a feminist book
in any sense. True enough, Stephen is as male-chauvinist as they come.
Joyce's conversion to the women's cause happened later with his play
Exiles. Indeed, one original part of Suzette Henke's thesis underlines the
change of tone and temper that can be detected in this play. Bertha is the

first heroine to force her way to the front of the stage, and thereafter his leading ladies have the last word in everything he wrote.

However, Joyce never leaves Byron for long and makes sure that all his reappearances are memorable. Molly Bloom pictures her young lover, Leopold, trying to pass himself off as Byron, and neither he nor she finds the comparison discomforting or absurd. Then Bloom has given Molly a copy of Byron's poems, the only such recorded literary gift, as far as I know. When he shows up elsewhere he's usually called 'Our Byron'. He was in the modern idiom, 'one of us', almost the only non-Jew in Bloom's carefully vetted Valhalla.

What this volume does more ambitiously than ever before is to show that James Joyce, in the full flower of his genius, was captured by the feminists' appeal. The writer has at her fingertips the complete equipment of a psychoanalytical expert, and at some stages the reader may feel overwhelmed by jargon, but Joyce himself comes to the rescue with moments of dazzling enlightenment. The 200 pages of argument and 60 packed pages of notes, and the excellent use made of Brenda Maddox's recent life of Nora Barnacle, describe how far-reaching the feminist hold on Joyce has become. Much of the debate turns on the character of Molly Bloom and her splendid, ineffable peroration, the final words of which appear scandalously on the dust jacket. Should such a stroke of provocative castration ever have been permitted? One doubts whether the author can have concurred. For surely, what Joyce intended was that the whole soliloquy should be read as the climax to the whole book: the happiest ending in sexual history.

However, the legion of Molly Bloomites in their large and, I trust, ever-growing number will never complain. Molly takes full command as she always should, scorning the male exhibitionists of the Blazes Boylan variety who present the phallus 'as if it was one of the seven wonders of the world', and preparing the way for her Byron's return with matchless, deflating good humour: 'He'd never find another woman like me to put up with him the way I do … nobody understands his cracked ideas but me.'

These immortal sentences might be thought to point to a less than ecstatic finale. But not at all. Molly is overjoyed again to note her husband's 'difference' from the others; he is warm, considerate, caring, sensitive, and 'polite to old women'.

He has no connection whatever with the patriarchal authoritarianism which she has learnt to despise. Above all, 'yes that was why I liked him because he understood or felt what a woman is ...'

Thus Suzette Henke clinches her feminist case. It is hard to believe that this same Molly was once seen by other critics as 'a slut, a sloven, a voracious sexual animal', one exhibiting 'the mind of a female gorilla who has been corrupted by contact with humans.' But then Henke adds, to make the cup run over, a picture of Anna Livia Plurabelle who takes over *Finnegans Wake* as Joyce's all-including, most farraginous archetype, outdoing even Molly in 'the semiotic rhythms of the capacious unconscious and the free flow of fertile libidinal desire.'

If you haven't read *Finnegans Wake* yet, I trust this will incite you, as it does me. Anyhow, even without this last magnificent bonus, Joyce's new womanly man has taken over so conclusively that he should never be dislodged from his pre-eminent glory again. Perhaps we should just alter the old cliché: behind every good man stands a good woman or, better still, beside every good man lies a good woman. Without one, no chance of the other: no Molly, no Bloom; no Nora, no Joyce; no liberated women, no liberated men either.

Joyce's best friend

Review of Frank Budgen, *Myselves when Young,*
in the *Evening Standard*, 12 March 1970

'And is he talking to you again about that old book of his, Mr Budgen? I don't know how you stand it. Jim, you ought not to do it. You'll bore

Mr Budgen stiff.' And then a bit later: 'What do you think, Mr Budgen, of a book with a big, fat, horrible married woman as the heroine?'

But the speaker was Mrs Joyce and Jim was James Joyce and the heroine was Molly Bloom, and Mr Budgen, now in his late eighties, despite his other capacities, must still regard his association with the creation of *Ulysses* as his chief claim to fame.

Way back in the 1930s, he tore himself momentarily away from an Homeric struggle of his own to make himself a painter in order to describe the Joyce he had known in Zurich and Paris, and he produced a miniature Boswellian masterpiece and still the best introduction to *Ulysses*. Anyone who ever read it will reach eagerly for the belated autobiography Frank Budgen now offers us, *Myselves when Young*. For a start there are additions to the Joycean saga which for obvious reasons Mr Budgen could not recite whilst his hero was alive.

What could seem shabbier than his conversation with the respectable Mrs Joyce, as they left their favourite café in Zurich one night? Tearfully she explained that Jim wanted her to 'go with other men so that he could have something to write about', while Joyce, pretending to be more drunk than he was, shuffled up in the rear, hoping to overhear the answer.

And was Joyce's affair with Marthe Fleischmann also a piece of calculated experimentation since, as Mr Budgen suggests, 'literary gentlemen's adventures with dark ladies are usually worth the fringe benefits of a sonnet or two'.

Anyhow, Budgen became an enforced accomplice in the seduction, even to the point of decorating his studio for the purpose, and the manner in which he describes the comic, matter-of-fact scene would alone make this volume a treasure.

'As soon as he came into the studio, I saw that he was in a mood, which, of all his moods and tenses, I found most agreeable. It was that of a small boy sprawled on the floor self-forgettingly trying out his Christmas gift Meccano. No mummery, only the project.' Mr Budgen, I trust it may be seen, weighs his words and rarely wastes any. To the passing world, he says, Joyce would show a 'considerable *liability*; like the Apostle Paul, he could admit to being all things to all men.' Certainly without Mr Budgen's testimony and for all his Joycean candour, Joyce himself would be a much less attractive figure.

But *Myselves When Young*, the reader must be reminded, is not primarily another memoir about the great man. It is the story of a poor and lonely but cheerful Cockney (Joyce called him 'his Cornishman' but he could scarcely claim that fine Celtic distinction) who battled his way to happy penury in the Paris of the 1920s via the merchant service and a host of odd jobs and the even more curious trail of Edwardian socialist politics.

He was pilloried by his fellow workers at the post office when he refused to join the rejoicing over the relief of Mafeking. He was present at the Holborn Hall on one momentous occasion when Jim Connell, author of the Labour anthem 'The Red Flag', rushed to the platform to assail the American Labour leader Daniel de Leon, who had dared to denounce the orthodox Labour leaders of the day as 'the labour lieutenants of the capitalist class'.

Budgen was a de Leonite; in Paris he first followed Jean Jaures; he can paint them both for the giants they were, and many others of lesser stature, from his drunken father and a religious-maniacal stepmother. Perhaps it was these last two who prepared the way for his immediate chemical affinity with Joyce. He tells it all with skill, even if this volume cannot equal the pre-eminence of that earlier one on the making of *Ulysses*.

And after all, Joyce said to him about that one, as they drove in a taxi up the Champs Elysées: 'I never knew you could write so well. It must be due to your association with me.' It was.

Oliver St John Gogarty

Review of Ulick O'Connor, *Oliver St John Gogarty: a life*, in the *Evening Standard*, 23 June 1964

Nothing fades on the printed page like conversational prowess. A man is acclaimed by his friends for his wit, but when the attempt is made to give it permanence, the result is usually stilted and musty. Without the spontaneity, the cadences, the timing, all is lost.

Anyone writing about Oliver St John Gogarty confronts this difficulty in an extreme form. He was a poet, playwright, surgeon, politician, athlete, aviator and much else. Yet he won his fame as a talker in an age of famous talkers among a nation of famous talkers.

He could talk for hours on end until, as happened on one occasion, Augustus John had to throw a bowl of nuts in his face as the only way of stopping him. He talked for seventy-odd years, holding his own against such legendary competitors as James Joyce, George Moore, W. B. Yeats and a host of others accepted by the connoisseurs in Dublin as proficient craftsmen.

How can such an ocean be contained in the pint pot of a one-volume biography? Mr O'Connor makes a valiant effort, starting with some of these competitors. There was, for example, J. P. Mahaffy, Oscar Wilde's old tutor at Trinity College. 'In Ireland', he said, 'the inevitable never happens, but the unexpected often occurs.' Or: 'An Irish atheist is one who wishes to God he could believe in God.' He was also, it seems, the originator of the jest attributed to others – the reply to the informant who came with the news of the sickness of a rival: 'Nothing trivial, I hope.'

Then there was Jimmy Montgomery, who when appointed film censor, announced that his task would be to prevent 'the Californication of Ireland', adding, 'I am between the devil and the Holy See.' Or there was Yeats himself, beloved by Gogarty and regarded by him not only as 'Ireland's greatest most powerful voice' but also the best talker of them all. Asked what he thought of a poet whom he accused of imitating him, Yeats replied: 'Why should a wild dog praise its fleas?'

Gogartyisms are on much the same level. When Sir William Orpen, the fashionable portrait painter, died, he lamented: 'He never got under the surface till he got under the sod.'

Of a social climber who was becoming notorious for the times he fell off his horse, he remarked: 'Acquired concussion won't open the doors of the country houses. The better classes are born concussed.'

Once when he was performing an operation a lesion burst and the young pupil at his side cried 'Jesus Christ!' 'Cease calling on your unqualified assistant,' said Gogarty, reaching for the necessary instruments himself.

Mr O'Connor has ransacked the memories of Gogarty's friends. But how could these passable quips have provoked such gargantuan laughter? Where has the magic gone? Oddly or not so oddly, it is not Gogarty's conversational wit which retains its vibrancy. His poems with their perfected rhythms, his Rabelaisian limericks, the furious but polished invectives he unleashed against de Valera, can survive on their own without the accent and the sparkling eye, and as a playwright he is a worthy precursor of Sean O'Casey.

His old charwoman condemns the Dublin hospitals: 'What's the good of feeding the little creatures for a few days and then throwing them back where they caught the diseases? It's like spittin', on a herrin', when the sea's dried up.' And his mob leader cries: 'We will shake capitalism off our backs as a terrier shakes canal water out of its hide.' The best parts of this book are the glimpses of Dublin at the turn of the century. Gogarty and his fellow medical students invaded the brothel area, known as the Kips, where business was transacted with full police approval.

The words he heard there enticed him as much as the orgies. 'Here', he wrote, 'nothing but the English language was undefiled.' He was overwhelmed by the madam, Mrs Mack. 'She had a brick red face, on which avarice was written like a hieroglyphic, and a laugh like a guffaw in hell.'

James Joyce came with him on these expeditions. Lacking Gogarty's nonchalance, he lectured the madams on points of Greek drama and whispered Gregorian psalms into the prostitutes' ears. Gogarty wrote:

There was a young fellow called Joyce
Who possesseth a sweet tenor voice.
He goes to the Kips
With a psalm on his lips
And biddeth the harlots rejoice.

Half-a-century later Gogarty was sitting in a bar in New York, still talking, and indeed just about to cap his story when a youth got off his stool, and put a coin in the juke box. 'Oh dear God in Heaven,' he bewailed, 'that I should find myself thousands of miles from home, at the mercy of every retarded son-of-a-bitch who has a nickel to drop in that bloody coal-scuttle.'

Mr O'Connor recites the intervening facts between these episodes with sympathetic care, but the miracle eludes him. Gogarty the conversationalist is dead and cannot be resurrected. The sad truth remains that to make a great talker sound and stay great is the rarest of gifts. There are quite a number of Dr Johnsons, but only one Boswell.

A real democrat

Review of Garret Fitzgerald, *All in a Life*, in the *Guardian*,
15 December 1987

I started writing this review in Charles Haughey's Dublin – by which I
mean no insult to the beautiful city and no reflection on his rival, the
author of this autobiography. I mean only that the sole topic of political
conversation here this week is Charles Haughey, and how he out-
Houdinied Houdini at the beginning of the week, and then fell flat on his
face on an IRA-planted banana skin at the end.

Charles Haughey, in similar contortions, naturally plays a leading
role in this book, right from the moment when Garret Fitzgerald first
hears that another Irish Taoiseach, Jack Lynch, has sacked 'Neil
Blaney, and Charles Haughey, apparently for gun-running.' Garret
made no accusations then; he describes how he went back to sleep.
But the rivalry between the two men became sharp and deep on
almost every count, and in these pages we are offered an absorbing
account of it.

Those particular charges against Haughey never came anywhere near to being proved, just as his latest gaffe of selecting a Defence Minister with distant IRA connections may be shown as nothing more sinister. But, of course, Garret Fitzgerald's abiding hatred of the IRA and all its works is something of a quite different order. He knows, and has always known, that the whole democratic case is at stake. So there can be compromise.

Not merely does he find it necessary to warn his own countrymen on the great matter. Sometimes the British could come near to being duped too. It is worth quoting the whole passage since it may have present applications: 'I am not sure that British politicians even today understand the extent to which this and similar contacts – secret contacts with the IRA – have contributed to the continuation of IRA violence over a long period by enabling that organisation to persuade its members that persistence in the campaign of terror will eventually lead to British–IRA negotiations for a British withdrawal.'

The warning should be repeated time and again, especially since Garret himself did momentarily believe that the British Labour Government at one stage did contemplate such a departure. To my knowledge they did nothing of the kind, for all the same good reasons which Garret formulates. But the fact that he should still retain such fears freshly underlines the peril.

To defeat these deadly enemies of democracy on both sides of the Irish Sea, it was necessary to seek a new relationship between London and Dublin, and Garret Fitzgerald did more than any other single man (or woman) to establish the Anglo–Irish Agreement and its kindred developments. He tells the whole story here with a most refreshing disregard for the normal rules of Cabinet secrecy. The achievement is a tribute to his candour, his integrity and his high intelligence.

Alas, the most recent, terrifying headlines in the newspapers, in Haughey's Dublin and back here in London, prove that Fitzgerald and all his confederates have not yet defeated the assault on democracy. A fresh outbreak of indiscriminate political murder by the IRA and the so-called loyalists seems to take command of events.

And alongside a picture of the Taoiseach, with two of his recently reappointed Ministers and the headline 'Stand by your Man,' reads another one: 'Renewed calls to close extradition loophole follow court judgement.' Two men facing prison terms in Northern Ireland have just been extradited because their offences were held to be 'politically motivated'.

I hope all concerned, especially the judges, find time to read Garret's book.

Part 5

Labour and the nation

Robert Owen

Review of Gregory Claeys, *Citizens and Saints: politics and anti-politics in early British socialism*, in the *Guardian*, 12 April 1990

Thomas Paine and his proper place in the history of political ideas was the theme of Professor Claeys's previous book, and a wealth of biographical detail combined with a grasp of larger perspectives so that a real contribution was made to the world-wide Paineite renaissance.

That there has been such a sensational rise in Paine's reputation is illustrated by recent events in Paris, where for so long his fame was wretchedly neglected. He has now been the subject of his first French biography by Professor Vincent, and thanks to his discoveries the place where Paine lived near the Luxembourg has been commemorated, with Madame Mitterrand officiating at the proceedings. She and her husband do understand the history of human rights (despite the ill-advised attempt of our own Prime Minister to instruct him in these intricate matters), and it is excellent that the Paineite revival should take place under the Mitterrand patronage.

Now Professor Claeys attempts a further reconstruction of a similar character. His title and subtitle need not conceal the fact that he is applying to Robert Owen and his ideas the technique he applied to Paine. Apart even from the title often accorded him as the father of British socialism, Owen did play a foremost role in several surging movements of his time – trade unions, co-operative societies, education – and the plan of exploring afresh these associations was a good one.

However, Claeys is also well aware of the criticisms, both contemporary and those coming later, which condemned Owen's outlook as being too paternalistic, too conservative in a sense, to deserve the title of radical, much less socialist. When his *New View of Society* was published in 1816, such a true radical observer as William Hazlitt protested that there was nothing new in it; it was as old as some other utopias, Godwin's, Harrington's or Sir Thomas More's. Owen, Hazlitt lamented, was much too ready to believe that kind words and his own inexhaustible good will would be able 'to make fools wise and knaves honest; in short, to make mankind understand their own interests, or those who govern them care for any interest but their own.'

But those words were written in 1816, at the time when his factories at New Lanark were the chief cause of his fame. He died forty-two years later and had time in the interval to develop his views on a whole range of topics on both sides of the Atlantic. Professor Claeys traces many of his ideas to their sources – for example, how much Owen learnt from Godwin on his frequent calls at the old man's house – and then underlines how original was the elaboration he gave to many of them. He was both citizen and saint; he had a capacious intellect as well as a compassionate heart; he had millennial aims but he also liked to pride himself as a much more practical man of action than many of his associates.

Despite his doubts about universal suffrage and his resultant arguments with the Chartist leaders, he stood for Parliament himself on ten occasions. Once in a contest at Marylebone he got just one vote, much to the amusement of his opponents. Of course he saw these campaigns as propaganda exercises. His election address in 1832 had several good points, including a few topical ones: a graduated property tax, the abolition of all other taxes, free trade, national education, employment for all, liberty of speech, writing and religion. Self-government for all British dependencies, plus a prospect of universal peace on earth, were also envisaged.

Sometimes he was accused, and especially by some of the Chartists, of showing much too little interest in Parliament. But he had his excuse. He saw his own proposed childhood employment bill mutilated by a parliamentary committee, and he reflected: 'I saw so much sacrifice of truth and correct feeling for supposed personal or class advantages that I became thoroughly cured of my veneration and high opinion of our legislators.' The last inflection shows that he did have a sense of humour. Somewhat earlier, and with savage effect, he had been prepared to denounce the British Parliament altogether as 'a complicated machine, to enable the useless non-producer of wealth to enslave, and to keep in ignorance and poverty, the actual producer of wealth.'

Robert Owen, as even his most fervent admirers must admit, had a slightly irritating habit of thinking he knew best. Among the Chartist leaders, he could stir resentment in the breast not only of the fiery Feargus O'Connor but hardly less from the gentler William Lovett. He in turn would question whether those same leaders understood the cause of the economic ills they saw all around them and the necessary remedies. And he too had a case; he understood just about a century before a British Government was driven to take the essential measures what was needed to tackle real destitution and ignorance, and most especially among the children who suffered most.

Professor Claeys abundantly proves his case that Robert Owen, like Thomas Paine, deserves a far-ranging reassessment. He did go to Paris in 1848 and hailed the new revolution there as a mighty event, but we can hardly expect President Mitterrand to do the honours again. It so happens that a book with the very best Robert Owen imprint has just been published. It is *Punishing The Poor: poverty under Thatcher* by Kay Andrews and John Jacobs. Once more the British socialist tradition and the British democratic tradition reunite, as happened in Chartist times, to the glory of our country.

William Morris

Review of L. Parry (ed.), *William Morris*, in the *Tate Gallery Magazine*, March 1996

The William Morris, who died a hundred years ago, is making more of a splash than many of his supposedly more eminent fellow Victorians, and thanks to the wonderful exhibition now being organised at the Victoria and Albert, of which this brochure is the appropriately beautiful introduction, the numbers of his admirers in the century to come will be greater still. None of us who still call ourselves socialists need be surprised or alarmed.

I may be excused for recalling vividly the tone of voice in which an up-and-coming young film director, Jill Craigie – the first woman in the business – announced, 'I'm a William Morris socialist myself', much to the scorn of some of the leading so-called Bevanites – followers of Aneurin Bevan – in her audience, headed by Dick Crossman, who could spread intellectual devastation at will. Morris, we were severely warned, had once led good socialists off the right road, and we'd better beware.

Aneurin Bevan, by the way, might overhear these debates without offering a verdict. Some of us suspected him of having a specifically soft spot for William Morris himself.

Indeed, across the Welsh mountains where he marched earlier in the century or across the Yorkshire moors where such rising stars as Barbara Castle learnt their socialism, it was the rhythm of his poetry with which they were first captivated. A socialist poet who opened before us the new world was indeed a phenomenon.

It was a poet that he first made his fame and yet, more curiously, if his reputation generally as an artist has declined, it is the poetry which showed the weakness. His mentor in so many other matters, John Ruskin, could have encouraged him to take Byron as his poetic model and thereby retain a more modern tone.

The way in which Morris extolled what he had learnt from Ruskin still retains its resonance. It was Ruskin who gave him a 'sort of revelation' when he gazed through Ruskin's eyes at the Gothic marvels in Venice, Ruskin who seemed to point out for him a new road on which the world should travel. Ruskin's Venice had been Turner's Venice, and indeed Turner's Venice had been Byron's before him. When in the 1890s Morris published, in his beautiful Kelmscott Press edition, the chapter on the nature of Gothic architecture, he called it 'one of the very few necessary and inevitable utterances of the century'. Morris had his own well-developed sense of history, which was partly no doubt what developed his interest in Marxism.

What he saw with his own eyes in the last century – the beauty and the horror – could have saved us from some of the worst infamies perpetuated in this one. And, maybe, it is not altogether too late. Ahead of his time, William Morris was a green revolutionary as well as a red one who always had the spirit to stir up countrymen and countrywomen from their shameful, ignorant slumbers.

None of these developments has happened by accident. The Morris revival owes most – everything, it might nearly be said – to Fiona

MacCarthy's magnificent biography. 'He was our best man,' wrote Robert Blatchford, and hers is our best biography of a socialist worthy of the name. She writes especially in this new volume of his work as a designer in so many multitudinous fields. It is hardly possible to imagine that she has added to her previous store of riches on offer, but there they are – thanks to the large visual innovations of which Morris was the author. It was the manner of daring with which he would seek to comprehend and express all forms of culture. He was derided by the so-called experts in so many fields, but now all of them are thrust back on the defensive in the face of this display. William Morris will be winning the prizes from the new disciples or the monstrous invectives from Philistine England ten, twenty, fifty years hence. It is easy to guess, but just before his own death, and just after the death of one of his closest Russian comrades, he wrote: 'I have not changed my mind about socialism.' What he meant by such a claim is now beautifully recorded in this exhibition as in Fiona MacCarthy's book. But to keep matters in proportion, proper space must be found for Blatchford's last word: 'Morris was not only a genius, he was a man. Strike at him where you would, at any time.'

The Webbs

Review of Royden Harrison, *The Life and Times of Sidney and Beatrice Webb, 1858–1905*, in the *Guardian*, 28 January 2000

'And what exactly is the daily life you ought to live if you wished to be, and to be thought to be, a genuine revolutionary?' Such was the question which Beatrice would occasionally address to Sidney Webb in the later years of their supposedly ideal marriage. A strong streak of irony must always have been present in the wife's enquiry, if not the husband's evasive reply. The two did contribute mightily to the socialist upheavals of the past century and, most directly, to the notorious Clause IV of the Labour Party's constitution which later leaders have found so offensive to their ideas or injurious to their electoral prospects.

Beatrice and Sidney were equally skilful in presenting their case for the kind of revolution in which they believed and the kind of institutions which would be necessary for the purpose – not merely the aforementioned Labour Party, but several others, such as the London School of Economics, the *New Statesman* and others still surviving to serve no less commendable purposes. At other equally presitigious institutions, the first introduction to the history of trade unions was Sidney's or Beatrice's on the Co-operative movement. A third volume entitled *Industrial Democracy* displayed their combined talents even more fruitfully. It is now hailed by such a leading historian as Eric Hobsbawn as the most lastingly significant of their writings and was also, by sheer accident, the first study of the Webbs by two would-be students of Labour politics in the 1930s – Barbara Betts (later Castle) and the writer of this review, who made these explorations together at her flat in Coram Street. Beatrice in that mood almost succeeded in distracting us away from our first thrilling introduction to Karl Marx.

Beatrice, indeed, kept a diary which she brilliantly transmuted much later into a volume proudly called *Our Partnership*. The most moving part of the diary, however, had to be suppressed until quite recently – the story of her passionate longing for Joseph Chamberlain when he was declaring war on all the most powerful institutions of the age with a fervour which Sidney never aspired to – royalty, the victims of the rich and, most especially since he knew them at first hand, the class which wielded both the power and the wealth. If Beatrice had gone off with him at that moment, it would indeed have been a sensation of the first order.

One of the reasons why the affair did not prosper, beneficially for humanity at large, was his attitude to women. He made it clear that despite his genuine radical instincts on so many other subjects, he had no sympathy with the women of those days who were starting to present their case on their own account with seemingly irresistible logic. But with Beatrice at that particular moment, this was no obstacle. Most curiously indeed, she seemed to share some of those strange inhibitions. It would take another kind of man altogether to challenge this strand in her nature.

All these various aspects of the story are freshly covered in Royden Harrison's long-awaited, authorised biography of the two of them. Don't be misled by the long wait or the official sanction. Every judgement in these pages has been weighed; every incident bears retelling, every word counts. This particular volume appears to take up the record no further than 1905, when the Fabians had not reached the peak of their influence; when indeed Beatrice's own natural generosity of spirit made her confess that she had changed her mind on that thorny question of women's rights. The man who did it was another famous Fabian, H. G. Wells. He sent her a copy of his *In the Days of the Comet* in which he presented the arguments that socialists of the modern age must also face the challenge of sexual politics. Sometimes he would say what he was doing was to put the case of the passionate daughter. He had no idea then how Beatrice had suppressed her own passions.

H. G. Wells' view on the whole Webb entourage was most famously presented in his novel *The New Machiaevelli,* which appeared in the pre-1914 period when the question about how the new idea of socialism, Fabian or of any other brand, was to be applied, in this country or across the rest of the planet, could not be dodged. Royden Harrison, with the full weight of evidence at his disposal, claims that the Beatrice–Sidney collaboration was 'the most fruitful partnership in the history of the British intellect'. Sometimes their methods of spreading their ideas succeeded, sometimes they failed. Royden Harrison examines the balance sheet with the unfailing fairness of the partnership itself at its most honest and lucid.

No doubt Royden himself, like H. G. Wells and other contemporary critics, would have wished to see the two revolutionaries moving much faster. It was the besetting sin of the Fabians to allow themselves to be too much enmeshed with existing institutions. Above all, youth cried out for something much more adventurous, truly revolutionary, not only in politics, but across the whole field of human relationships. Such was the message which HG sent Beatrice in his *Days of the Comet*: he had somehow broken down altogether her prejudices about the activities of the women's movement. Again and again, he put the plea for the passionate daughter.

But did Beatrice read the climax of the lovers' story in *The New Machiaevelli,* which was also more significant than the notorious criticisms of the Webbs in their respectable home life? Page after page records how a loving, a truly revolutionary partnership was born and how indeed it had the vitality to carry the crusade further afield. Just at the book's climax, when it seems that a conventional scandal may wreck the hero's parliamentary career, the woman takes command – 'she was amazingly sharp and quick and good. I have never dreamt there was such talk in the world.' She drilled sense into his stubborn head on the women's question and a host of other aspects of every kindred question. The Wells who had sent his *Comet* to Beatrice some years before was entitled to claim that he had applied his adventurous mind to the subject as well as any rival in the same line of business. *The New Machiaevelli* was the proof that he understood the truly revolutionary nature of the women's movement in the best sense of the word and how nothing must be allowed to block its path.

After her own style, Beatrice did understand that too, and careful readers of these volumes today may see how Beatrice understood, and HG shared her understanding. Royden Harrison's book makes a most notable addition to the riches in our socialist library. It shows how partners can act together and how indeed they will be needed to save our stricken world.

North Cornwall 1939

Yorkshire Post, 27 March 1989

I re-read for the purposes of this article the record of what happened in this country just fifty years ago, in March 1939, when the Spanish Civil War came to its pitiful end. No one, certainly no one with any appreciation of his country's honour, can read the story without a rising sense of shame. It was the most shameful decade in our history, and those last diplomatic or parliamentary rites at the Spanish graveside had some claim to be the most wretched of all.

Other events in Europe throughout that February and March quite dwarfed the Spanish scene. Hitler was preparing for his seizure of Prague, in defiance of all the promises of peace in our time which Chamberlain had accepted at Munich less than six months before. Stalin made a speech, little recognised for its momentous implications by political leaders in the West, that he might not be prepared to pull capitalist chestnuts out of the fire. He did refer directly to the consequences of the non-intervention policy in Spain. But no Western leader, least of all the British Prime Minister, Neville Chamberlain, would respond. Spain for them had always been a sideshow, a distraction.

They were just glad to see the end of it. But even leaving aside the monstrous misjudgement of our own national interest, the world's interest, involved in the so-called non-intervention policy to be considered in a moment, we might have been spared the last indignities, the last infamies.

Britain rushed to bestow official recognition on the nationalist regime of General Franco even before the ink was available to sign the undertakings between his military forces and those of the defeated Spanish Republic. Franco despatched a telegram to Chamberlain promising that after the surrender only criminals would suffer reprisals. This was considered to be the only condition Britain could extract. Lord Halifax, our compliant Foreign Secretary in the House of Lords, was somewhat more explicit. No country outside Spain, he said, could judge whether any Spaniard was guilty of a crime or not, and any offer of British help in the evacuation of the Republicans would prejudice the British reconciliation with the victors.

In fact, the indiscriminate vengeance against all those considered guilty of 'subversive activities' had been started much earlier. One Italian general reported to Count Ciano, Mussolini's Foreign Minister, that Franco had already launched in Barcelona 'a very thorough and drastic purge'. Many Italians, including several imprisoned by the Republicans, were among those executed. Mussolini himself, as reported by Ciano, was more realistic than the British Ministers. 'Let them all be shot. Dead men tell no tales.'

A last remnant of British honour was rescued by the debate which the Labour and Liberal Parties forced in the House of Commons. Chamberlain had deviously agreed to the recognition more with the French premier before the Commons was informed. 'We see in this action', said Clement Attlee, leader of the Labour Party, 'a gross betrayal of democracy, the consummation of two and a half years of the hypocritical pretence of non-intervention and a connivance all the time at aggression. And this is only one step further in the downward march of His Majesty's Government in which at every stage they do not sell, but give away, the permanent interests of this country. They do not do anything to build up peace or stop war, but merely announce to the whole world that anyone who is out to use force can always be sure he will have a friend in the British Prime Minister.'

And Chamberlain could reply only that Franco had given pledges of mercy and that Britain could enforce no conditions upon him. True enough. And that refusal and incapacity to exert any British restraint on Franco's repression continued from that moment, throughout the long years of the Second World War itself, until Franco's death forty years later. Only in these last few years has the world had a fresh chance to see what Spanish democracy can achieve.

But wait. Spanish democracy: was there any such a species? The Spanish Civil War: was it not always an inscrutable Spanish affair, 'a faction fight', as another notable member of Chamberlain's pre-war Cabinet, Sir Samuel Hoare, dubbed it at the time? Were not the poets and others (80 per cent working class, by the way) who went off to fight in the International Brigade, were they not just a bunch of eccentrics, tricked by an international conspiracy or Communist plotters or their own leftish hallucinations? How could they see England's freedom too swaying in the Spanish scales?

The modern craving for cynicism is often fed by the official histories, whether written in Chamberlainite or Churchillian terms. For Winston Churchill himself, along with the others, was blinded by his class prejudice in the early days of the war and he was a notable absentee from that debate in March 1939 when the last act of dishonour was approved.

Beware of all such prevarications, old or new; they are just the latest versions of the big lie we were told in the 1930s. Dig a little deeper into the archives and it will be discovered that Hitler and Mussolini had been ready to retreat if the British or French Governments had shown one small part of the courage of the International Brigaders who came from the beleagured democratic states of those times and from some of the dictatorships too. Fascism could have been destroyed on Spanish battle-fields. Considering the scale of the Second World War, here is surely the greatest might-have-been in all history, and if the claim is still dismissed, something near proof about the actual date of the turning point may be offered to clinch the case.

When the Franco revolt against the democratically elected govern-ment of Spain was launched in June 1936, the military advantages lay with the rebel forces and they carried their assault to the precincts of Madrid. The prize was almost within their grasp. They were thwarted then and for the next two and a half years by great sections of the Spanish people, by the strength of Spanish democracy. 'Had Spain been left to herself,' reported an eminent reporter of *The Times* on the spot on 7 January 1937, 'the war would have been over long ago.'

Spanish courage and Spanish endurance did all that could be expected of them. Even the fearful internal divisions within the ranks of the defenders of Spanish democracy, which George Orwell and others chronicled with such pitiless objectivity, could not destroy the cause. Spain was betrayed in London and in the most respectable accents of Sir Anthony Eden. 'The British Government was throughout the real inspi-ration of non-intervention ' wrote Hugh Thomas in his classic history of the war.

Some of us, piecing together the evidence available from many quarters, tried to say as much in 1936 and 1937. Spanish democracy held its own against all that European fascism could mobilise against it for nearly three years, as long almost as, say, the Americans were involved in the Second World War. Madrid was held by the democratic forces all through the period of the fascist conquest of Austria and the Munich sell-out, right up to 1939 when Dr Negrin's duly-elected Government was at last forced to surrender to the fascist onslaught without a whimper of protest from official circles in London.

I recall that time quite well, partly because some of us participated in the last by-election conducted in Britain before the actual outbreak of war. It took place in North Cornwall in 1939, and the Conservative candidate plastered the hoardings with the poster: "YOU ARE READING THIS IN PEACE BECAUSE YOU LIVE UNDER A NATIONAL GOVERNMENT". It was all part of the campaign against the socialist (or Liberal) warmongers who had wanted to send aid to Spain, and the posters were still there, slightly tattered, when war came to Britain on 3 September 1939.

Never again

Review of Peter Hennessy, *Never Again: Britain 1945–1951*, in the *Times Educational Supplement*, 15 September 1992

What happened to George Orwell's Englishmen? The sentence, with or without the question mark, might be taken as a further subtitle for this book. Neither the master nor his pupil would complain. Indeed, Peter Hennessy reveals on his first page how it was the reading of Orwell's *The Lion and the Unicorn* which gave him the idea of writing an intelligent, intelligible history of our own times. Orwell's brand of patriotism, which he had expressed best in that volume written in the beleaguered, battered London of 1940, suffuses every chapter here – making an allowance of course for the fact, as Orwell certainly did not, that English patriotism must be accepted as a quality shared by the Welsh, the Scots, and even the Irish.

Certainly the story of Britain in this period could not be told without some pre-eminence being given to the Welsh in particular. After 1918, it was the Scots who provided leadership for the Labour Party; the whole flavour of it came from the Clydeside. But after 1945, the special drive and imaginative momentum came from Wales, with James Griffiths and Aneurin Bevan, by luck or accident or Attlee's design, given their chance to carry through the most far-reaching measures of domestic reform. They each brought their differing styles of Celtic flair to their tasks, and sometimes 'the bovine Anglo-Saxons', as Bevan might call them when provoked, were compelled to marvel at their audacity of word and deed.

However, this preliminary Celtic diversion is prompted only by a desire to forestall any quibbling about Orwell's original essay. He knew what he meant by his Englishmen; they were the salt of the earth. They had been most shamefully betrayed by their leaders in the 1930s, and had been forced to live in a most unjust, inefficient, degrading society. But they were the people (men and women) who won the war and resolved to make a peace quite different from the one which had betrayed the homecoming heroes of 1918. The dust-jacket on this volume shows, with brilliant appositeness, the soldier, in 1945, coming home to greet his wife and son in their hastily-modelled prefab, flaunting its Union Jack. He and his wife have just voted to elect a Labour Government with a true Orwellian, iconoclastic enthusiasm.

No sense of strain indeed is involved in associating Orwell's name with Bevan's. He had read *The Lion and the Unicorn* at the moment of its publication and shared every mood it sought to express. Orwell's breed of Englishmen were the same whom Bevan especially honoured. Orwell defined them better than anyone else; Bevan could speak for them better than anyone else, but their common aspiration was that, one way or another, the people's demand for fair play and justice and common decency should be made articulate and effective. The original thrill of those times – first, the war years properly covered in these pages and then the period of the victory and the peace – was that the people's voice seemed to be expressed more powerfully and passionately and persistently than ever before.

Peter Hennessy constantly passes judgement, as a good historian should, on the successes and the failures of his characters and, not surprisingly, he awards the palm to the establishment of the National Health Service. He cites a remark from Sir Roy Griffiths, called in from Sainsbury's to advise on the present-day structure, who is alleged to have said: 'If Florence Nightingale were carrying her lamp through the corridors of the NHS today, she would almost certainly be searching for the people in charge' – presumably intending to suggest that the whole command structure was out of control, irresponsible, unworkable.

But Florence Nightingale was a much more ruthless politician than that: she would have forced her way into Number 10 Downing Street and confronted that real enemy of the NHS with all her unleashed feminist fury, and even Mrs Thatcher might have quailed and drawn back from the most foolish and doctrinaire of her assaults on socialist achievement. As it is, not even the most enthusiastic supporter of the Service need cavil with Hennessy's conclusion: 'Yes, 5 July 1948 was the second of Britain's finest hours in the brave and high-minded 1940s. Like the Battle of Britain it was a statement of intent, a symbol of hope in a formidable, self-confident nation. The NHS was and remains one of the finest institutions ever built by anybody anywhere.'

So far, so exciting. Aneurin Bevan himself might be satisfied that such a verdict on his achievement of July 1948 could be passed in September 1992. But he, like his Cabinet colleagues or the later leaders of his party in opposition, had to witness, too, a series of retreats both ideological and electoral. Never again would the party command such a parliamentary majority as it did in 1945.

But that is not the meaning of the book's title. What the 'Never Again' was supposed to mean in particular, in the mind of the British electorate, was that never again would the horror of mass unemployment be allowed to return on the scale which was accepted with such shameless complacency in the 1930s. Never again would it be said that such a waste of national and human resources would be a price worth paying to balance a budget or to secure some even more obscure aim.

Peter Hennessy has no doubt what an important business writing history may be. 'History for me,' he insists, 'is the Queen of the Arts.' He understands that it is the drive of the narrative that must govern everything else. Occasionally he permits himself a few too many hind-sighted glances, but never to diminish or qualify his great achievement: a real history of our own times to rival any other.

Maybe he hoped, as did many of his readers, that his publication date would roughly coincide with the arrival in power of a new Labour Government. But anyhow, even without that beneficent accompaniment, this volume and the ones which are to follow offer a feast of political instruction.

The theme which he has not yet fully examined or exhausted is what happened to Orwell's Englishmen: the decency-loving, freedom-choosing, community-caring English patriots who won the war and then hoped to win the peace, and then built the National Health Service, and then hoped to build much more on the same magnificent model. When were they finally beaten – if they have been? Maybe the chief significance of the Thatcherite counter-revolution was that it did mark the extermination of Orwell's Englishman, and the substitution of the money-grubbing Essex monster, part Norman Tebbit, part Teresa Gorman, but anyhow with all mitigating human features finally removed.

These harsh comparisons are for the future, but meanwhile our historian offers his considered judgement on Attlee's Britain in 1951. It was, he claims, making comparisons with the past, 'a kinder, gentler, and a far, far better place in which to be born, to grow up, to live, love, work, and even to die.' Such an epitaph – and this is also part of his judgement – 'cannot be placed with conviction on the plinths of any of the eras to come as Mr Attlee's Britain gave way to Mr Churchill's.'

Quite a claim indeed to be made for the Englishmen and their fellow Welsh, Scots, etc., who had had to fight a longer war than any other people on the planet, and then emerged to make a decent peace and the beginnings of a decent society. The more that history is told, the better for us all.

Labour's war

Review of Stephen Brooke, *Labour's War: the Labour Party and the Second World War,* in the *Guardian*, 30 July 1992

Once upon a time the writing of Labour history was left to the propagandists, the diarists, the biographers and (most suspect of all) the autobiographers. More recently some real historians like Ken Morgan or Ben Pimlott have raised standards and expectations. Stephen Brooke is a good recruit to this company. He retraces some well-beaten tracks, but his discoveries are genuine, original and far-reaching.

His chief challenge is to the general thesis that in the period from 1939 to 1945 and soon after – the high noon of accommodation between the political parties in Britain – there was a real *consensus*, to use the term which has been invoked much more retrospectively than ever it was at the time. There was no such word, no such thing, no such conception. Indeed, it could be said that 1945 was the year when the so-called consensus was most magnificently broken and such, moreover, are many of the greatest moments in our political history. But stick with Brooke and the facts for a while; that' what he does and that's how he draws his original conclusions.

The more he examines the post-1931 Labour Party – and that's the right moment to start the story, since the whole of Labour's mood and spirit were governed by memories of that hour of defeat and betrayal – the more he and everybody else could be persuaded that no Labour Party, no Labour leader, could easily contemplate a fresh accommodation with the class enemy, particularly when that same enemy had led the country into the national calamities and humiliations of 1938 and 1939 and 1940.

Brooke, the historian, has the sense to judge Labour's real moods at the time from what they were actually saying, the real words. If any Labour leader had used the non-existent word *consensus* then, he would have been torn limb from limb. But there was no such peril. Whatever the differences between the Labour rank and file and their leaders throughout the 1930s, none of them – the Attlees, the Bevins, the Morrisons, the Daltons, the Lansburys – had a good word to offer the ruling Conservative Party which so nearly led us to our ruin. So when the catastrophe did come, the leaders couldn't change the language: why should they? The invectives of the mid-1930s fitted so well the crisis of 1940. And if the leaders had wanted to change their tone, why should the rank and file, many of whom had been repudiating the infamous doctrines of surrender and appeasement long before they were bombed out of their homes in London, Coventry and Plymouth?

Here the real words used by the contestants are constantly cited, and they can sound like a pistol shot in the modern ear. Clem Attlee believed that one highly dangerous element in our society was 'the greed of ruthless profiteers and property owners', that the application of socialist economics would be needed to win the war, that he would be ready at the end of it to establish 'a socialist Commonwealth'. He and his party entered the Churchill coalition to save the country but to serve these longer prospects too. And coalition did not mean consensus.

One curious consequence of Brooke's fresh interpretation is that both left and right of the party may draw some ideological consolation. During the earlier years treated here, the rank and file found their best spokesmen in Harold Laski on the National Executive and Aneurin Bevan in the House of Commons, but these were by no means lone voices. They represented a widespread discontent, especially when the leaders had agreed to an inept and unworkable electoral truce. Nothing could hold in check the potent left-wing ferment which spread into every aspect of our national life.

However, one persistent complaint from the left was that their leaders in the government machine exercised their influence much too timo- rously, and the associated fear was that this weakness might fatally frustrate Labour's victory when the war was over. Brooke's examination covers the whole range of policy-making, and he shows much more convincingly than ever before how the Labour leaders helped to produce the radical achievements of 1945. To sustain Labour's independence had always been the aim of the left; the legitimacy of that demand could not be denied by the leadership, and when the chance came the whole party could profit from the common strategy.

It might be supposed from this enthusiastic reception that our author had written an immaculate Bevanite treatise; but not at all. In ideolog- ical terms, he is much more in what might be defined as the Evan Durbin–Tony Crosland–Roy Hattersley camp and he writes a brilliant chapter on these themes, including some marvellously modern instruc- tion on the libertarian aspects of the subject from Barbara Wootton, Michael Young and, most topically, G. D. H. Cole.

His whole book could be read as a subtle and comprehensive contri- bution to present-day Labour Party debates. But maybe Brooke, the historian, is even more persuasive than Brooke the philosopher. In my estimate the one failing of this book is that the whole of it should have been written as a narrative and not as separate theses. That is how the greatest history books are written, not with hindsight, but by the recreation of the hearts and minds of living men and women. The men and women of the Labour Party, the leaders and the led, saved their cause and the country and the wider world in these historic years. Stephen Brooke shows how they did it.

Ideals and raw deals

Review of Kenneth O. Morgan, *Labour People*, in the *Guardian*,
10 April 1987

When the historian Kenneth Morgan transferred his attention from
Lloyd George studies to the Labour movement at large he brought with
him one of the great Welshman's own strongest passions: an insatiable
zest for politics.

Weary titans, or misplaced bureaucrats, or would-be philosophers, or
bungling idealists exclude themselves from any claim to the highest
honour. That must be kept for those who serve no other god whatsoever.
I once heard Lloyd George himself berate a company of high-falutin'
Oxford undergraduates for neglecting the immediate, supreme, all-else
consuming task – to get the Tories out, Neville Chamberlain at their
head. Who could challenge his sense of priorities?

But was not the Labour Party brought into being for the very purpose
of raising politics to loftier altitudes? Was not the vision of the new
Jerusalem something which the Labour movement pursued as never

before? Were not all, or almost all, the leading figures among the pioneers, or their successors, touched at some moment by this same dream? Was not part of their appeal the rejection of sordid practicalities, including many of the lowly arts with which Lloyd George had debased, perhaps fatally, his own glory.

Kenneth Morgan knows all about these tender matters, as he shows in almost every one of these portraits of would-be Labour leaders. Each drew some of his strength from the common socialist source, from the proposition which Morgan states so bluntly and justly: 'The British Labour movement has always venerated the collective ideal. Its key images have focused on solidarity, mass endeavour, the common good.'

This shared history and aspiration between the party workers and the trade unions especially, but in many other common endeavours as well, is what gave, and still gives, to our movement its distinction and its staying power.

How the leaders and the led sometimes got diverted into pragmatic byways or blind alleys; how they weathered the storms, discovered new places to bivouac on the way to the promised land, and mixed their metaphors; how cowards flinched and traitors sneered; all this is recited here with real insight and freshness.

Occasionally the arch apparatchiks – Arthur Henderson, Herbert Morrison, Morgan Phillips – reveal their allegiance to the romantic ideal. Sometimes the most successful leaders – Attlee, for instance, 'a modest little man with much to be modest about', are caught red-handed in a shameful plot against their own rank and file. 'It is hard to acquit Attlee, Morrison and Gaitskell', concludes the matter-of-fact historian, 'of charges of conspiracy to remove Bevan from the Government' – the same Aneurin Bevan who revealed himself, like Lloyd George, 'an artist in the uses of power'. Attlee indeed might have required some further scrutiny, if the portrait gallery had included George Lansbury. Morgan acknowledges some of his other omissions: Blatchford, Snowden, the Clydesiders, Jack Jones.

Without Wells and Shaw two vital strands in the making of the party are missing. And the rebuilding of the party after the 1931 catastrophe was truly heroic; a combined feat of idealism and pragmatism, and George Lansbury was its embodiment, however much Bevin and Dalton poured scorn on his exertions.

The same Attlee, however, receives his final glowing Attlee-esque accolade from an unexpected quarter. 'Attlee grows on you' says A. J. P. Taylor, a tribute, as Morgan calls it, from 'our greatest living historian, our most incorrigible of academic rebels.' Morgan himself of course is what he defines, in another context altogether, 'a trained historian from the A. J. P. Taylor stable of Thoroughbreds.'

Ken Morgan's own assortment of qualities grows with each new book. An absorption with politics, like Lloyd George's; a Taylorite taste for mixing reckless, revealing judgements with the narrative; a hard independent judgement for most occasions and a soft spot for a few such as the present reviewer, whose interest must be declared, like an MP's.

Yet even all this he knows is not enough. He understands the moods and eccentricities of the Labour movement, as maybe only the Celts who did so much to create it can. The Gaitskells, the Crippses, the Attlees even, never could know. No amount of instruction on the playing fields of Eton and Winchester could ever be a substitute for the lore to be learnt at Cardiff Arms Park, White Hart Lane, Highbury or Home Park.

Harold Laski

Review of Michael Newman, *Harold Laski: a political biography,* and
Isaac Kramwick and Barry Sheerman, *Harold Laski: a life on the left,*
in *History Today* October 1983

When Harold Laski died suddenly at the age of fifty-six, in 1950, the
Labour Party's National Executive Committee passed a resolution
expressing gratitude for his 'outstanding service' and promising to
establish a permanent memorial to his memory. No doubt was possible
about his eminence or notoriety: he was better known on both sides of
the Atlantic than most of the official leaders of the Labour Party. No
doubt was possible about the sincerity of those who moved the resolution: a few of them revered him as a political thinker of the first order
and he had been constantly re-elected by the Labour Party's rank and
file to take his seat on that NEC. But his last few years were darkened
by quarrels with some of the other party leaders, notably Clement Attlee
and Ernest Bevin. The end might almost have come as a kind of political
heart attack, the more poignant in Laski's case since all who knew him

knew especially that in his frail body he had carried from infancy a passionate political heart. The NEC's commitment to establish a permanent memorial has hitherto been set aside. However, a ceremony at the National Museum of Labour History in Manchester offered an occasion of which Laski would surely have approved.

Two excellent biographies appeared in the autumn of 1993, one by Michael Newman (*Harold Laski: a political biography*, the other by Isaac Kramwick and Barry Sheerman (*Harold Laski: a life on the left.* Both are worthy of their subject. Each reopens the question about the true greatness of Harold Laski. Each puts to shame the general verdict about him which the Attlees and the Bevins were quite ready to disseminate and which respectable historians were much too eager to accept in turn. Thus Clement Attlee, the laconic Attlee, offered his fresh verdict in 1960: 'People who talk too much soon find themselves up against it. Harold Laski, for instance. A brilliant chap but he talked too much. A wonderful teacher. You must be able to talk to teach and we need all the teachers we can get, but he had no political judgement.'

It so happens that Laski's period of full activity in the politics of our century roughly corresponds with Attlee's and Bevin's and, although he came from a quite different background, his contribution to the British Labour movement can bear comparison with theirs. Both these volumes supply the detailed evidence.

The young rebellious Laski made his first incursion into British politics in Oxford and London in the years before 1914. He broke away from his rich Jewish Manchester family and married the gentile Frida, who happened also to be a passionate feminist. Each helped further to convert the other to some form of socialism or rather the particular brand of socialism which George Lansbury was preaching in the East End of London. Lansbury had jeopardised his political career rather than betray the women's cause, but he also fought for his East End workers with the same unflinching loyalty. Lansbury taught Laski how to fight for his socialism: he was no bad tutor for sure and Laski never forgot. He judged that the George Lansbury whom he saw in action was one of the two greatest men he ever knew – the other was H. W. Nevinson, the liberal journalist (with the small 'l') who also understood the women's cause. Little Laski hurled himself into the battle and the limelight against Lloyd George at the Oxford Union and so militantly in London that for a while he had to escape from the police to Paris. Maybe it was his love of Frida, his love of Lansbury, which made him so passionate, even reckless in the excellent cause. Neither Attlee nor Bevin, so far as 1 know, risked being guilty of some misjudgement on that account; they just kept silent on the subject. It was Laski's form of advocacy and his readiness to join with others equally outspoken which eventually won the day. Hardly less notable, as revealed in these biographies, is the way the young intellectual recruit to the Labour movement recognised the essential role which the trade unions must be allowed to play in the building of a free society.

Laski, the political philosopher and teacher, was constantly discussing what was the nature of the sovereign state and how it should be adapted, or revolutionised, to meet the demands of a true democracy. Both in the United States, where he was teaching, and in the Britain of the 1920s when he returned, Laski saw how essential it was for political freedom that those industrial battles should be fought and won. He appreciated the role which Ernest Bevin played in several of these contests and, most especially, the part which he played in rescuing the Labour Government from the disaster of 1931. Attlee's role was not so notable – or noticeable. But he too should have known enough of what Laski was writing and saying (he was always doing both in language which everyone could understand) to appreciate how valuable was Laski's contribution to the general political debate in the late 1920s or the early 1930s which helped ultimately to lead to the great Labour victory of 1945.

Two other great themes came to dominate Laski's political life where his judgement may now be weighed against the Attlee–Bevin conduct of affairs. The most flagrant clash between them – the one which touched

Laski most sorely – was the British Labour Government's glaring departure from its declared policy towards Palestine after 1945. That it was such a departure cannot be denied. Of course, it is also true that the pre-war, pre-1945 Labour Party should have understood better, should have made better efforts to understand, what was and would be the strength of the Arab case in any dispute about Palestine. But at the, moment of betrayal that was not the issue at stake. Of course, Laski's Jewishness and, more especially, his friendship with leading Jewish figures in the United States intensified his bitterness. But, unlike most of them, he himself had not been a Zionist. Like so many others, he was converted by the Hitler terror. Maybe he and others in the Labour Party should not have been so swayed, but they were, left, right and centre in the party, leaders and led: they made the pledge to the Jewish people in Palestine and across the world absolute. And then they broke it, and the final breach added a last touch of horror. When the British House of Commons passed the resolution which ended the British mandate and ordered the withdrawal of British troops, no one could know, no one at the British Foreign Office could know, that the Jewish fighting forces would be so effective, that they would save themselves and their state. It might have been another Holocaust.

Considering all these implications, Laski and the others who shared his commitment might marvel at their moderation. And whatever else might be questioned in his conduct, it was not a matter of misjudgement. Laski thought deeply and argued freely throughout his whole adult life on the great interlocking subjects of Jewish freedom and assimilation. Most of what he said or wrote is worth reading. The same cannot be said for Attlee's casual comments or his excuse for the final catastrophic intervention.

Another great matter on which both men were called to pass judgement and which seemed to be ironically interwoven with their individual performance was India. It was during the first years of the 1945 Attlee Government that the independence of India was established, and both at the time when the commitment was made (under Laski's direct inspiration) and when it was carried through, Laski was eager to give Attlee considerable personal credit. He had reserves of magnanimity which both Attlee and Bevin found it hard to muster. But the full definition of Laski's vision on this subject shows how unwise the pragmatists may be to assume that all the good judgement is on their side. Attlee's own introduction to India was in the 1920s when he was one of the Labour MPs who formed part of the Simon Commission. He signed that report which so gravely disappointed Indian hopes of self-government; his outlook seemed to be hopelessly inhibited. Until the great opportunity came in 1945 he seemed to concur with the prevailing orthodox view of successive British Governments, both before and during the war.

Laski had the good luck – and India shared the luck too – to have had a different introduction. He was appointed to a jury in a libel case featuring Sir Michael O'Dwyer of Amritsar. O'Dwyer, the British general who had conducted the massacre, was dead, but the case was reopened. Laski's heart was shaken and he had soon turned to study the whole background of the case. Such was the process whereby he usually developed his political allegiances. He was convinced that Britain could not continue to govern India and at every available opportunity – in 1931 at the Round Table Conferences, throughout the 1930s, in the early years of the war, in the 1940s when the Churchill Government put the Indian leaders in prison – he preached the cause of a peaceful, constitutional transfer of power, so necessary for India's unity and the avoidance of collapse into religious persecutions. If his studied advice over the years had been properly heeded, a world of dissension in the process of Indian liberation might have been avoided. He had some good allies in India and Britain: Jawaharlal Nehru and Krishna Menon and some English journalists headed by H. N.Brailsford. But Laski was the one whom they acknowledged as their inspiration, not just as a talkative teacher who happened to bring his mind to bear on the problem but as a political thinker of the first order who gave to the Indian problem his highest thought.

Many of the other arguments which developed between Laski and his leaders concerned so-called pragmatic questions about the pace and methods of the advance towards a democratic socialist state. Of course, Attlee, Bevin and Co. had to deal with the realities but even here they were not always infallible. 'It is the fashion now'. Bevin replied to them on one occasion, 'for men like Harold Laski, Aneurin Bevan and Silverman, the intelligentsia of those people who claim to be members of our party, to ridicule us, to denounce us, to say we are slow, to say that we are conservative, to say we are reactionary. After all, we are the Labour Party.' And once Bevin had spoken in those terms, Attlee was inclined to follow suit. Neither of them could have taken much trouble to see – as Laski's pupils could – how deep was his loyalty to the party of his adoption.

Harold Laski paid us – that is, the whole nation as well as the Labour Party – a compliment of assuming that we truly meant it when we talked about freedom in general and free speech and free writing in particular. He was constantly arguing about how we could extend these glorious benefits for all mankind and womankind, best developed in the France of the Revolution, in the Britain of the Labour movement, in the rising, democratic republic of Thomas Jefferson and Franklin Roosevelt across the Atlantic which he honoured hardly less. Looking back now, we may see that it was often not a question of his talking too much but more that we, and especially our leaders, listened too little. He was also, as Attlee somewhat patronisingly acknowledged, a great teacher. But he himself would never draw too sharp a distinction between the different roles. He could infuriate the academics no less than the politicians: 'No one can teach politics who does not know politics at first hand.' Another of his constant battles was to persuade the so-called great liberals – among them William Beveridge at his own London School of Economics – not to be so sensitive or startled about the expression of furiously unorthodox opinions, especially when the orthodox economists had helped to plunge our world into Hitlerism and all its kindred horrors.

Nothing could soften for long the voice within him which would speak out against every kind of injustice, every kind of cruelty, every kind of tyranny which blocked the path to a decent society. This was his teaching; these were his politics. And his Frida enshrined it best of all when she insisted, at the end, on inscribing the words from his favourite Heinrich Heine: 'If you would honour me, lay a sword rather than a wreath upon my coffin, for I was, first of all, a soldier in the war for the liberation of humanity.'

Heine was the foremost upholder of that great Jewish tradition in the last century; he won respect for his view almost everywhere but in his native Germany. Laski also won international respect for his fight for freedom except at last, momentarily, in the British Labour movement to which he had given most of all. It was good that that injury was at last remedied in these two books and by the National Museum of Labour History in Manchester. It would be better still if the party's National Executive Committee carried forward its 1950 resolution.

The Stalin myth

Tribune, 13 March 1953

Stalin, the man, is dead. What about Stalin, the myth? It is as well that the myth should be buried in the same coffin. Of course, the achievements of the Stalin era were monumental in scale. Under his guidance the Soviet Union was collectivised and a largely peasant people were made literate.

Thanks to these achievements, the Russian armies which were broken by the Germans in the First World War repelled and destroyed them in the Second. Since then, Communist power has been extended to the China seas and to the centre of Europe. Who, in the face of these colossal events, will dare to question Stalin's greatness? How superhuman must be the mind which presided over these world-shattering developments?

At first glance these questions appear to make only one answer possible. But there are other scenes in the drama which should not be forgotten. The Nazi–Soviet Pact and the frightening sycophancy towards

Hitler which Stalin displayed in the two subsequent years still stand as probably the most grievous and colossal blunder of the century.

The same blindness still afflicted him after 1945. He was busy clamping his power on the satellite states which had been allotted to his sphere of influence, busy despatching Marshall Zhukov to obscurity for fear that he should challenge his own prestige, busy no doubt on many indispensable tasks, but amazingly unaware of the greatest event of the post-war epoch.

China was preparing to shake the world on a scale not known since the Russian Revolution of 1917. But Stalin still believed in the star of Chiang Kai-shek! As little perhaps as the planners in Washington did the great revolutionary leader understand that the operations of revolution were still engulfing the world.

The old society is collapsing over large stretches of the planet. Vast masses of people in Asia, Africa, the Middle East and elsewhere are not content to submit to the old poverty and the old imperialism. They are shaking these burdens off their backs and nothing will stop them.

It is at least arguable that these commotions might be more intense and widespread if it had not been for the stolid, brutal determination of Stalinism to fit every social and national uprising into the same harsh, fixed pattern. It should at least be evident that the attempt to denounce and destroy each such rising as a Kremlin plot is the one way to construct the world Communist conspiracy which is so much feared.

As for Russia itself, the question remains open whether Stalin's dictatorship has been sufficient to destroy the constructive momentum of the Revolution which gave him the real sinews of Soviet strength. But it may be that socialist regeneration in Russia itself is just another of the world developments which the infallible Stalin could not foresee.

The trouble with Victor

Review of Ruth Dudley Edwards, *Victor Gollancz: a biography,* in the *Guardian*, 7 December 1987

Victor Gollancz rebelled against his Jewish father before he'd reached his teens and the somewhat ungainly reconciliation was postponed, almost literally, until the old man was on his deathbed. Soon after that first assault on Jewish tradition, the boy was able to design a religion of his own serving almost every purpose, high or low, which he might require until his own dying day.

Victor's religion, in which he was always able to find sanctuary, particularly at moments of political crisis or personal collapse, may not at first sight strike those who knew and worked with him or for him, authors or politicians or wage slaves in his office, as what we most wanted to know about this extraordinary man. Indeed, his attempt to escape into Christian mysticism, or whatever it was, was often the reason why the charge of hypocrite or humbug was levelled against him.

That terrible accusation had to be wiped away; so his new biographer is right to give the theme such pre-eminence. But let we secularists, religious and political, have no fear; the rest of the picture is painted in no less lavish detail.

Here is the whole man, his touch of genius rekindled, with the author matching the intelligence, the eloquence, the assiduity, the passion, the overbearing charm of her subject, in just the manner which he could exert on some newly acquired literary property or some newly encountered young beauty.

Victor, by the way, I was amazed to learn, regarded himself as a devoted feminist, and his very first book *The Making of Woman,* written in 1914, had this as its main point of interest. And, by the way again, in the sentence before the one containing this information, may be re-read the passage which he is marking for quotation with his celestial pencil for the advertisement in next Sunday's *Observer*. It tells all that readers, booksellers, rival publishers, need to know about the latest masterpiece and the only publisher who could present it.

Most publishing houses, pious about their proprietors if little else, would stop there, and so would Victor himself, if he had had the choice. Ruth Dudley Edwards starts off her story with the tale of Victor bringing home the manuscript of Francoise Gilot's *My Life with Picasso*, and then telephoning a colleague: 'We can't publish this! Supposing someone wrote like that about Beethoven ... or me!' Well, someone has, and with Victor the most revealing or enlivening moments are not those, as he presumably intended to imply with Picasso or Beethoven, concerned with sexual diversions or embarrassments, although there are some of those too; they are the moments of high political tragedy or challenge when Victor had to face, often in a more exposed position than anyone else, thanks to his publishing successes or his own intellectual arrogance, a sudden disruption of the world around him, his own faith. Sometimes he could act, through these periods of pressure, with nobility and courage and a driving zest all his own. No one who saw him in action in the Save Europe Now campaign, in the starving, war-torn Continent after 1945, saving us from some of the long-enduring, self-inflicted horrors of the post-1918 period, could doubt his good faith and his rare talent. And there were many such crises, mostly great redeeming moments in the twentieth-century history of our country or our Labour movement, when Victor played a leading almost indispensable role in the redemption.

But at other times he refused to face horrifying realities about the world he claimed to save, or personal appeals which he had no right, as a socialist, a publisher, a man, to brush aside with the shoddy excuses which contented him. Yes, occasionally even he would allow his judgement as a publisher to be cast down from high ground of principle where it was supposed to be established. Vanity, cheerleaders at public meetings, intellectual conceit could all play their part in the pitiful spectacle.

The most notable example concerned his treatment of George Orwell, one of his own discoveries whom he ought to have been especially eager to protect. But Orwell came into his own without Victor's aid. Not quite so happy an outcome was reserved for Noel Brailsford, the bravest, the foremost of all the socialist publicists of the Thirties. He was made to pay the penalty for exposing the reality of the Soviet trials while Victor himself, as his present biographer concludes, 'had been supremely effective as a propagandist during that very period when he had been gulled.' No soft impeachment indeed.

And throughout the whole book, so far as I see, no awkward dilemmas are dodged, no important truths are suppressed, no Picasso-like oddities or weaknesses are washed away. It is hard to know which to admire the more; the discernment of the biographer or the courage of the publisher. As a longstanding member of the National Secular Society myself, I have often thought that the surest proof of the absence of an afterlife is the fact that my old, easily provoked employer, Lord Beaverbrook, has not taken steps to express his displeasure with the present degradation of the

Express newspapers; if he had the chance, I am sure he would not have hesitated. Now, immediately on re-reading the last of these wonderful 750 pages, I made a special expedition to Henrietta Street to make sure no thunderbolt had hit those rickety, building walls which looked, half a century ago, as if they could never withstand another of Victor's tempestuous outbursts. The place still stands, I can assure you, a truer emblem even than ever before of everything that is best in liberal publishing – or liberal England, for that matter. The chief credit is due to his daughter Livia. I hope that she and that author she has backed and inspired will get all the prizes they deserve in this world and the next, from her father and his grandfather too.

George Lansbury

Review of John Shepherd, *George Lansbury – at the heart of Old Labour,* in *Tribune*, 19 September 2002

A few of us who are still alive and kicking – I think I mentioned the point at the memorial meeting for Barbara Castle – joined the Labour Party when George Lansbury was leader. He was such a man that, once having met him and heard him speak from a platform, you would never forget.

Barbara had been brought up in a Labour household. Lansbury was for me one of the reasons for joining. Just at that moment the party was facing the most dangerous crisis in its history. Of course, we didn't know that at the time. But without Lansbury and what he stood for, the whole Labour movement would have been wiped off the map.

Quite a few people who should have known better, including some eminent historians, wrote about the period as if Lansbury was part of the problem, not the solution. Most of these misleading, malevolent suggestions came from the diaries of the period, most notably Hugh Dalton's. He, along with many other leading figures in the party, had lost his seat in the 1931 electoral catastrophe and he could not imagine how the few accidental survivors could sustain an intelligent opposition, much less help rebuild the Labour Party outside.

But, against all the odds, the deed was done. Not immediately, of course, but within months the Labour Party in the House of Commons was conducting its affairs much more effectively than the old party under Ramsay MacDonald. Some were previously quite unknown figures: Stafford Cripps and Clement Attlee on the front bench and a few others on the back benches, such as Aneurin Bevan from Wales and George Buchanan from Scotland.

The unemployment crisis in the country was cutting ever more sharply into the lives of the people, particularly in parts of Wales and Scotland. Lansbury himself retained to his dying day (which was not far off) the socialist inspiration he derived from his own people in London's East End. He had done as much as any individual leader could to preserve what was best in the Labour Party's tradition and to prepare the way for the recovery of 1945.

The quality of the writing of Labour's history has vastly increased in recent years, thanks chiefly maybe to the influence of Peter Hennessy and his pupils. Most of the leading figures have been fortunate with their biographers, such as *James Callaghan* with Ken Morgan or *Hugh Gaitskell* with Brian Brivati. But Lansbury was not so lucky. The first books about him became embroiled in disputes about the Official Secrets Act.

Against all the odds, he had made himself into a great journalist. The Lansbury who had made his *Daily Herald* into the best newspaper the Labour movement had ever had could have produced a masterpiece. But, unlike so many of his contemporaries inside or outside the Labour movement, he had his own ego under strict control. He was that rare phenomenon, a truly disinterested politician whose aim was to serve faithfully the people of Bow and Bromley whom he loved and who came to love him.

The whole of that story deserves to be told and our new author, John Shepherd, does it magnificently. The London where Lansbury was reared was gripped by poverty, descriptions of which can still turn the stomach. Men, and more especially women, had to endure unspeakable hardships. Sooner and more clearly than many of his fellow socialists, Lansbury understood that and that the denial of the vote to women was a monstrous insult. Indeed, he sacrificed his own seat in Parliament in the women's cause and then devoted no small part of his energy and knowledge to ensure a victory.

That intricate story and his part in it is better told here than ever before. His *Daily Herald,* with the brilliant cartoonist Will Dyson at his side, sustained the socialist cause through the darkest years and made the prophecy that the boastful victors of Versailles would condemn mankind and womankind to another bloodbath. Thus, too, Lansbury made another contribution to the victory of 1945.

According to Alan Taylor's peroration, the England that arose then was not only that of the wartime victors: it was the one the Labour movement had sung about a century before and nowhere more lustily than in Lansbury's Bow and Bromley. Of course, Lansbury was a pacifist as well as a socialist. But in the age of Hitler and, even more so, it might be said, for socialists in the age of the Spanish Civil War, pacifism was not a sufficient creed to meet the challenge.

Lansbury hated to make any such admission but he did offer his resignation as party leader. At first the party refused to accept it but then Ernest Bevin accused him of 'hawking his conscience from conference to conference'. It is a terrible insult. George Lansbury's service to the Labour movement had been as great as Ernest Bevin's, not least as we saw in 1931 when he summoned to our rescue the whole rich tradition of the worldwide Labour movement.

Tribune at that time was leading the campaign against fascism but it was always proud to print the writings of George Lansbury.

Aneurin Bevan

Obituary in *Tribune*, 8 July 1960

Aneurin Bevan was unique. There was no one else even remotely like him. As a man, a speaker and a political leader he always acted in a style completely individual to himself.

He was, I believe, the most principled great political leader of the century in the sense that to sustain and apply his principles in practice was the motive power of his life, the passion that absorbed him while others were engaged in the darker corners of the political workshop.

His eyes were fixed on the horizons of politics. He was obsessed by the broad tumultuous movements in society and the world at large. Ideas were his passion and he was interested in power as a vehicle for ideas.

He was indeed a rarity, for although born and bred in politics he had many other loves besides. He loved the soil with the heart of a peasant; hence his life-long desire, which he eventually fulfilled on his farm in Buckinghamshire, to escape from the smoke and rattle of London he detested. He loved music and paintings. He could recite the poets and acclaimed them as the greatest of the species; do they not see further and deeper than the rest of mankind?

Most adept of all, perhaps, was his taste for argument philosophical argument. In another incarnation he might have been the founder of a new school of logic and, whenever the opportunity occurred, he could confound the latest authority from the university with his nimble brilliance in disputation.

In short, Aneurin Bevan always thought for himself and usually preferred his own conclusions. Others did their homework with blue books and statistics; he chose to think, or to think through, argument.

This was his strength; some called it his weakness. Rarely was he content with the beaten path. Since the problems of socialism, no less those of world peace, are novel, he was convinced that new ways must be sought. The fertile brain was rarely inactive; the subtle tongue was always searching for new phrases and formulations to awaken the imagination.

The curiosity was, I suppose, not that such a man had to spend the bulk of his life in dispute with his own colleagues and in his own party, but that he survived so successfully and influenced his times so powerfully. The reason for the achievement was the amazing combination of talents, talents of the brain, charm and speech, which even his fiercest enemies never denied him – these plus the correct estimate of his political character always accepted in the Welsh home town from which he came and so widely shared throughout the Labour movement as a whole in his stormiest trials.

Aneurin Bevan, I believe, did more than any other man of his time to keep alive democratic socialism as the most adventurous, ambitious, intelligent, civilised and truly liberal of modern doctrines. This, the triumph of his whole life and personality, was the greatest of his achievements.

He wanted a Labour Party seriously determined to change society to its foundations and a Britain sufficiently independent and sceptical of all the clichés of the Cold War to guide and lead the nations to a genuine peace.

These were the kind of causes which he served more eloquently, more subtly, more faithfully and, we must add, in view of the long hostility he encountered and surmounted, more courageously than any other British citizen of his time.

Ernest Bevin

Review of Alan Bullock, *The Life and Times of Ernest Bevin, Volume II, Minister of Labour 1940–1945*, in the *Evening Standard*, 18 April 1967

Ernest Bevin was a great Minister of Labour. He held this office during five years of the most terrible war in history, raised it to a peak of influence never previously conceived possible, and left it with his own personal reputation immeasurably enhanced.

He was responsible for the biggest mobilisation of manpower and woman-power for war purposes carried through by any of the belligerent nations.

An unflagging interest in all the other normal and abnormal facets of his department's work confirmed that he had an administrative gift of the first order. He must, in addition, have been a foremost member of the War Cabinet. Or, at least, his role in this respect won Churchill's fulsome commendation. But here the whole truth is not available to scholars.

Enough is certainly known of those heroic years to prove what many who had come in contact or conflict with him before 1940 had realised:

that he was a giant of a man, with some qualities of head and heart equal to the most striking aspect of his demeanour, described by his friends as a vast self-confidence or by his enemies as a gnawing gargantuan egotism.

All these accomplishments and characteristics are properly chronicled in the new volume of Mr Alan Bullock's biography. The story is told with complete clarity, intelligence and mastery of often tedious detail. No other biographer is likely to tread this same road for a long time. On Bevin, especially as a few warts are allowed to adorn the portrait, the book will doubtless be accepted as definitive.

All the greater, then, is the need to assert that the final effect of this apparently fair-minded recital is lopsided and inadequate.

And it will be melancholy as well as misleading if the tumultuous controversies of the Second World War are to be fitted into such an orderly, prosaic pattern as Mr Bullock presents. Among those with whom he worked most closely, Bevin always made – and kept – enemies.

A short list of them appearing in these pages includes Beaverbrook, Citrine, Morrison, Shinwell, Aneurin Bevan and Percy Cudlipp, at that time editor of the *Daily Herald*. Mr Bullock's usual inference about these quarrels is that the superior wisdom and foresight rested with Bevin.

Bevin himself would press this point more aggressively. He would claim that all the public spirit, patriotism and devotion to the cause of the people rested with him too. His opponents were always conspirators, stabbers-in-the back, Communists-under-the-bed, playboys, saboteurs or worse.

To make such a case plausible, it would be necessary for Mr Bullock at least to indicate the real strength of what could be said by these not inconsiderable opponents. Little of the sort is attempted. What they did actually say is occasionally abbreviated or summarised almost to the point of distortion.

The first quarrel with Beaverbrook, for instance, concerned the pace at which things could or should be done in 1940. The author mentions, without recapturing it, the tempo and tension of those times. Thereafter, Beaverbrook's biggest quarrel with Churchill concerned the major strategy of the war.

Bevin, on Mr Bullock's testimony, had nothing to contribute on these themes, which was doubtless one reason why the Chiefs of Staff no less than Churchill found him such an agreeable colleague. Beaverbrook was left to fight the critical battle for urgent aid to Russia, without assistance from the far-sighted Bevin.

The same absurd bias affects the account given here of the Bevan–Bevin controversies. Aneurin Bevan knew the miners; Ernest Bevin thought he knew them.

The awkward consequence was that Bevan's advice to the House of Commons on the coal problem – the most serious industrial problem of the war – was consistently right but rejected, while Bevin's advice to the Cabinet was usually wrong, but usually followed.

Or consider the case of Percy Cudlipp. He is left exposed as a target for Bevin's wrath and abuse while the merits of the dispute remain invidiously undiscussed. Bevin accused him of pursuing 'a nagging, Quisling policy', clearly a defamatory accusation. Or rather Bevin claimed to have been misreported and withdrew the charge in private. But now something approaching the same accusations are repeated in Bevin's quoted correspondence. Any fair-minded observer of the affair, I believe, should have concluded that Cudlipp deserved the credit for producing a brilliant and independent newspaper in defiance of Bevin's bullying.

These, however, are no more than bare examples of a general truth about the Second World War which Mr Bullock's book, like so many of the official histories, refuses to acknowledge. The men at the top, Bevin included, became more and more out of touch with the spirit of the times. Hence the constant rows of Ministers with the newspapers, the defeats for the Government at by-elections, the events leading up to and the results of the 1945 election. The evidence of this mounting, radical ferment is massive.

Bevin was baffled and exasperated by many of these developments. He was all too ready to regard criticism as treachery. He was furious when journalists would not bow to his bullying, outraged when he discovered that a few members of the Parliamentary Labour Party would not allow Parliament to be manipulated in the style Bevin used elsewhere. There the majority, however huge, had to argue their case with the minority, however small.

The process became all the more offensive to his taste when the critics could prove the wisdom of their prophecies and when the evidence grew that popular feeling was on their side. On such occasions Bevin often did what lesser men have done. He would sulk, rant or threaten or, taking a leaf from the book of his later enemy Stalin, he would accuse others of contemplating or perpetuating the backstairs manoeuvres in which he himself indulged. For he was also, as Mr Bullock scarcely even hints, a persistent and often vindictive intriguer.

Yes, he was still a giant, but he often used that giant's strength tyrannically. And the rest of the nation, including those who questioned his infallibility, were not pigmies. It was, after all, the British people, not any handful of their leaders, who won the war.

Tom Driberg

Review of Francis Wheen, *Tom Driberg: his life and indiscretions,* in the *Guardian,* 26 April 1990

A certain brand of modern biography, said Hazlitt, could add a new terror to death, and that was before the age of Chapman Pincher. The felicitously named Pincher, as Francis Wheen wittily calls him – and this book is stuffed with wit both from subject and author – has made a speciality of libelling the dead. Sir Roger Hollis was the most notorious case but Tom Driberg was another victim of the same treatment from the same hand. The first of the many virtues of this book is that it should kill for ever, in Tom's case and some others, the cowardly Pincher perversion.

When I first heard the tale that my old friend Tom Driberg had been employed both by the Soviet KGB and our own MI5, I thought that each of these organisations had just about an equal right to feel outraged or to roar with laughter. Tom loved to court danger, but by the same reckoning he invited blackmail at every turn, almost literally from the cradle to the grave. He could never keep a secret anyhow; he was much too knowledgeable about edition times.

To suggest that any secret service – let alone our rabidly anti-red, anti-homosexual British contraption – would ever entrust him with one is richly comic. Tom himself would have enjoyed and exploited the joke. If the charge had ever been printed in his lifetime, he would have sued, and what a splendid array of witnesses or backers he could have summoned to his defence.

Tom kept his friends, male friends at least, on the short list: Auden, Betjeman, Evelyn Waugh, Mountbatten, Beaverbrook even. Several of these associations are unravelled by this biographer with intricate sensitivity. If not the poet he longed to be himself, he was a great provoker of poetry in others and some excellent, if not easily repeatable pieces appear in these pages. As for Beaverbrook, the account given here of how a rasping hatred ended in a calculated but honourable rapprochement, initiated by Tom, kills off some other lies.

However, we must not be distracted too soon from the Pincher saga, for which we are offered a happily conclusive exposure. Apparently Pincher suggested to Wheen that one reason why the combined Hollis–Driberg treachery was concealed from the public was because Margaret Thatcher, as Prime Minister, made a private compact with me, as Leader of the Opposition at the time. I am supposed to have agreed not to press the charge against Hollis if she would show equal restraint in protecting my friend Tom.

Such are the fantasies of the secret service world which now seem to have taken total possession of the Pincher mind. Any such approach by me would surely have been counterproductive; any fool could see that. Moreover, if Pincher had troubled to study the published facts, he would know that I have constantly protested about the monstrous injustice done to the Hollis family against which apparently there is no protection whatever. Every inquiry into the subject has shown that Hollis was not a spy; but still Pincher and Co. make their miserable living by saying that he was.

The basis for the Pincher charge against Tom – not that he usually requires any facility so formal – were the arrangements made for Tom's visit to see Guy Burgess in Moscow in 1956. The affair suited both sides and therefore, deduced Pincher, must have had the connivance of each. This book explodes the whole of this particular claim in detail.

Tom was a free agent, on this journey and all the others. He had always been much too ready to look forgivingly on Communist misdeeds, but this attitude was combined with an absolutely genuine devotion to the cause of peace.

Anyone who knew him could easily put this claim to the test. Among his assortment of qualities, he had a simple, Sermon-on-the-Mount approach to public affairs. He thought there was such a thing as Christian socialism, and that he was an exponent of it.

But Tom could combine his qualities with deeds of inexcusable depravity. His cruelty to his wife Ena, who had committed no crime but her desire to help him, can still leave the readers gasping with horror. He could treat other human beings, waiters or waitresses, even more unpardonably. A well-known psychoanalyst called him evil: he did have a satanic streak. No one who knew him would be likely to deny that either.

Sex dominated Tom's life much more than we casual participants in his political diversions ever knew, and the topic is rightly given in these pages its persistent, shocking, risible pre-eminence. Laughter as well as tears may follow, and the whole tone of the book keeps a proper balance between the two, thereby helping to sustain Tom's protestations about his political allegiance and his religious faith. No small accomplishment indeed: one which we puritan sceptics would never be willing to underrate. Francis Wheen has written a truly great biography, one which takes full advantage of the fashion of recent years to write without inhibition about homosexual matters, but one which presents the rest of the man too. Tom Driberg had gifts of the first order as a journalist and a political observer. He saw the wickedness of the world all around him, and was not afraid to expose it, whatever the cost or risk to himself. Tom's own combined, resilient courage and craft shine through these pages; he has been lucky at last.

Richard Crossman

Review of Anthony Howard, *Crossman: the pursuit of power,* in the *Observer*, 21 October 1990

Dick Crossman had the rare gift of a Rolls Royce mind, by which I mean that his intellectual mechanism worked with a smoothness, efficiency and precision not possessed by lesser mortals. The only other politician with the same equipment whom I saw in action at close quarters was Stafford Cripps. The word *mercurial* applied to both, and could be taken as a compliment or a criticism.

Stafford Cripps combined a deep religious conviction with a brilliant mastery of any brief set before him. The two qualities together meant that with the same gesture he would brush aside the wicked, the fools, and the occasional wise man into the bargain. Dick could do the same with an even greater boldness or brusqueness, and as this biography shows had acquired the habit at school. He soon discovered that he had a brain to beat anyone else's, and was ready to make the most of it.

But what could be Dick's substitute for Stafford's direct line to the Almighty? He certainly had not a scrap of religion of his own, and his abandonment of it was one cause of his deep quarrel with his parents. The seemingly harsh title of this book might be taken to imply that Crossman's religion was the ruthless pursuit of his own interest, and of course the charge of political opportunitism was one constantly levelled against him throughout his life by enemies and friends alike.

Anthony Howard faithfully examines, as a biographer should, the series of notorious occasions when Dick seemed to expose his own readiness to change his mind and to berate those who would not perform the somersault with the same agility. Indeed, he adds a few to the list. All of us may treasure the moment in the Spanish Civil War when the young WEA lecturer at Chorley, seeking to emphasise his impartiality above the battle and to escape the charge of fellow-travelling, remarked: 'In Spanish affairs I trust Communists and Catholics about the same' – only to discover that his chairman was himself a Catholic.

But faced with a real task or a real challenge he could bring to bear his outstanding capacities with an intellectual courage for which he was seldom given credit. He did so during the war when, as his chief Bruce Lockhart said, he deserved a prize not for good conduct but for distinguished service. Wars, and more especially that one, were not to be won by sticking to the rules.

More spectacular still was the way he applied his original mind to the problem of Palestine and offered a solution which could have saved that post-1945 Labour Government from what must still be seen as its most serious and most shameful failure. There could have been a peaceful partition of Palestine, with a just recognition of the rights of both Jews and Arabs: what a prize! That was the supreme moment when the chance for genuine statesmanship appeared, and Dick Crossman became its chief advocate, with all the detailed knowledge he had acquired on the spot and on both sides of the Atlantic.

Many observers then and thereafter wondered why the Crossman who displayed such abilities was given no advancement by his leader Clem Attlee, and some abstruse reasons have been discovered in the old family relationships between the Attlees and the Crossmans. A more plausible psychoanalytical explanation is that Attlee and Bevin, who acted as unshakable allies in this wretched affair, could never forgive Dick for having been right.

However, these were individual cases, separate problems to which he applied his own peculiar inventiveness. What about the larger question of his political philosophy, his understanding of what democratic socialism meant or what it could be? Where, if anywhere, some of his irreverent contemporaries would ask, did Dick get his socialist faith?

Here, I fear, his ever-candid biographer is not so explicit as he should be. He tells of a mock election held at Winchester in 1924, and recalls 'how it was Dick, predictably, who was the Labour candidate.' But there's no predictably about it. Not even a remote clue is given us how the idea of becoming a Labour supporter was borne in upon him.

This point is stressed in no sense of mockery. To me what impressed over the years was the strength of his reforming zeal, his hatred of accepting conventional ideas, or muddled solutions. It is fascinating to see in Anthony Howard's intricate account of his dealings say, with Aneurin Bevan and Hugh Gaitskell, how it was, in the end, the deeply-rooted conservative élitism of Gaitskellite (and eventually of Wilsonian) politics, which offended him. He had not devoted his political life to war on the English Establishment – yes, right from the predictable choice of his party colours in 1924 – just to submit tamely to the same forces in his own party.

The curious truth is that Dick's religion was the Labour Party, and he expounded his faith in the magnificent letter of protest printed and sent to Harold Wilson at Prime Minister in June 1969. The accusation was that so many of the strategic decisions which had shaped the fate of the Government since 1964 had been taken in small conclaves without prior Cabinet consultation.

Of course, it wasn't the denial of the Cabinet's rights which offended him so much, although he wrote better on this subject than almost anybody since Bagehot. It was the associated denial of rights to people outside, to the members of Coventry Labour Party management committee. This was the spur to the publication of his own diaries, and he did that deed too with a relish and a bravado which was all his own.

How he must have enjoyed the joke on his arrival in the Elysian fields, although there too, I suspect, born reformer that he was, his energies were soon diverted to some long overdue work of irrigation.

Jack Jones

Review of Jack Jones, *Union Man: the autobiography of Jack Jones*, in the *Observer*, 31 August 1986

Where to start: with the man or the book? Jack Jones's autobiography is no pallid, ghost-written formality; it is the man himself, strong, direct, dedicated, learning from history and quite prepared to teach it at the same time – a book therefore to take its proper place in the library of the British Labour movement.

The story starts in Liverpool with a bare, blistering tale of childhood, and then the first union battles on the docks. No time was allowed for growing up in between. He recalls the books he read and his soapbox heroes from an earlier time, headed by Tom Mann, Ben Tillett and Jimmy Sexton. The young Jack Jones, reared among the barbarities of Liverpool dockland where the system of hiring set every man's hand against his neighbour's, lived on to play a leading part in establishing civilised work conditions for dock workers. He went to fight in Spain, speeded on his way from Transport House by a surly, ever-suspicious

Ernest Bevin: 'Have the Communists been after you?' Jones, as it turned out, had a better understanding than Bevin of the stakes involved in the Spanish Civil War; he had too, what he never lost, a youthful, idealist ardour. But Bevin also commanded the respect of a whole new generation of trade unionists, even those who might resent his bullying and his egotism. Both Frank Cousins and Jack Jones learned from Bevin, and that tradition has helped shape all our worlds.

For Jack Jones, as for the bulk of the British Labour movement, the Second World War was a continuation of the Spanish struggle against fascism; he needed no instruction from patriotic Tory appeasers. And he spent much of the war and the first years of the peace in Coventry, learning how the productive process could be improved in the teeth of Hitler's bombs or bovine managements.

These are the most original pages in the book, telling a tale not told before: how the trade unions in general and shop stewards in particular were thrust forward into the modern age.

'Always', says Jack, 'I was encouraging greater involvement of members in the work of the union. Democracy, in that sense, was not strong in the TGWU.' Indeed: but still a confession which may baffle those who never heard of the Age of Arthur Deakin and how he and his like were sustained by the Thatchers and Tebbits of earlier times. The real struggle for trade union democracy is told here with authentic, first-hand knowledge.

And here too, Jack Jones acquired his faith in the doctrine which in later years he preached more passionately and imaginatively than anyone else – his belief that the trade unions must advance towards industrial democracy. When that cause foundered so wretchedly in the last years of the last Labour Government, Jack Jones was one of the hardest hit – 'It meant a lot to me personally,' he says.

He gives a candid record of his dealings with Labour Governments, and this must be the section which will attract most public attention. It would be no bad idea for every prospective Minister in the next Labour

Cabinet to be supplied with a copy, especially since he quotes one of them as having said in 1966 that the Cabinet should act 'unclouded by sentiment and unprejudiced by history'. That would never suit the Jack Jones philosophy: he would dismiss it as a device for refusing to learn the lessons of the past.

Jack Jones preached – and practised – democracy in the conduct of the affairs of his own great trade union, never ceasing to invoke the principle that people in good jobs must discharge their debt to the lowest paid, the elderly, the unemployed. A socialism which forgot that, he argued, would not be worthy of the name. As men and women strive to recover the way we lost along that road, they will turn back to this book and the man who wrote it.

Denis Healey

Review of Denis Healey, *The Time of My Life,* in the *Observer,*
15 October 1989

I recall a Cabinet meeting at which Roy Jenkins threw across the table
at Denis Healey a variation of the insult once levelled against Macaulay:
he wished he was as certain about *anything* as Denis was about *everything.* And, of course, there always was that air about him. Fools were
not suffered at all; wise men had to watch their step; he was forever
formidably right in his own estimate, even on those occasions when he
might be executing an extraordinary, even Crossman-like, change of
political direction.

However, the Denis Healey I saw in operation at close quarters did
not fit the Jenkins caricature. He had a clear idea of the objectives he
wanted to secure, and mostly, from a socialist point of view, they
were good ones. He would listen; he could be endlessly patient in
negotiations, which is the only way to negotiate with would-be
friends or allies; he had an irrepressible intellectual curiosity

deriving partly from his interest in matters which touched only the fringe of politics.

All these qualities are brought to bear in the writing of this book, which means that it is a very good one indeed: exciting, revealing, ambitiously tackling the largest themes, self-justificatory but not offensively so. If the rest of my space is devoted to critical observation, the balance is not intended to diminish this first judgement but rather to protect the truth about the Labour Party's history in this momentous epoch.

Ernest Bevin was the young Denis's hero, and no one should complain on that score: he *was* a great man. Denis served him first as International Secretary and the period is fascinatingly recorded here. But Ernest Bevin also involved that great Labour Government in one act of eternal dishonour with painful consequences for our world today: the manner in which we scuttled from Palestine. Denis in these pages sidesteps the issue; he should have had the candour to face it head on, all the more so since he finds space on this and other issues to deride those who did recognise the reality at the time or at least sought to devise an alternative better than Bevin's – notably Dick Crossman, or *Tribune*, or Aneurin Bevan within the Cabinet.

The same sin of omission, and occasionally something worse, applies to the recollection Denis would leave us of Aneurin Bevan himself. Bevan, he implies or even insists, was a splendid rhetorician and not much else. Even his last speech at the Blackpool Conference in 1959 he describes as one devoid of real political content. Indeed. How was it, then, that so brilliant a rhetorician failed to penetrate so sensitive a skull as Denis's – particularly as their minds happen to be more closely attuned than most observers might suppose on the recurrent controversy of the Cold War?

Running constantly through the book – from Denis Healey's early membership of the Communist Party to his truly imaginative review of the Gorbachev era – is the mighty question of how the West should deal with the Soviet Union. These pages are packed with the evidence that his was never just the response of the orthodox Western cold warrior. He was always searching for a more sophisticated strategy for the West: he helped devise Labour's welcome to the Rapacki plan in the 1950s; he wanted a much better response to Khruschev; he recognised how tragically a real moment for rapprochement was so wickedly cast aside at Suez.

There are two notable examples here of Healeyite soul-searching, two occasions when, with the assistance of hindsight, he now acknowledges that he was wrong. One concerns the whole period when Western observers thought Stalin's behaviour meant he was bent on the military conquest of Western Europe – 'I now think we were all mistaken.' A mighty admission, but Denis should have had the grace to acknowledge that the *we* did not include Aneurin Bevan, whose very different estimate of Soviet intentions was presented in the teeth of official strategic thinking.

A second, even more conclusive, confession concerns the debate in the Commons on 2 March 1955 when Churchill spoke of his horror of the development of nuclear weapons and how he had been thwarted in his efforts to secure a meeting with Stalin's successor soon after Stalin's death. 'I opposed it at the time,' confesses Healey, 'but now regard it as an historic opportunity lost.'

It was truly an historic parliamentary occasion when the two protagonists, Churchill and Bevan, debated the theme of our nuclear weapon-threatened world, and when Bevan elicited Churchill's extraordinary declaration. Just at that very moment the Gaitskellites (with Healey's assistance) were trying to drive him out of the party and out of politics altogether. His larger vision about relations with the Soviet Union could not save him; rather, in Gaitskell's eyes, it was a major item on the charge sheet.

However, I would not end on this sad note. Denis himself can apply his own unforgettable verdict. Reporting on a sequence of slightly less historic events, when he and his fellow Treasury Ministers had to endure the consequences of the Lib–Lab Pact, he remarks of John Pardoe: 'He was robust and intelligent enough but sometimes I felt he was simply Denis Healey with no redeeming features.' No such apparition appears in these pages.

Politics is a good profession, and Denis Healey has written as persuasive a defence of it in the modern age as any democratic socialist could wish. He illustrates how both Bevinites and Bevanites are necessary to make a successful Labour Party, and how the true natural Bevanites have usually had enough magnaminity to recognise as much. Bennfoolery, also treated here, is something different altogether, which Healey played a most honourable part in extirpating.

John Smith

Observer, 15 May 1994

John Smith's combination of gifts and qualities was winning an extraordinary response, not only within the Labour Party but among a steadily growing section of a much wider public. Even the host of natural rebels in our midst held their breath and their tongues. He was doing it his way, and the performance looked more and more sure-footed but still ambitious enough to meet the challenge ahead. His natural good humour and high spirits, never suppressed for long even in the direst circumstances, seemed to be more than ever both justified and infectious. I saw him last at a memorial meeting a week ago for Jo Richardson. He limped onto the stage and we warned him to take care of his injured foot. 'But my heart's all right,' he insisted. And that was truly the most important part of his political anatomy.

Everyone who had ever worked closely with him discovered how clever he was, quick on the uptake but even quicker to detect a political folly or absurdity. His debating mastery in the House of

Commons was a phenomenon, but it was not gained or sustained easily. A determined effort was made, sometimes by the most puerile methods, to cripple his effectiveness. Outside observers may not always appreciate how oafish can be the conduct of the gentlemen of England, especially when backed by the newly-raucous types from the secondary professions.

Once they saw how good he was, they tried to destroy him, and, if he had led us into the next election, no doubt these sleazy methods would have been intensified. We should not be too much misled by the soft-spoken amenities of recent days. Dead Labour leaders somehow develop more rounded characters than live ones. And John Smith's character was becoming one of our strongest assets.

He could measure the political prospect with long-term acumen. One of the most courageous acts in his whole career was taken just after he had arrived in the Commons: he voted, against the majority of his own party, for entry to the European Community. He had acted from principle; he was an international socialist.

Yet he seemed to feel all the more strongly the obligation to repay the debt which he, like so many of his generation, owed to his party. If John Smith's example had been followed by others, the whole Thatcherite calamity could have been avoided.

At the last general election, he showed the same dedication to honest politics which modern politicians are not supposed to understand. His detailed budget was an attempt to present fairly the nation's real economic situation. And the nation should now be able to recall how bitterly and shamefully he was defamed.

John Major as Prime Minister did not seem to comprehend that it was his own demagogic lies about his taxation programme and ours which was the chief cause of the destruction of his authority.

It was that great spirit more even than the brilliant head which made John Smith such a splendid leader, so well qualified to lead us into the next century.

His cool calculation could be forced to boiling point when he saw tens of thousands of his countrymen driven from their jobs, the poorest families in the land hit hardest, the squandering of our precious resources, especially the oil off the Scottish coast, and the creeping or galloping corruption which both the Thatcher and Major regimes allowed to poison almost every aspect of our political life.

John Smith was resolved to change the whole prospect. Above all, maybe, he would have striven to transform Britain's status in the world: to play a full, magnaminous defeatism of the Douglas Hurd–John Major epoch. Having played a proper role in the ending of South African apartheid, no Labour Party led by John Smith would accept the enforcement of similar infamies in Europe itself.

People said he had no ideology; but for him the greatest questions were moral no less than political. He was an unashamed Tawneyite, a sworn enemy of the acquisitive society, with a strong trade union association and a Scottish accent – no bad philosophy, with pardonable improvements.

Without Scotland, there could be no good government at Westminster. John Smith, the devolution expert, knew that too. He was a genuine creation of the whole British Labour movement, which is the reason why, despite the unspeakable tragedy of his death, we should still be able to find, for our party and the country, a good successor.

Part 6

Voices for freedom

Charles James Fox

Review of David Powell, *Charles James Fox,* in the *Guardian,*
25 November 1990

Of all the British parliamentary figures who deserve to be acclaimed in
this year of revolutionary commemoration, pride of place must surely go
to Charles James Fox. Most famously, he hailed the fall of the Bastille
as a victory for freedom everywhere and, even more significantly, he
devoted his next ten years to defending English liberties, against fearful
odds, amid hysterical war fever.

How gracious and sensitive and apposite it would have been if our
Prime Minister, on her visit to Paris for this year's Bastille Day junket-
ings, had been provided with a quotation from Fox, as she was once
supplied by a speech writer, as she entered Downing Street, with the
words of St Francis of Assisi. How President Mitterrand would have
responded; he does know his history. How a warmth could have been
instilled into Anglo–French relations, and how honour would have been
done to a real defender of English freedom.

Since that opportunity was lost, we may welcome all the more David Powell's excellent new biography which tells the story for a new generation in a most direct and effective manner. He knows well, as all Fox-lovers must, that he is the subject of one of the greatest biographies in the language, *The Early History* by Sir George Trevelyan. It is not easy to tread in those footsteps, but the task should be constantly attempted.

In Trevelyan's hands, the charm of Charles Fox was conveyed, the combination of gifts which made him the most attractive Englishman who ever gave his mind to parliamentary politics. Somehow the influence which persuaded Edward Gibbon to say, 'Let him do what he will; I must still love the dog,' has been transmitted down to us, and somehow, too, the cause of English liberty which he made peculiarly his own embodies the glow of his personality.

True, this portrait was not accepted in all quarters; indeed, a few decades ago a most deliberate attempt was made to exterminate it altogether. The Namier school of history sought to banish honour and principle from the records along with all the Whig interpretations. All politicians of that age, like most others, had their price, all had their snouts in the trough of corruption. Fox, in particular, therefore must be knocked off his pedestal as 'the man of the people', David Powell's subtitle, and reduced to the same office-seeking, treasure-hunting, backstairs-intriguing habits as the rest.

Indeed, for the Namierites and their near-nihilist hangers-on, he became the principal villain. How they hated his great moments of magnanimity, and deluged themselves, if they could, in his rare hours of debasement. Out of office for all but two of his thirty-five years' parliamentary life, and forfeiting so many easy chances to get his fingers in the till, he was the perpetual contradiction of their theory.

Some part of the credit is due, as David Powell shows, to the influence of the American War of Independence which first stirred his liberal sympathies. But why did those events impel him much faster and further leftwards that the others who challenged George III? How was it this spendthrift, rampaging, spoilt son of the aristocracy had his 'inmost soul', in Gibbon's horrified words, 'deeply tinged with democracy' at a time when democracy was a dirty word?

One crucial part of the answer derives from the tumultuous London of the time, the great mass meetings of the Westminster elections, in Westminster Hall, in Covent Garden, in Palace Yard. Often the glorious gossip of those occasions has been recalled: how the ravishing Georgiana, Duchess of Devonshire, canvassing for Fox, bought a butcher's vote with a kiss (a tale, alas, denied by Georgiana herself, at least in reports to her mother).

But Fox himself felt the democratic potency of those contests and gave emphasis to it in his own words: 'It is the energy, the boldness of a man's mind, which prompts him to speak, not in private but in large and popular assemblies, that constitutes, that creates in a state, the spirit of freedom.' He drew strength and courage from the vast London crowds who swayed before him, and it was there he learned his hatred of censorship, repression, informers; his trust in the people.

Both before and after those memorable encounters on the hustings he had made himself the greatest parliamentary debater of all time: first, in his youth, when he would dare anything against any assortment of opponents, and, later, even more honourably, when he was the spokesman of a tiny minority which confronted the war hysteria.

Only the merest scraps remain of those unreportable speeches, lasting maybe for two or three hours, delivered without a note, transformed in mid-flight to seize a sudden advantage, rising and falling in tone and speed, at one moment appealing and analytical, at the next unloosing impetuous torrents.

One part of that gift, both on and off the platform, was discerned by the same Georgiana: 'I have always thought', she said, quite early in their acquaintance, 'that the great merit of C. Fox is his amazing quickness in seizing any subject – he seems to have the peculiar talent of knowing more about what he is saying and with less pains than anybody else – his conversation is like a brilliant player of billiards, the strokes follow one another, piff, paff.' And yet she who saw him so discerningly at close quarters showed her larger comprehension too.

Charles Fox, on the hustings outside St Paul's Church, Covent Garden, could sound like a twentieth-century radical, a real radical, before the word was debased with Thatcherite associations, like Lloyd George at Limehouse. But he was an eighteenth-century rake who could lose £5,000 a night at Almacks or win £50,000 in a year at Newmarket – at 1780 prices, what's more. He was reared in the narrowest of oligarchies, and lived to enlarge the meaning of freedom for all Englishmen and women thereafter. 'His standard is in the hearts of men'; yes, that was his proper democratic epitaph, spoken appropriately by that best of canvassers, the gorgeous Georgiana.

Citizen Paine

Review of Gregory Claeys, *Tom Paine: social and political thought,*
in the *Guardian*, 16 November 1989

Thomas Paine to the Pantheon! This splendid cry, I must in fairness
acknowledge to *Guardian* readers, is not one prompted by this latest
book about him, although it might well have been. I first heard it, most
appropriately, in the Paris of the pre-14 July celebrations when a number
of French historians assembled at a special seminar in the French
National Assembly to discuss the theme in strictly academic terms.
Suddenly, after all the debate, the proposal for action seemed to light up
the affair with a revolutionary blaze.

And such a development, quite unforeseen by the seminar organisers,
was indeed an event of real historical interest. One of the most curious,
persistent aspects of the Thomas Paine saga – another theme properly
emphasised in this new book – is the way in which his great achievements have periodically been the subject of bitter, deadly denigration. It
was happening every few years in his own lifetime, and the pattern has

been repeated every few decades ever since, on both sides of the Atlantic, in the land of his birth and the land of his adoption.

Both the British Establishment and its American counterpart, if there is such a definable body, have always had their reasons for defaming Thomas Paine; these were tributes to the potency of his still highly combustible revolutionary thought. But why the French?

In one sense his neglect there was all the more inexplicable, since his *Rights of Man* was, and remains, the most powerful defence of the Revolution. Somehow the true role of Thomas Paine in those mighty events became so buried beneath the debris that even the greatest of French Revolutionary historians, Jules Michelet, could make mistakes about his name, his nationality, his true glory.

One cause of the change was the publication of the first French biography of Paine. Napoleon, in his revolutionary days, is supposed to have said that a statue to him should be erected in every country in the universe, and then did nothing about it when he had the chance.

Professor Bernard Vincent's book *Thomas Paine ou la Religious de la Liberté*, published in 1987, at last made some French recompense for the Napoleonic bombast or, rather, placed Paine in his proper French setting of the Condorcet household, 'the hearth of the Revolution,' as Michelet called it. Condorcet and his beautiful, feminist wife have recently experienced a revival in their fame, and it is most fitting that all these reappraisals should synchronise.

It is indeed the international reputation of Thomas Paine which this new volume constantly examines and extols. As a man of words and a man of action combined, no other figure of the century could match the way he would take all national frontiers in his stride. He was the first who could properly call himself a citizen of the world, and who sought to translate his claim into action.

Amazingly, some of his supposedly less well-educated contemporaries saw all this quite clearly when it was concealed from their terrified rulers. Soon after the publication of *The Rights of Man* in 1791 one of his Yorkshire disciples wrote: 'Our views of *The Rights of Man* are not confined solely to this small island but are extended to the whole human race, black or white, high or low.'

That was the true Paineite doctrine; it was no accident that the American Paine was one of the first to denounce slavery and the English Paine one of the first to describe the lineaments of the welfare state.

Yet, side by side with these spacious visions went Paine's fury about the obstacles which blocked the path to reform. It was the combination of the two which made the true Paineite message, and Gregory Claeys has a real gift for ensuring that the connection is never neglected.

What Paine did in his *Rights of Man*, he says, was to challenge as never before 'the bonds of deference and hierarchy which were the sinews of an aristocratic, agricultural and Anglican nation.' No one before has shown so well how servility could be, must be, perpetually despised and assaulted. One radical, quoted by Claeys, wrote for many besides himself to some so-called loyalist society which would burn both the book and the man: 'Men and Angels sing the eternal immortal praises of *The Rights of Man*', and signed himself, 'Not your humble servant, but the contrary.' These were Paine's own words with which he signed his own most far-reaching democratic document of the French period. Altogether, this volume makes a most welcome American contribution to the Pantheon campaign, to set beside Professor Vincent's French initiative.

Must we English always lag behind? Not at all, or at least the Welsh can make amends. Earlier this year, Gwyn Williams wrote a new preface to his classic *Artisans and Sans Culottes* in which the role of Paine was once again properly celebrated. 'His insolence was the best cure for deference,' wrote Gwyn. 'His subversive presence seemed to be every-where. Wales, Ireland, Scotland, each experienced their Paineite introduction to the new world, and never allowed these honourable traces of democratic manhood (and womanhood) to be wiped from their records.'

All devoted Paineites should also be eager to acknowledge, as I fear Gregory Claeys does not, that the true revival in his reputation was the work of an English writer. H. N. Brailsford started his essay on the subject with the exchange which Professor Vincent adopts as his epigraph: 'Where Liberty is, there is my country,' said Benjamin Franklin. 'Where Liberty is not, there is mine,' replied Thomas Paine. He never forgot that his most devoted readers might be those for whom even the right to read would be denied. I suppose he had more of his books burnt in one place or another than any other English writer, even though he took the precaution of calling his *Satanic Verses*, *The Age of Reason*.

Amartya Sen

Review of Amartya Sen, *Development as Freedom*, in *Tribune*,
1 September 1999

Little Jamaica and monstrous India have this in common – after hellish long years of suffering at the hands of their imperial masters, each set off on its own path of democratic hope, fifty-two or fifty-three years ago. I myself had a ringside seat to mark these great events, having witnessed the final exchanges between Alexander Bustamente and Norman Manley on the Kingston election hustings in 1946 and having been instructed on the supreme questions of Indian independence way back in the 1930s by Krishna Menon, secretary of the long ostracised India League, soon to reappear in London as the first High Commissioner for his newly demo-cratic independent India. Never before had the voters, men and women, been able to use their power to such purpose. They have been doing it ever since, not solely for their own benefit but for the world at large. To prove how democracy works can truly be said to be the paramount question for civilised people everywhere.

A good rule for democratic travellers is to take the best books with you. No one should cross the Atlantic without a copy of Thomas Paine's *Rights of Man*, or maybe his earlier ones which first taught the Americans how to use the word independence. Previously, *en route* to other parts of the American hemisphere, I have often recommended C. L. R. James's *The Black Jacobins*. That volume tells most wondrously how the revolutionary leaders of those times fought for their own rights and set the pattern for rebellious followers across Africa and America ever afterwards

But this time I took with me a quite different volume: the treatise of an economist turned philosopher or political pundit, perhaps you may call him. At first hearing it may sound dry as dust but I tell you it is nothing of the kind. It is the best democratic manifesto since the great French philosophers tried their hands at the same art in the eighteenth century. If we could persuade the politicians to listen now, we could protect and enlarge the lives of millions of men and, more especially even, millions of women.

The country our author loves best, the democracy he knows best, is his India: come to his analysis and indeed his grand solutions in a minute. Immediately it is the tragic similarity of the terrible problems in the different hemispheres which hits the traveller in the eye and is never allowed to escape his attention.

Poverty, a deeply entrenched poverty seemingly incurable, seems to affect some sixty per cent of the Jamaican population and in recent times, say in the last decade, Jamaica has been shocked to experience the combined explosions of crime and corruption famous in some other parts of our drug-addicted world, but still deeply offensive to the vast majority of democratic Jamaicans.

Each week a new crime of hideous proportions, posing equal problems for the police and the government, hits the headlines. It is not racist in the sense known in Britain or indeed India. The modern Jamaicans are much too much a multi-coloured lot to fall for such absurdity. But that, in another sense, makes the terrible Jamaican murder rate even more inexplicable or dangerous. Politicians and offenders confront one another with ever more offensive propositions. The crowded prisons are to be made even more bestially deterrent. The guns are to become more plentiful in everyone's hands.

But suddenly too we have signs of another dispensation. The same forbidden ground, Kingston's Trench Town, which was supposed to breed nothing but guns and criminals, is the place where the Jamaican love of music and books merge together and dedicated teachers find their reward. Bob Marley's songs were first sung here but were soon recorded across the world wherever new voices were being heard. Little Jamaica uses its own voice no less confidently than the wonderful airline, Air Jamaica, which they have fashioned for themselves to bind together the West Indian islands and give them their bond with the new century.

Sometimes the modern disease of combined crime and corruption is interpreted by interested parties as if it is solely the responsibility of the governments in the individual countries: the particular administrations in charge in Kingston, New Delhi or London. Some of the real criminals have a special interest in fostering the idea that the world-wide disease is ineradicable. Amartya Sen's book is the best civilising response to this particular line of reactionary nonsense. And this amazing streak of topicality is only one reason that his voice must be heard.

A world-wide disease which if it were not properly detected and the remedy sought could indeed overwhelm us or, even before that, destroy any claim that we have built a real and lasting civilised society. It is the old horror described by Karl Marx but quite often also by other socialist philosophers both before and after him – the deepening poverty which seems to afflict societies which take no adequate measures to combat it. Jamaica is thus afflicted, India even more so. Here in our own country we had made some advances in closing the gap between rich and poor but in recent times the progress has shamefully been put in reverse. As for the supposedly invulnerable American continent, there too the gap widens which may be the reason that nearly half of that country's population fails to use their vote to stop the hideous development.

Sometimes political philosophers, usually of a deeply reactionary nature, have sought to use this supposedly incontrovertible evidence to prophesy disaster if their reactionary policies are not meticulously followed. One of the most prominent of these was the Right Reverend Thomas Robert Malthus, who prophesied round about the year 1800 that food supplies would infallibly be outstripped by the growth in populations. Malthus was hailed as number one hero by the Tories of his day. He is Amartya Sen's chief *bête noire* – or just one of them at any rate. He himself offers instead a range of combined civilising voices from France and England to defeat the whole challenge.

Amartya Sen indeed offers a quite different prospect for the human species. Wherever men and more especially women have been able to choose for themselves, a great new prospect of freedom has opened before them. The liberation of women and the practical evidence of the fruits of it, say in his own Indian state of Kerala, is one of his principal themes. He rediscovers the truest humanist strands in our own philosopher-economists, say Adam Smith or John Stuart Mill, and presents them in a new synthesis. His title only is too modest. *Development as Freedom* is accurate enough, but here also are described in these pages the practical means whereby mankind and womankind can set out on a new course. Among the authorities Amartya Sen calls in aid is 'my illustrious countryman, Gautama Buddha'. Indeed, a new lustre runs through every page in this book. Not a trace of the old religions may be detected in it. It is indeed a new voice for humankind as a whole. He writes with a new authority not only about the wealth of nations but the even greater wealth of our single humanity.

As I finished reading this book, the terrible news was coming through of the Gujarat earthquake. Whatever the contribution human failings may have made to the disaster, it is the terrible 'act of God' which reduces every other factor to insignificance. But Amartya Sen has some highly pertinent comments to make on a kindred topic: the fact that independent India has succeeded in preventing the kind of famines which caused devastation before, as recently as 1943. Since then there has been no famine, thanks to India's democracy. Amartya Sen himself witnessed that as a boy and he records here what Winston Churchill, who was still in charge of policies for India, had to say in London. It will make you as ashamed as we should be of the whole imperialist story.

Salman Rushdie

Guardian, 3 March 1989

If people are now being killed in Salman Rushdie's native Bombay because of his book, is it not time to cry halt, time for Rushdie and his publishers to call the whole thing off, recall copies and promise never to commit the same offence again?

To which the short, and the long, answer must be: the killings are not attributable to Rushdie's book; not a single sentence within it incites people to kill or offers excuse for the killers.

On the contrary, the reason for the killing is to be found in the religion of the killers or those who have incited them to kill, or in the measures of the police who felt required to take protective action against the peril of even more widespread killings, inspired by the same religious appeal or provocation.

And please don't tell us, for a start, that the idea of such religious-inspired killing becoming more extensive is a fanciful excuse. It is nothing of the sort. It has been happening before our eyes, over the past seven or eight years, on a large, nearly unprecedented scale, without a murmur of objection from those who claim to be outraged by Rushdie.

The killings in the Iran–Iraq war have been so huge that they are literally incalculable, and they have had the added indecency on the Iranian side that tens of thousands of boys have been sent to their deaths with keys of paradise around their necks. How many others have been killed in Iran itself without this happy consolation, no one knows, and few people seem to care except the brave Iranian dissidents who have long warned us about the scale of the Ayatollah Khomeini horror. For them – and for us, maybe – it is a threat on the Hitler dimension. But for the moment I'm concerned about the numbers and the wantonness of the killings. It would be a strange world which drew the contrasted conclusion that the trouble comes from Rushdie and not at all from Khomeini.

Most Muslims throughout the world, and most especially, we might say, those settled in this country, have every interest and duty to say how strongly and unshakably they oppose the Ayatollah and all his works, both his death threats beyond his frontiers and his murderous methods at home. Many have done so without hesitation or equivocation. When the horror has passed, they will deserve the highest credit – as did the trade unionists, socialists and Jews who resisted Hitler in the back streets of Berlin and Munich when Chamberlain and Co. were still engaged in their appeasement act. These are truly the best spokesmen of their Muslim cause.

But these voices are drowned or at least subdued by others. I quote from Dr Shabbir Akhtar of Bradford's Council of Mosques (*Agenda*, 27 February) who doubtless approved the shameful book burning in that city: 'Any faith which compromises its internal temper of militant wrath is destined for the dustbin of history, for it can no longer preserve its faithful heritage in face of the corrosive influences.' Dr Akhtar professes a fundamentalist, absolute religious allegiance which would permit no argument with Rushdie. He or, at least his book, must be destroyed.

However, Dr Akhtar's case gives us the opportunity to introduce Christianity and all its kindred intolerances into the debate. 'Many writers,' he continues, 'often condescendingly imply that Muslims should become as tolerant as modern Christians. After all, the Christian faith has not been undermined. But the truth is, of course, too obviously, all the other way. The continual blasphemies against the Christian faith have totally undermined it.' Indeed, there is a measure of twisted sense in the Doctor's analysis: the survival of Christianity has been due in part to its newfound mildness, its tolerance of other creeds, an ending or at least a mitigation of the old rivalries, say, between Protestant and Catholic. Once those contents led to unending killings too.

For Dr Akhtar's benefit, and indeed for the general enlightenment of mankind, we might put the case the other way round. Once upon a time there was little to choose between Christian and Muslim or Protestant, in what Dr Akhtar now calls an 'internal temper of militant wrath' or the preserving of 'the faithful heritage'. Each side could be indiscriminate killers, and they did it in the name of religion.

How the world in general, and Western Europe in particular, escaped from this predicament, this seemingly endless confrontation, is one of the real miracles of western civilisation, and it was certainly not the work of the fundamentalists on either side. It was done by those who dared to deny the absolute authority of their respective gods; the sceptics, the doubters, the mockers even, the men like Montaigne who saw where the endless bloodletting would lead, and how each side must be ready to abjure absolute victory.

The great, persisting threat to our world derives from this pursuit of absolute victory. Once it was Hitler's creed, and once it was Stalin's, and once it was called the Dulles doctrine, and once it came near to being adopted by a President Reagan launching fundamentalist anathemas against the evil empire. It is too soon to say that all these perils have passed, but on the intercontinental stage they have been miraculously reduced, with mankind able to breathe again – as they did when the crusaders and their enemies became exhausted by their mad expeditions or when Catholic and Protestant reached their sixteenth-century compromise.

How strident or absurd or indeed wicked were the fundamentalist voices of those times, the Khomeinis and the Akhtars, who denounced any move towards détente or rapprochement as blasphemy or treachery or godlessness. How much wiser and braver were the Montaignes, the Jonathan Swifts, the Voltaires, the Salman Rushdies, who knew that if such insanities were to be stopped, they must be mocked in the name of a common human decency with a claim to take precedence over any religion. Montaigne's books were put on the Papal Index; Swift was accused, on the highest regal or ecclesiastical authority, of defaming all religions; many of Voltaire's volumes were actually burnt.

So Salman Rushdie keeps good company. He is a great artist, even if, like Swift or Voltaire himself, he does not possess all the virtues too. But no shield against religious intolerance off the leash can always prevail, as Voltaire himself explained in his epitaph on the Saint Zapata:

He isolated truth from falsehood and separated religion from fanaticisms. He taught and practised virtue. He was gentle, benevolent and modest, and was roasted at Valladolid in the year of grace, 1631.

Comrades all

Review of Paul Preston, *Comrades!: portraits from the Spanish Civil War,* in the *Observer*, 2 May 1999

A few weeks ago, at the height of the controversy about British participation in the Balkan war, Correlli Barnett, the military expert, wrote a letter to the newspapers advising all concerned, especially – by implication – meddlesome, muddleheaded British Cabinet Ministers, to mark the example of their predecessors in office at the time of the Spanish Civil War. Since no British interest was directly involved and since no obvious merit could be detected in either of the parties engaged, the Cabinet of that period applied a policy of non-intervention from the start and stuck to it. The implication was that from the British standpoint the policy was a roaring success. However, Barnett failed to mention one matter which might have upset his non-intervention balance of profit and loss – the Second World War, which followed soon after.

Some of us are old enough to recall how that Spanish controversy felt at first hand. It was the most significant ideological argument of the

1930s. Before the outbreak of war in July 1936, it looked as if the fascist regimes in Italy, Germany and Austria were to be allowed to sweep all before them without any effective resistance, with the elected rulers of the supposedly democratic states in London and Paris looking for every excuse to avoid a military response. But this was the only kind of action which would have impressed Hitler in Berlin or Mussolini in Rome or, most recently, the fascist machine guns used in Vienna to wipe off the map one of the finest social achievements of the age.

But Spain was different. The newly established government in Madrid was democratically elected. The administration in Madrid, combined with the recently established republican president, represented the Spanish people more faithfully than ever before. When, so shortly after the election, they found their legitimate authority challenged by a military conspiracy, they resolved to defend themselves and their democracy. Military rebellion had often played a conspicuous part in Spanish history; doubtless the successes of Mussolini and Dollfuss had encouraged Franco to embark on his adventure. He thought he would be parading through the streets of Madrid in a few days. Instead, he had to wait three years.

How the people of Spain and their new government conducted themselves, and how the rest of the world reacted, is the story which Paul Preston tells in presenting nine skilful portraits of particular combatants or non-combatants in that momentous three-year period. At first glance, it may be supposed that he is subscribing to the Correlli Barnett doctrine, expressed by the then Foreign Secretary, Samuel Hoare, as a 'faction fight'. The ironic title may help to fortify the suspicion; is he not suggesting that some of the most fervent comrades conducted themselves in the most uncomradely manner. But we must turn to clear Preston's name. He is not searching for any fresh excuse for surrender. He is a true historian and he loves Spain, as did one of his particular chosen heroes in this volume, Indalecio Prieto.

Prieto played a most honourable part in the whole story. He helped to construct a truly democratic socialist Party, playing an essential role in the creation of the democratic republic, both in the 1930s and again in the recreation of Spanish democracy in the 1970s. Without the socialist Party and Prieto's stamp upon it, neither achievement would have been possible. He has often been the victim of Communist vilification and deserves his rehabilitation here.

And before Communist sympathisers jump to the conclusion that Preston is unfair to them, let them reserve their judgements till they have read his final glowing portrait of *la Pasionaria*. The woman who stirred the world from its slumbers has, as Preston illustrates, made her own contribution to the new spirit of reconciliation in modern Spain.

One significant portrait is missing: Dr Juan Negrin, who succeeded Prieto in his leadership of the socialists. Journalists who had the chance, as I did, to meet him during his exile in London, could not mistake his qualities. If he had been able to take over the premiership earlier, he might have been better able to save the whole enterprise. One chapter is called 'The Discreet Charm of Dictator Francisco Franco'. Charm of a sort was there but it concealed a ruthlessness which could shock even the emissaries of Hitler and Mussolini. However, his methods won approbation from English aristocrat circles; they could admire his prowess on the hunting field and his diplomacy. His admiration for his own survival never faltered, and this feature of his character becomes all the more odious when it is recalled that the blood-letting was almost exclusively Spanish. Maybe that's where Milosevic learnt his way of charming the Hurds, Majors and Carringtons.

Ian Gilmour

Review of Ian Gilmour, *Riots, Risings and Revolutions*,
in the *Observer*, 24 May 1992

Ian Gilmour has the distinction of being the first offender thrown out of
a Thatcherite Cabinet for ideological incompatibility. Readers of this
wonderful book may pause to consider how he ever became ensnared in
such an unlikely contraption, and how this product of his enforced
leisure might be viewed by his political executioner.

Riots, Risings and Revolutions is a masterly piece of historical
writing; an historical treatise but one which in passing puts the historians in their place along with the politicians. Not a single, dry-as-dust,
irrelevant passage is permitted, and the modern implications of these
ancient debates are spaciously displayed.

For instance, page 1 of the brilliant preface, which poses the question
whether England was truly such a violent society as it has been
portrayed, refers to Milton's heaven, where the angels happily resorted
to gunpowder, to the Jesuit priest (quite a modern one) who thought that

men were often more squeamish than God about the use of force, to the Mussolini who believed that only blood made the wheels of history turn, or to the Pope of the pusillanimous period who gave him his blessing on behalf of a Divine Providence.

Yet Gilmour is perfectly aware that the men and women of that century should be properly judged by their own tests. The talent he shares with the greatest historians such as E. P. Thompson or Christopher Hill is the gift of historical imagination. The new discoveries in so many fields are made only by the historians equipped with such iconoclastic honesty.

Time and again Ian Gilmour establishes original interpretations – for example, in his portrait of the Glorious Revolution of 1688, which offers the proper prelude to his whole story. He weaves all the various interpretations, Whig, Tory and the rest, into one brilliant tapestry but shows also – *proves* is not too strong a word – how the decisive action was taken by the people whom Tom Paine described as being always 'left out of the question': the rabble, the rioters, the mob. The word 'mob', as Gilmour mentions, is abbreviated from *mobile vulgus*, and the abbreviation itself came into popular use, most appropriately, in 1688. It was touch and go whether the infamous James II would be kicked out: he himself contributed to the outcome by his own cowardice or folly, but several of the leading figures in the drama behaved with a similar lack of cunning or courage. In the end, the tender balance was tipped – by the mob. Without them, there would have been no Glorious Revolution, and English statesmen would never have been able to give lectures about liberty to the French and other breeds.

Such legitimate boasting, prompted by Ian Gilmour's astonishing revelations about the true nature of English liberty, will, I trust, encourage Denis Thatcher to buy a copy of this book to read to his wife in bed. Hitherto, I had thought that my choice of reading for this pastime would always be *The Collected Works of Julian Critchley*. But here is a worthy companion volume. It concludes with a quotation from a previous British Prime Minister whom I had always thought offered the nearest likeness to Mrs Thatcher herself, apart from Neville Chamberlain: William Pitt, the younger.

Pitt described how perfectly he had conducted the affairs of the nation, protecting property, liberty and everything Englishmen and women held dear and how, by implication, no one could have done the job better. The date of this utterance, as Gilmour illustrates in his epigraph, was 17 February 1792 – just before England was plunged into the most wretched of wars, with appalling consequences for the mass of our people, and most especially, the rabble who had been responsible for the glories of 1688.

Postscript

Ian Gilmour repeats the sucess of *Riots, Risings and Revolutions* with his *The Making of the Poets: Byron and Shelley* in their time (2002). He captures the spirit of the age in a style worthy of Hazlitt.

Martin Gilbert's Churchill

Review of Martin Gilbert, *Finest Hour: Winston S. Churchill,
1939–1941,* in the *Jewish Chronicle,* 22 July 1983

Churchill's finest hour? No doubt whatever. Britain's finest hour? A
good bid for sure, since the survival of freedom everywhere against the
assault from the most infamous tyranny ever devised by man hinged
upon Britain's resistance during those crucial months. Martin Gilbert's
finest hour, too? Let us see.

Reviewers of books should not allow their judgements to be influenced by reading the reviews of other reviewers. But I must at once
confess that I have grossly offended against the golden rule. After one
of my oldest friends, Tosco Fyvel, invited me to review this latest
volume for the *Jewish Chronicle*, other events intervened. I could not
resist the temptation to read some of those other verdicts which
happened to find their way under my nose and eyes.

Mostly they acclaim Martin Gilbert's achievement without qualification, and here surely is a wonderful story re-told with skill, scruple,

elaboration and indeed fresh knowledge. Who could ask for more? The short and shoddy answer is Mr John Vincent, fresh from his triumphs in expounding the modern Conservative cause in the Murdoch press, *The Times* or the *Sun*, and who also for some still inexplicable reason has been invited to parade his prejudices in the *Standard*, once a great newspaper with a most discriminating books page.

However, against the writer's intention perhaps, the Vincent review may serve a useful purpose. Having sought to damn the latest Gilbert volume as 'ponderous' and much else quite inappropriate, he seeks to intrude his own superior intelligence with the demand that many more interpretative judgements should have been offered.

Leave aside for a moment the obvious retort that Mr Gilbert's manner of selection – even in 1,248 pages – is a form of interpretation: turn instead to the question posed by Mr Vincent which casts a gleam of light over Conservatism past and present, both the brand with which Churchill (and the rest of us) had to contend in the 1930s, and which, alas, has re-emerged to take command today.

'Above all' – yes, exactly, *above all* – Mr Vincent asks, 'we need to know why we did not make peace in 1940 – and whether Churchill's assumptions in continuing the war were sensible.' And then, in extending that question, defined as supreme, Mr Vincent describes how the making of such a peace could have been considered excusable, feasible, honourable.

Not for years have I seen the old appeasement argument of the 1930s and 1940s so brazenly reopened, and the deed has an added interest when it is done by a Conservative historian putting Churchill in his place and right off his pedestal – the Churchill of 1940, mind you, and not the Churchill of earlier or later years whose feet of clay are more excusably exposed.

And, of course, there was an argument. 'Churchill was a leader imposed on the Tories by the nation,' writes Mr Vincent – quite true, and he might just have added: by the nation, on the Labour Party's initiative, in the critical House of Commons Norway debate, backed by a few others like Lloyd George and the for-ever-to-be-honoured handful of Tory rebels.

Then Mr Vincent describes how sullenly the bulk of the Tories in the Lords and Commons welcomes their new leader. Right again. But then he re-states the tell-tale question: how far were the Tory doubters right?

Yes, rub your eyes and read those words again. The Tory doubters of 1940; how can history, Mr Vincent's kind of history, be said to justify *them*? As Mr Gilbert explains, with ponderous but still startling accuracy, there were such Tory doubters not merely in the months of the phoney war, prior to Churchill's appointment as premier, but in the critical weeks and months thereafter, in the period of our greatest national peril ever.

The most prominent of the waverers was Lord Halifax, the Foreign Secretary still in Churchill's Cabinet, and whom indeed George VI and the bulk of the Tories in both Houses would have preferred instead of Churchill as Chamberlain's successor. Halifax wanted to use Mussolini as a mediator. He believed some kind of settlement with Hitler might be attainable. He could not see how the war could be fought and won. And the inescapable inference of Mr Vincent's question is that Halifax was right. A fresh essay in appeasement was truly the most 'sensible' course for Britain to seek to follow.

So why did this sensible policy get such little support? It was Churchill, in the nearest Mr Vincent strays towards a coherent explanation, 'looking at the war through the rose-coloured spectacles of genius'. who constructed his victory and our salvation on a splendid foundation of error.

And indeed this much *is* true. Churchill was a romantic, and it was that quality more than any other which served him and us so well in 1940. A much more astute observer than Mr Vincent saw and said as much: 'Being a great artist,' wrote Aneurin Bevan, 'Churchill was not a great man of action. He always thought he was, but this was another of his characteristic illusions. He could he be? A man of action must be a realist. He may dream and have visions, but for him two and two must necessarily make four, and the facts of life must be the stuff with which he works ... Churchill's contribution was to fling a Union Jack over five tanks and get people to behave as though they had become fifteen.'

But back to 1940, and what saved us. It is all there, in Mr Gilbert's compilation, if only Mr Vincent, instead of flaunting his own second-rate paradoxes, had been a little more interested to learn. Most of us who were round about at the time understood. Tens of millions of our people understood. Churchill understood. It was the great source of his strength in 1940, the real measure of that genius.

Churchill understood that by that time the British people were not going to give in to Hitler and Hitlerism, whatever happened. Any politician, himself included, who suggested yielding an inch would have been torn limb from limb.

Churchill knew as much and said as much, as Mr Gilbert faithfully records. He does not attempt to surmise what would have happened if Halifax's fresh lapse into his pre-war postures had been made public, but it is interesting to recall how pardonable was the suspicion about the old Chamberlainite appeasers, expressed in such volumes as *Guilty Men*, published just about the time when Halifax was recommending Mr Vincent's 'sensible' course to Mr Vincent's self-deluded Churchill.

Churchill made many errors in the conduct of the war, and he had many strokes of luck, and sometimes the misjudgements and the good fortune combined together to enable him – and the rest of us – to escape from some wretched predicament. The most notable example, also discussed although necessarily not exhausted in this volume, concerns his giant misapprehension about the capacity of the Russians to fight and survive. Churchill believed that the Soviet resistance would collapse, and yet, if it had collapsed, what would have been left of the Churchill strategy?

Churchill's would-be critics should concentrate on some of these issues; there is plentiful scope for investigation and reassessment, and most notably in this all-important field of Anglo–Soviet relationships. Some critics, notably Aneurin Bevan, conducted those scrutinies at the time, and it is fascinating to see how some awkward and risky exercises in wartime criticism are now vindicated.

But let the new breed of Chamberlainites and Halifaxites lay off 1940. That was the year of years, the hour of hours, the moment when the British people much more surely than their leaders (on Churchill's own testimony) decided to expiate all the crimes and follies of those who had fed the fascist monster. It was done magnificently and, more than ever before or after, Churchill's language fitted the time.

Nigel Nicolson

Review of Nigel Nicolson, *Long Life: memoirs,* in the
Evening Standard, 17 August 1997

Snobbery in all its grotesque English manifestations is one of the themes
tackled in these pages. Throughout most of the century, Nigel Nicolson
had a special ringside seat for studying the phenomenon, but let us hasten
to add that he has several other themes which he interweaves with
unfailing skill. His memoirs are among the very best covering the period.
His wit, his candour, his special insights offer a brew all its own. Read
every page with delight, but he will also guide you towards unexpected
discoveries, as in his mother's famous garden at Sissinghurst.

He was outraged when one quite prominent American critic sought to
devalue the work of both his father, Harold Nicolson, and his mother,
Vita Sackville-West, by branding them both as snobs. Whatever might
be their other failings, their writings were there to disprove the accusation. Nigel himself got into a quite different kind of trouble through
painting the portrait of that marriage never attempted before. He was

viciously accused of having betrayed both of them, but no one who reads these pages will accept that any single item on the charge sheet still stands.

He did know, by the way, what real snobbery was. Vita's mother, Lady Sackville, ran her estate at Knole in the manner in which she thought all estates in England should be conducted. When, on the outbreak of war in 1914, all her male staff were called up, she protested to Lord Kitchener, the Minister of War: 'I think you may not realise, my dear Lord K., that we employ five carpenters and four painters and two black-smiths and two footmen, and you are taking them all from us. I never thought I would see parlour maids at Knole ...'

Considering the kind of places where Harold and Vita were reared and where indeed they sought to bring up Nigel and his brother Ben, it is all the more amazing that any kind of liberal ideas about the relationship between men and women were allowed to penetrate. 'We were not easy children,' writes Nigel at one stage, but Harold and Vita could not be called easy parents either. No one could call them that, not even the ever compliant Nigel himself. His father's homosexuality and his mother's lesbianism combined to challenge all the other orthodoxies, and Nigel's composure in overcoming these discoveries is a wonder all on its own.

He describes, for example, the exact moment – he was eleven years old at the time – when he and Ben discovered that the formidable Virginia Woolf, who could sometimes treat their mother quite kindly despite other disturbing moments, was actually writing a book about her. 'Virginia was writing my mother's life. She took my brother and me to Knole, walked us through the galleries, interrogated us about the portraits and, taking our ignorance for granted, supplied her own make-believe answers on the spot. Some of the characters in *Orlando* were born that day but we did not know it, and the two fantasies, that Orlando aged twenty years in 350 and to change from man into woman half the way through, were hidden not only from us but from Vita too, until a finished copy, and the manuscript, arrived by post on publication day.'

Vita was 'dazzled, bewitched, enchanted', and quickly communicated her excitement to Virginia in person. Ben and Nigel were not so pleased when they discovered that Orlando had only one son in the book. 'There are two of us.' To which Virginia is alleged to have replied, like Humpty Dumpty might have done: 'In my books one person counts as two.' Nigel lived to describe *Orlando* as 'the longest and most charming love letter in literature'. Vita was no less excited at the time, and no wonder.

Virginia herself was sometimes accused of snobbery and, as Nigel reveals, she could make the charge herself in a manner most hurtful. 'What a damn snob he is,' she wrote of his father's best friend, Raymond Mortimer. 'Raymond I can't cotton to, though his virtues are as prominent as his nose.'

Such exchanges may seem too petty even to be recorded, but what Bloomsbury did achieve, and we are all the beneficiaries of it, was the overthrow of the whole monstrous edifice of Victorian sexual hypocrisy.

But again, I insist: don't miss a word. He weighs them in those same special scales where his mother and father used to weigh theirs.

Bob Boothby

Review of Robert Rhodes James, *Bob Boothby*, in the *Observer*,
14 July 1991

Sometimes the lesser lights, properly displayed, can illumine the
political scene better than the blazing assurance of their leaders when
presented by biographers – or autobiographers. Robert Rhodes James
can never have hit upon a subject so good as Bob Boothby, and Bob in
turn can thank his lucky stars, a constellation whose worth he has
already tested in his lifetime.

Bob had everything: good looks, high spirits, a beautiful voice, a first-
class brain, an athlete's frame which no punishment could injure. He
had an adoring mother and father who thought that nothing would be
beyond his capacity: he soon acquired the impregnable base of a
constituency which thought the same. He had courage and independence
to match his ambition: what could stop him?

Here, it might be gracelessly interpolated that a long-lasting love
affair with the wife of one of his future party leaders might have seemed

to provide one obstacle, but the short answer is that it didn't. The full, real story is told here for the first time and with proper sensitivity. Bob comes out of it well, and in any case a previous would-be Tory leader risked a much more questionable adultery in equally eminent circles, and finished up as Queen Victoria's favourite Prime Minister.

Bob entered politics in the 1920s when the Conservative Party seemed to offer advantageous opportunity for its young adventurers. He became associated with a number of them nicknamed the YMCA: Anthony Eden, Harold Macmillan, Duff Cooper, etc. Boothby was as good as any of them, and in most respects better.

Indeed, as this volume brilliantly illustrates, he had a special relationship with the two greatest political figures of the century. Boothby served the two masters, Lloyd George and Churchill: he honoured both, learnt his politics from both, found that their paths kept crossing his own. Most of us who knew Bob had heard him talk on this theme, and here is the proof, if any were needed, in his elaborate correspondence, of how well-founded was his claim of political intimacy with them, how he never lacked the courage to tell them what he taught and to learn in return.

As we knew, Boothby came to believe that Lloyd George was the greater of the two. As we also knew, another observer–participant, Aneurin Bevan, made the same judgement for the same reasons. This did not mean that either man disputed the crowning services to the nation which Churchill gave in 1940 especially. It did mean that they were not prepared to accept all the other qualities sometimes attributed to him: his supposed magnanimity to his enemies and his supposed loyalty to his friends. Both Bevan and Boothby knew better.

However, on a few memorable occasions – they happened also to be the most dangerous in our history, dangerous for the survival of the British state and the British people – all these leading political figures were on the same side, with Boothby putting the case as eloquently and persistently as any of them. But huge Conservative majorities voted them down, and they had to conspire and regroup and be voted down again.

Precisely because Boothby was in the thick of it, his biographer must recite the story of how the Conservative Party machine, in the Commons and the country, used every foul means to destroy opposition. If the machine had had its way, Boothby, Eden and Churchill would have been destroyed, and 1940 would have been not our finest hour but the year of infamy. Here you may read how that machine operated right up till the moment when Hitler's tanks crashed through the Ardennes, and how it even continued to operate afterwards. It was not quite power enough to challenge Churchill again, but was powerful enough to pursue poor Bob.

Some latter-day readers may suppose that these strictures are too severe, that they are coloured by a false sentiment about Boothby. Perhaps they would accept the verdict of what other YMCA product (the 'C' here stands for Conservative, not Christian), Anthony Eden. 'You have no idea' he said to one of his secretaries, 'how awful they were,' Here, thanks to the combined effort of Boothby and his biographer, the omission is repaired, and no one should ever be allowed to plead ignorance again.

Ironically, there was one other occasion when Boothby, the ever-popular and highly-esteemed Member for East Aberdeenshire, found himself fighting for his political life. He voted against Suez as he did against Munich, and they almost upset him. But 1956, with all its shame and squalor, was not 1938 or 1940. Those were the two terrible years, and Bob Boothby had the distinction of saying so at the time.

He said much else too. Of course, he was not always wise or right but he was almost always decent and brave, and he showed how the House of Commons could be used for these decent and brave purposes. To have such a life faithfully recorded makes a splendid contribution to our political literature.

When he failed to ask Boothby to join his Government in 1955, Eden is supposed to have said: 'We don't want Charles James Fox, do we?' He might have saved himself if he had. Few parliamentarians of modern times had a better claim to the proud Foxite label.

Beaverbrook's seductions

Review of Anne Chisholm and Michael Davie, *Beaverbrook: a life,*
in the *Evening Standard*, 1 October 1992

A comprehensive verdict on the subject of this biography is given in a
quotation on the dust cover. Since this particular comment was made by
one of the most eminent of Conservative Prime Ministers, I suppose we
must take it seriously. It was Harold Macmillan who said: 'He couldn't
resist seducing men in the same way he seduced women. And once a
man was seduced by him, he was finished.'

Just about the time when Macmillan recorded these words privately,
he was appointed as under-secretary to Beaverbrook at the Ministry of
Supply, and I happened to bump into him in the room in Beaverbrook's
country house where we were both waiting for an audience with the man
himself.

Macmillan knew I was a journalist working on Beaverbrook's
Evening Standard, and unloosed upon me a fulsome tribute to the part
which Beaverbrook had already played in helping to win the war and the

even nobler achievements which might come to him in the future. He obviously intended these casual remarks to be passed on in the right quarter.

Ever afterwards, I suspected that Macmillan was something of a phoney, and the impression was not removed by his handling of such events as Suez, Profumo and a few other scandals and follies. His taste for grandiloquence always jarred, even when it took him to Number 10: most of us in the Labour Party thought the Tories had made a fatuous choice, both from their point of view and ours, in preferring him to R. A. Butler. And his judgement on Beaverbrook today is no more to be trusted than the sycophantic tones which he contrived to advance his own interests in 1942.

Anyhow, Beaverbrook himself loved argument but hated sycophancy. However, let us take the Macmillan tests head on. One of the good reasons for a new book on Beaverbrook today, as the new authors have appreciated, is that his dealing with women can be covered more frankly and extensively than previous biographers have had the chance, or inclination, to do. And the subject is utterly absorbing. Women played an all-important part in his life. Those who knew him best knew that, and some of the most extraordinary revelations have only become available, by accident almost, in the past few years. Beaverbrook loved several lovely women, and several lovely women loved him. (It wasn't only, or even often – I would guess – a matter of seduction, according to the crude Macmillan indictment.) One of these – one of the most dazzling women of the century, for both brain and beauty – was Rebecca West. She did not tell the story while he was alive or she was alive, but it has appeared now in her posthumous novel, *Sunflower*, published in 1989.

Rebecca wrote to a woman friend in 1922: 'I found him one of the most fascinating talkers I've ever met, and full of the real vitality – the genius that exists mystically apart from all physical conditions, just as it does in HG.' HG, of course, was H. G. Wells, no mean performer as

Rebecca herself testifies in this same magical sentence. Several other women were captivated – by the Rebecca West, not the Macmillan method. Once the *Sunflower* revelations became available, no excuse was left for reprinting all the old libels. And similar deductions may be made in the case of the other alleged seductions. Beaverbrook, the journalist, may not always have been able to exercise the same arts at Beaverbrook, the lover, but he was as much absorbed in his journalism as he was in his affairs.

He happened to have the good fortune to be both the proprietor and editor of his newspapers; but he was a newspaperman in every fibre, obsessed by the news, how to get it, how to print it, and how to argue about it. Most of the journalists he seduced became much better journalists in the process. And some of the best of these came from *Tribune*, or returned there soon after their healthy period of Beaverbrook tuition.

Our new biographers devote a whole chapter to this theme but somehow fail to tell a part of it in which the *Evening Standard* figured most prominently and disgracefully. So now the suppression can be repaired. On 2 March 1950 the front page of the *Evening Standard* ran as follows:

Fuchs and Strachey. A Great New Crisis
War Minister has never disavowed Communism
Now involved in MI5 efficiency probe

The whole contrivance was of course a most scandalous one. Strachey was no spy, and *Tribune* hit back in his defence more furiously than anyone else. When I'd written the article, someone in the office suggested the title: 'Prostitutes of the Press'. I thought that too banal, or too defamatory, and suggested instead the no less insulting: 'Lower than Kemsley' – Lord Kemsley being at that time the proprietor of the *Daily Sketch* and the *Sunday Times*, and held to be, in our estimation, the criterion of low Tory journalism.

Since the authors of this new biography explore in some detail my own relations with Beaverbrook, it is strange that they show no interest in this story which, I would have thought, reflects considerable credit on Beaverbrook, and *Tribune*, and the kind of journalism he taught us.

Whatever else he was or was not, he was a great journalist. Upstarts like Lloyd George and Churchill understood, even if the point escaped such fine old fake aristocrats as Harold Macmillan.

My Egyptian hero

Review of Keith Kyle, *Suez*, in the *Observer*, 14 July 1991

Suez is not some mere canal; it signifies a political event of world-wide consequence, the most humiliating defeat suffered by our country in modern times. The single word stands out here on a brilliantly designed dustcover, and offers a fitting introduction to 620 packed pages, almost every one of which cries aloud for quotation or comment.

That same sharp word recalls for me also the occasion in 1986 when I attended in Cairo a seminar on the 1956 affair. At the end of the proceedings the Egyptian organisers took us to Ismailia to see the canal for ourselves, and to meet in particular Mohamed Ezzat Adel, chairman of the Suez Canal Authority, the Egyptian director of the business who was ensuring that the canal was being run more successfully than ever before.

He was one of the most impressive lovers of his own job I have met, professional, confident, knowledgeable on all nautical matters, but also a dedicated Egyptian patriot who had been posted there by President Nasser, and shared the general Egyptian respect for him. A constant claim of the British Cabinet in 1956 – the voice of Lord Hailsham, visibly making his appearance as our First Lord of the Admiralty, was the most raucous of the lot – was that Egyptians could not be expected to run canals.

Hailsham survived his Suez participation: he lived to bluster another day. But some others were broken, most spectacularly and legitimately Sir Anthony Eden. Keith Kyle, who now assesses the evidence more microscopically than ever before, reminds us from what a height Sir Anthony fell.

Not merely had he been given a longer training in the rare business of managing great diplomatic crises than any other British Prime Minister of the century. He had also displayed, in the very months before he took over the top job from Churchill, an aptitude for one of the most essential aspects of the task: how to deal with our dear American allies. Since we, the resilient British, knew more about the real world than the brusque Americans, it was desirable that we should be able to secure their backing and esteem while exercising our independent judgement.

How could such a man with such genuine achievements to his credit contrive such an almighty catastrophe as Suez? Some close observers attributed everything to the flaws in Sir Anthony's own character: the vanity, the restlessness, the absence of what Churchill had: an innermost conviction of his own long-term wisdom, his sense of proportion. Churchill would hardly have mistaken Nasser for Hitler.

All the leading British performers in the tragedy strut on to the stage: Harold Macmillan plays an Iago – or perhaps Edmund the Bastard was, more suitably, his model. And as the terrible events and the aftermath unfolded, the worst aspect of the affair was the way all the main partici-pants lied to save their political skins. The collusion with Israel was not the only or even the most monstrous deception. As Foster Dulles infuri-ated Eden and Co. with his moralising, they tried to pretend that he had started it, against British advice, by withdrawing the money for the Aswan Dam. That too was a lie, although only one among legion.

Which brings us to the other protagonist, Gamal Abdul Nasser who, according to Eden, was the major cause of all the troubles and whose physical removal was contemplated by our law-loving Christian rulers. Keith Kyle makes no attempt to remove the warts from the portrait, nor does he disguise how widespread was the belief that Nasser was another Mussolini, if not Hitler. If they had been looking for a real historical parallel they might have found a much more likely one in Arabi, the leader of Egyptian nationalism in the 1880s – but that would have involved reading the kind of history not taught in British public schools.

But we should have known better. Nasser was no saint; but nor was he some fascist ideologue or any kind of fascist. He believed that Israel's expansion must be resisted, but he himself had not excluded the possibility of an eventual settlement with Israel, and if the Aswan Dam had been built with eastern backing, as it so nearly was, his retaliation over the canal might have been postponed or the whole operation could have been conducted by other means.

Nasser hated the great empires – the old English one, the new American one, and the rising Soviet one. He refused to submit to any of them, although he felt compelled to deal with them all.

As for the canal itself, the revered Arabi had described those patriotic Egyptian aims in the 1880s and set out the simple proposition which Eden, Hailsham and Co. so signally failed to grasp nearly a century later: 'The Suez Canal cannot be better protected for England, as for the rest of the world, than by the admission of the Egyptian people into the comity of nations.'

The writer of those words was Arabi's chief English friend, Wilfrid Scawen Blunt, the most dedicated or at least the most flamboyant anti-imperialist of his day. He could see the truth, nearly a hundred years before, and I am glad to say that his portrait now hangs in the British Embassy in Cairo, where once Eden and Nasser shook hands, and where the whole senseless, bloody tragedy was so nearly avoided. The failure was not all on one side, but Nasser at least understood his world better than Eden.

Willy Brandt

Tribune, 16 October 1992

Willy Brandt was a real international socialist; he understood in every fibre of his being – his mind, his heart, his spirit – what the words meant and how the cause should be served.

In the achievement of most of the good things which have happened in the post-1945 Europe, he played the leading part, and most of the worst things happened when his advice was spurned or derided.

More than any other single man, but with the assistance of his fellow Social Democrats, as he would have been the first to testify, he saved Berlin from the shameful Soviet siege of the city after 1945. But he would not have been able to play his part there if it had not been for his heroic opposition to the attempted Nazi conquest of Europe during the war itself.

When the Berlin Wall was finally knocked down, he more than any other citizen of our Europe had the right to lead the rejoicing.

Indeed his life exemplified the two sides of the kind of policy which post-1945 Europe most sorely needed but did not always get – resistance to tyranny in every shape and guise combined with a constructive policy to escape from the diplomatic deadlock which threatened to push the world into nuclear catastrophe.

His *Ostpolitik* paved the way for everything which others were to achieve later.

These were achievements on a world-wide scale and socialists everywhere can take pride in the fact that Willy Brandt brought such fresh honour to the name. But he also played the main part in guiding the Socialist International to undertake a more ambitious world-wide role.

He used the resources of existing parties to help the parties which still lived under dictatorships in the old world or the new, in Franco's Spain and Salazar's Portugal or across the Atlantic in Latin America.

He always wanted to see the Socialist International throw its resources and intelligence to these new tasks.

It was an ironic tragedy that the new united Germany which he and his party had done so much to establish turned its back – momentarily at least – on the collective socialist action which was so sorely needed.

Some of these recent events in Eastern Europe, and in particular the rise of the old terrors which he had resisted so valiantly in his youth, might have broken his heart. But that wonderful organ was not constituted that way.

He always looked for new ways in which the democratic socialist cause could be served. He knew better than any other European leader of his generation what a rich and wonderful tradition that was.

I am sure he did that to the end.

Noel Malcolm

Review of Noel Malcolm, *Kosovo: a short history,* in the *Guardian,*
19 April 1998

A book to stop a massacre! It is impossible even to read a few pages here
without attention being distracted by the latest news from the place itself
and its next-door neighbour. Will the masterminds in Belgrade be able
to apply their final solution? Noel Malcolm applies his own well-
stocked mind to these latest questions, and we must return to them. But
readers may be advised that once they start reading, they won't be able
to stop. What we are offered here is not some hastily contrived pamphlet
dealing with the topic of the moment – not that those productions should
be condemned – but an inspired application of the historian's art. It is as
if some new Edward Gibbon had appeared to instruct us in these matters
and to restore a sense of human decency amid the crimes and horrors of
our century.

Kosovo is a place with a thousand years of history of its own, which
is what Malcolm recites for us. However, it is not like his *Bosnia* which

he wrote about previously and which had had for so long a separate political existence, the additional fact which made the Serbian aggression against it so scandalous and the Western world's toleration of the attack so inexcusable. The offence against Kosovo is of a different character, but no less horrific – much more like what imperialist masters have sought traditionally to impose on their neighbours – what the British did in Ireland, say, or what the Stadt-upholders did in South Africa, or what some new breed of tyrant is now attempting in Burma or Algeria. Our civilised century, with two great victories for freedom, should have been the one when all master-race doctrines were banished for ever. Alas, it is taking a little longer than we thought. As far as can be seen from all the available evidence – our up-to-date historian gives it all – the people of Kosovo want to run their own affairs, like their neighbours in Macedonia, Croatia, Bosnia, Slovenia, or indeed their neighbours in the north, the Serbs. But there the objection arises. Whatever else develops in the Balkans, the decree comes from Belgrade – the Serbs must keep Kosovo. Whenever there is trouble there, the rulers in Belgrade send in their strong man. Some of the most prominent war criminals still wanted for their genocidal crimes in the later war learnt their trade in Kosovo ten years ago. That was one moment when the developing horror could have been stopped. Most of Europe turned a blind eye then, which should increase our awareness now.

Kosovo is not only a place where people live now, but a sacred name in Serbian history, the place where Serbian valour, despite its defeat, saved the day for civilisation against the monstrous Muslim power, the Ottoman Empire which sought to engulf Europe itself. The actual date of the battle was supposed to be 15 June 1389, but even that is uncertain. For sure, it was fought on Kosovar soil, but that's about all. Noel Malcolm's chapter on 'The Battle and The Myth' is a treasure all on its own, a wondrous exposition of how the historians themselves may become not merely the most powerful exponents of a myth but the actual creators of it.

For us socialists, if I may be permitted such a clumsy intrusion, one of the mysteries is how, in modern Belgrade, the Serbian monarchy seems to have gathered such prestige to itself, starting with its personal exploits at Kosovo, but offering the cloak, too, for all later nationalist expeditions. What actually seems to have happened in 1389 is that one Serbian king fought and lost his life in single combat with the Turkish commander, whereas the brother who succeeded him soon preferred to make deals with the conqueror. As with other monarchies, having it both ways was the road to survival. The Serb kings were still at it in 1941 when Hitler presented his ultimatum to Serbia and the Serbian monarch sought to emulate the role of the 1389 traitor, Vuk Brankovic.

Such indeed were the crimes committed by the Serbian monarchy against their people that it used to be one of the proudest boasts of the Yugoslav Communist Party that they played a leading role in their overthrow. Now they discover that the royal standard has its uses.

The other leading expert on the subject is Slobodan Milosevic who, despite all the disasters he has brought upon his own people, still retains a final control over the political levers in Belgrade. He made his fame and name over Kosovo, being the first to concoct the fatal potion: a rabid Serbian nationalism combined with a rampant Marxist militarism. 'Every nation had a place in which it eternally warms its heart,' he once told a cheering audience years ago. 'For Serbia, it is Kosovo.' He thought then that he had the military power to do anything he wanted in that part of the world, starting with Kosovo, but then turning elsewhere. Tragically, most of the rest of the world believed him and made their shameful dispositions to be on the victor's side.

Leaders of the people in Kosovo made a different, much braver decision, but still one which is unresolved in its consequences. They renewed their demand for an independent republic, but emphasised that they did not wish to secure it by an armed rising which might be so easily crushed by that same military power. Tender questions arise now about how much reliance should be placed on the chastened leader in

Belgrade or the resolution of the so-called international community, which did, most belatedly, check the earlier Serbian aggression.

Noel Malcolm's history is short enough to be read by Foreign Secretaries but explicit enough to stop a repetition of the surrender to force which still leaves its evil consequences in his beloved Bosnia.

A special Hyde Park victory

Review of David Cannadine, *The Decline and Fall of the British Aristocracy,* in the *Guardian*, 18 October 1990

The best political song I was ever taught to sing was not the 'The Red Flag' or 'Jerusalem' or 'England Arise' or the *Internationale* but the old radical land song which first became popular in Edwardian times:

Why should we be beggars with the ballot in our hand?
God gave the land to the People.

All those other anthems had their own special delights, but none could surpass the democratic resonance of the one which stressed at the same time, in the same rhythmic breath, the identity of the real enemy and the means for his overthrow. I am fascinated to learn from the 790 pages of David Cannadine's survey that that rousing chorus is based on an unshakable historical foundation. The unknown author who wrote the words and the well-known public figures who made them so topical and effective had discerned exactly, amid all other distractions, the presiding political reality of these past hundred years.

In the 1880s, when Cannadine sets his scene, the gods seemed still to be ordering matters quite differently: no sign whatever appeared of a popular dispensation. All the best land in England, and even more so in neighbouring Ireland, Wales and Soctland, was owned by a tiny group of top people, who had inherited it. No record of these land holdings had been kept since the Domesday Book. Indeed, the unique feature of the British land system, ancient and modern, was that no intrusive eye was allowed to investigate.

What the figures, published first in the 1870s in a book called *The Acreocracy Of England*, disclosed was that nearly three-quarters of the British Isles was owned by fewer than 5,000 people, that one quarter of the land of England and Wales was owned by 710 individuals, and that twelve men between them possessed more than four million acres. Moreover, comparisons with other countries showed that land ownership was much more concentrated here than anywhere else.

Never before had so much economic power and political prestige and exclusive access to high living been assembled in such few hands. The British aristocracy was, according to its own tests and estimation, the most successful of all time. It had gathered to its bosom the material means to guarantee survival; it had devised political institutions to suit its long-term purposes, a House of Lords and a House of Commons stuffed with its own nominees; it had steered clear of all such follies and fatalities as French Revolutions or American Mammon-worshipping; it knew what the menace of democracy was and how to strangle the infant in the cradle.

Then suddenly, in a matter of a few decades, the whole mighty contraption of pomp and authority was dissipated, scattered, smashed. All three verbs are needed to describe the process, since what Cannadine offers is a vast parade of how each new development brought its series of unforeseen consequences. He knows how real history should be written: the mixture of dashing judgements and riveting detail.

Some of the greatest leaders of the aristocrats helped to bring the calamity on themselves; it is instructive to recall that Lord Salisbury, often hailed, and not only by Tory historians, as the foremost Conservative statesman of the century, was there in charge with a full majority in both Houses when some of the most fatal errors of judgement were made. The trouble was that he hated democracy so much he could never come to terms with it, much less teach his followers the necessary lessons. He would have done better to advise them to heed Oscar Wilde, who gave his political warning at the critical moment: 'What between the duties expected of one during one's lifetime, and the duties exacted from one after one's death, land has ceased to be either a profit or pleasure. It gives one a position and prevents one from keeping it up. That's all that can be said about land.'

Just a few years earlier the open assault on landlordism had been unleashed, and Cannadine allots proper credit among three leaders who introduced a new temper into the debate. Michael Davitt founded his Land League to tackle the problem in Ireland, where the oppression was most severe but he himself carried the campaign to Scotland, Wales, and Salisbury's England, too. One of his pupils was Joseph Chamberlain, who learnt how to deal with landlords in proper biblical terms: 'They toil not, neither do they spin.'

But it was Lloyd George, the third of the triumvirate, who took up the cry with the most relish and effect. 'Oh these dukes, how they oppress us ... How could 500 ordinary men, chosen accidentally from the unemployed, overrule the judgement of millions, those who make the country's wealth?' The aristocracy was like cheese: 'The older it is, the higher it becomes.' Sometimes ridicule can be the most powerful of political weapons. Cannadine notes justly: 'After Limehouse, the House of Lords was never quite the same again.'

The full story he has to tell is the unmaking of the British upper classes, and it is much more wonderfully intricate than these few paragraphs can suggest. The phrase is consciously adopted from Edward

Thompson's classic *The Making Of The English Working Class,* and the two books can decently be mentioned together.

Scene after scene here is imprinted indelibly on the reader's mind; for example, the decisive moment, in the 1880s, not always appreciated, when the most important of all Reform Bills opened the floodgates to democracy by giving the vote to men who actually worked on the land and not Lloyd George's lordly unemployed; when the Lords, advised by the all-wise Salisbury, still sought to resist; and when the outbreak of popular protest was the strongest since 'the days of May' in 1832. The great Hyde Park meeting of 26 July 1884 tipped the balance at last. Before that date, to sing the song of the ballot would have been a mockery; thereafter, it was the direct summons to action.

Part 7

The poetry of places

Venice

My only Venice

Art Quarterly, Volume 1 (New Series), Number 1, 1988

All true lovers of Venice come to imagine that she reveals her last, secret charms only to them, and there is indeed a foundation of fact for the way she will forever capture her victims with this flattering illusion. Venice offers such a vast and variegated parade of every different form of art and culture and historical achievement and reflection that the individual observer can make his own selection and imagine that no one else has seen it just that way before. Then he stumbles on, say, a sentence from some fifteenth-century diarist or gets a glimpse of an old master from a new angle which seems to anticipate his own brilliant discovery. Then he may be reassured again: no one should be misled by the three-quarter truth that everything worth writing on the subject has been written already. As in the city itself, it is the forgotten corners which captivate most, the gleams and glimpses which can suddenly appear without a second's notice.

All that Venice asks in return is that those she seeks to seduce should not merely yield or submit; they must swoon. They must pitch their response on that proper note of ecstasy which alone suits the style of Venice through the ages. A true son of Venice had the root, or rather the thousand-year-old pile, of the matter in him when, quite recently, he called his book: *Venice, A Thousand Years of Culture and Civilisation*. No other city could say the same with the same assurance, and yet the whole edifice seems still to tremble in the soft Venetian breeze.

The whole intricate affair contrived by Peter Lauritzen in this volume resembles one of those curved and twisted chandeliers from Murano which could be dismantled piece by piece and dispatched safely, for the proper price, anywhere in the eighteenth-century world. Architecture and painting seem at first best suited to his methods but he is skilful too in noting how one art slides into another. Once he is in his stride, Venetian musicians take their proper place alongside the Palladios and the Tintorettos and not merely the Monteverdis and Vivaldis who have long since staged their own revivals, but a select host of others such as Baldassare Galuppi from Burano which, I am glad to say, is not here allowed to be overshadowed by the other 117 islands – the official figure – of the lagoons. Given half a chance, I will entice you on a special excursion to an unspoiled and unspoilable twentieth-century paradise in the company of another expert who loves Venice with a true Lauritzenian fervour.

However, we must not be distracted from the music, and the instruction here which Peter Lauritzen himself offers better than anyone else. I am happy to learn that, from the year 1527 to be exact, with the appointment of Adrian Willaert as *maestro di capella* at San Marco, Venice became the seat of Western music. Now 1527 is a date famous for something else: the sack of Rome following misdemeanours by the papacy, and Peter Lauritzen properly regards these event as a judgement on 'the infamous league' against Venice contrived by Pope Julius II and his hangers-on and expertly thwarted by Venetian diplomacy. And what a moment in the history of culture and civilisation it was when Rome believed that it could excommunicate Venice! Giogione had died a few years before, but Titian was at his peak. Exiles from all over Italy crowded to find shelter from the storm in the secular cloisters of San Marco.

Pietro Aretino came in search of books; no bad notion since one quarter of the books printed in the civilised world were printed in Venice. Danese Catteneo came to study the Gothic tradition of stone-cutting in the place that knew it best. Jacopo Sansovino came to learn architecture from the Lombardos and the Rizzis. The Greeks bought land for their own church, and the Jews for theirs, for their building which stood near the site of the old bronze foundries, and so the Venetian word for casting gave its name to their quarter, *il ghetto*: not at all, be it noted, in tolerant Venice a word of ill repute or fear. Titian, by the way, was called in a year or two later to turn his hand to diplomacy, and flatter the Emperor Charles V; and neither the Medicis of Florence nor the Popes of Rome could quite hold their own in such company. Once more, the intellect of Italy crowded into Venice; one among them Galileo Galilei, Professor of Mathematics at Padua, formerly from Florence and later to face the Inquisition in Rome, who in Venice, however, was escorted by the Signoria up their Campanile to see his telescope demonstrated.

In the end, the maiden city which had so bravely resisted Emperors and Princes, Turks and Spaniards, pirates and popes, was raped by Napoleon. Many observant, modern visitors (meaning myself) may have been tempted to view Napoleon's conquest with an acquiescent eye, since he did build the Ala Navoleonica at the western end of the Piazza and thereby complete the best drawing room in Europe, and he did improve the vantage point for seeing the Guidecca and he did open the ghettos, old and new. But he destroyed more than forty churches and more than eighty palaces (if Mr Lauritzen's figures are correct).

It is a deadly indictment. This was the end. But it wasn't. What riches there were still to come: Byron's Venice, Hazlitt's Venice, Stendhal's

Venice, Heine's Venice, Rossini's Venice, Turner's Venice, Ruskin's Venice, George Sands's Venice, Browning's Venice, Proust's Venice, Verdi's Venice, Wagner's Venice, Stravinsky's Venice and how many more: Shirley Guiton's Venice, for she can take us on that excursion to paradise which I had promised you.

Allegedly, it was round about the year 1800 when the matchless beauty of Venice started to fade. But the claim is hard to believe since the glories of the present are still overpowering; and anyhow what was good enough for Byron should be good enough for everyone else. He puts his stamp on that impressionable Venetian stone more indelibly than any other post-Napoleonic conqueror.

Yet even he did not see everything. If you can still imagine a modern earthly paradise to be possible, get up early in the morning, unlike Byron, make sure that the soft but sharp spring sunshine is there for the rest of the day, and wander by whatever route you choose to the 400-year-old Fondamenta Nuova to catch the No. 12 vaporetto. Don't be sidetracked by the San Michele cemetery where Stravinsky was buried flamboyantly a few years ago, or to glass-blowing *Murano*, or to momentarily more fashionable Torcello where there were once, before Venice was ever heard of, 100 churches and where now the sense of doom and decay is too suffocating to be endured.

The paradise I speak of is only just around the corner. It has glittered in the sun with its present incomparable brightness for roughly the past two decades and, come hell or high water, and especially the last which unavailingly did its worst in the Venetian floods of 1966, is likely to retain its individual glory until the end of the century and beyond.

But first let us make good the claim to modernity for our wondrous Burano. No doubt the foundations were laid by Venetian-style island-makers of 1,000 or more years ago; no doubt the founders were fishermen–sailors like everyone else who scoured the lagoon for refuge and livelihood. But somehow, while aristocratic Venice scaled the heights, proletarian Burano stayed stuck in the mud and sand. Apart from a few waylaid saints clasped to her bosom and stolen for the purpose in the best San Marco manner, Burano had to be content with her own single crooked campanile and a society based, literally century after century, on the same hard, bare, unyielding struggle for existence which the first benighted Buranelli must have encountered.

Then suddenly in the early 1960s or thereabouts, out of the bright blue Burano sky a meteor seemed to fall and to transform the island into the beatific, man-made vision which it is today. The post-war prosperity of Italy and the western world was gleefully seized by the intelligent workers of Burano and transmuted into a genuine boon of loveliness and beneficence.

They grasped the moment to clean, paint, own and elevate their beloved township in one single motion. They did it all themselves, even though they seemed to act more by instinct than design. The good taste, like the communal spirit, was something deep inside them, but how it burst into such activity and achievement is truly one of the wonders of our modern world. The story might never have been told; it would surely have passed into oblivion if ever Venice is finally swamped and destroyed, as the modern prophets perhaps too tragically prophesy, by the looters of the lagoon.

But fortunately, whatever happens, the records of this magic era in the history of Burano will never be allowed to be suppressed altogether. They were preserved for the benefit of the world in general and the special breed of Venice lovers in particular by the aforementioned Shirley Guiton in a little Venetian classic called *A World by Itself.* Thanks to her, many wise thousands will hasten to embark on that No. 12 vaporetto and see how little Burano made a world by itself to catch and hold the eye for ever and ever and to achieve several other miracles besides, even in the shadow of Venice herself. Venice, as we have insisted, demands from her lovers absolute, hyperbolic submission. Clearly Shirley Guiton's work passes the test. She even qualifies for entry into an even more exclusive company.

A very few of the visitors to, and writers about, and painters of Venice have given back to the city some of the reflected glory which they have taken away in such superabundant armfuls, and two Englishmen, I chauvinistically assert, take the first two places in this most glamorous of competitions. Forget about the Goethes and Wagners and the Alfred de Mussets and the Thomas Manns and the rest. The two men who folded wilting Venice to their bosoms and then transformed her by their art into something lovelier still are two tourist-cum-exiles from England: Turner himself and the man who taught Turner more than anyone else about the city, Byron.

The cry came from one of his characters who had played his part in earlier times, but Byron changed the way the whole world would imagine his adopted city, the place where his liberal spirit was reborn.

My beautiful, my own
My only Venice, – this is breath!
Thine Adrian sea-breeze, how it fans my face
The very winds feel native to my veins
And cool them into calmness.

Bathing in glory

Review of Tony Tanner, *Venice Desired*, in the *Evening Standard*, 2 April 1992

One of the charms of Venice is that she seems to stir poets, painters, philosophers, printers, and anyone else qualifying for the proud title of artist, to heights of achievement which they can never touch elsewhere. Indeed, Peter Lauritzen, the most perceptive modern lover of the maiden city, claims she has been performing this role with careless, seductive ease for a thousand years.

However, the Philistine English – or perhaps we might better call them in this setting the Visigoth, misogynist British – have been following this Venetian fashion only for the past couple of centuries. It was Lord Byron who put Venice in her proper context for us. And it is good to see that Tony Tanner, in a dazzling essay in literary criticism which proves to be the most original of his writings, gives the place of honour to Byron.

At first hearing, such a plea may be dismissed as a piece of Byronic special pleading. But not at all: nineteenth century England freely acknowledged that its view of the city had been Ruskinised. But even before then Ruskin applied his peculiar talents to the task, the place, in English eyes, had been Turnerised, and even before Ruskin had sought to educate the ignorant English about their greatest painter – 'His imagination is Shakespearean in its mightiness' – he eagerly acknowledged their common debt to Byron. 'My Venice, like Turner's, had been chiefly created for us by Byron,' insists Ruskin in one of Tanner's epigraphs. Quite a creation indeed.

Ruskin made discoveries about the place which we take for granted, but which still offer a delightful instruction. He noted that it was the only important city in the world where the cathedral was not the principal feature. 'The Ducal Palace is the Parthenon of Venice, and Gradenigo is its Pericles.'

It was, alleged Ruskin, with breathtaking falsity, 'the great and sudden invention of one man'. But Ruskin does indeed make the palace more magnificent than ever. And neighbouring St Mark's, less she takes offence, was given a consolation prize: 'Never had a city a more glorious Bible.' Ruskin, on his hands and knees, told us how to read every individual verse.

He supposed that he was describing Venice in its full historical perspective. He was rather, as Tanner defines it, 'inventing a personal myth of his own, of quite extraordinary power and utterly incalculable influence.'

Ruskin said elsewhere that 'a nation's art is its only reliable biography.' History, biography, art of every form were moulded together to make the whole 'radiant mystery' of Ruskin's style.

He was sometimes thought to be lacking in potency in other fields, but no one could make that charge against his prose. He could at will give it a quickening self-excitation which, in Tanner's phrase, is 'little short of orgasmic'. Who else can write about the painters as he can? 'Perhaps when you see one of Titian's splendidly passionate subjects and find Veronese making the Marriage of Cana one blaze of worldly pomp, you might imagine that Titian must have been a sensualist, and Veronese an unbeliever.'

Your salacious suspicions can be transformed into sensual virtues, and you may find yourself exulting in the same kind of conversion as Ruskin himself experienced when he set eyes on Veronese's *Presentation of the Queen of Sheba*.

Hampstead for all

Hampstead and Highgate Express, 31 December 1999

'Who is the sorrel nag?' I heard a familiar voice, half knowing, half curious, cry out across the Heath. Perhaps there was a touch of mockery too, and that should have put me on my guard. It was the voice of John Hillaby, who knows every twist and turn of Hampstead Heath and, best of all, as the greatest of all Heath-lovers, Leigh Hunt, put it:

And that clear path through all, where daily meet
Cool cheeks and brilliant eyes, and morn-elastic feet.

He is also, let me remind you – Hillaby, not Hunt – the most formidable collector of miscellaneous, useless knowledge. Each adjective is intended as a compliment. He was now parading his comprehension of *Gulliver's Travels*, a theme on which I counted myself the expert, at least in our part of the Heath near South End Green, if not across the whole 800-odd acres of holy ground.

Who was the sorrel nag? I palmed him off on our next exchange with a reference to the dictionary. Jonathan Swift himself used the term to describe 'a bright chestnut coloured horse' even before he had ever journeyed to the land of the Houyhnhyms. 'A sorrel gelding of a monstrous size' makes its appearance years before.

However, the point can be dodged no longer. The question of the sorrel nag may be properly regarded as the most crucial and captivating of all Swiftian mysteries. In the bleak and suffocating utopia described in the fourth book of *Gulliver's Travels*, it is 'the sorrel nag (who always loved me)' who at last helps organise his departure and cries out from the shore: 'Take care of thyself, gentle Yahoo' – a note of humanity quite unlike the accent usually attributed to Swift. It was Stella or Vanessa or maybe a composite of the two.

Hampstead Heath, as I will soon be eager to illustrate, has been the scene of encounters even more memorable than this one, with men, women and animals all playing their allotted parts. But first I must acknowledge the excuse for all these revelries: the millennium, the determination of the citizens of Hampstead to celebrate properly the indisputable fact that in the year 986 the manor of Hampstead was granted by King Ethelred to the monks of Westminster.

Did I read aright in the brochure the name King Ethelred? Yes indeed, and every schoolchild, I'm sure, would shout as I did: Ethelred the Unready! I looked him up in the *Dictionary of National Biography* and, since he sat on the English throne for nearly fifty years, he is entitled to his twelve columns. But he is still, in the first sentence, Ethelred the Unready, and even Thomas J. Barratt, author of *The Annals of Hampstead* and one of the most kindly and considerate of men, cannot suppress the title altogether. 'A nickname', wrote Hazlitt, 'is the hardest stone to be thrown at a man.' I once heard Seymour Cocks, a brilliant Labour wit of the 1930s, refer to Sir John Simon as the worst Foreign Secretary since Ethelred the Unready. Everyone thought the insult most apt; no one stopped to consider the ill-usage of poor Ethelred.

Anyhow, one of the beneficent acts hitherto not properly recognised in that long reign was not merely the assignment of the manor of Hampstead into what he hoped were safe and pious hands, but an attempted definition of boundaries much more skilfully executed than anything seen in recent local government legislation. Not for Ethelred the crude butchery of a Patrick Jenkin or a Conservative manifesto.

Most of the guide books tell us how the limits of the grant were set 'from the Hanger West to Watling Street to the Cucking pool'. The cucking pool by the way, I learn from the all-observant Thomas Barratt, received its name from the old-time custom of *ducking* scolding women in a pond as a punishment for transgressing against the peace of their households; and some of these cuckings and duckings – I hope my NGA comrades in the printing shop are exercising their usual immaculate care for the *Ham and High*'s reputation – were still in operation when Dr Johnson became for a while a resident among us, when he wrote *The Vanity of Human Wishes* and a few other cheerless pieces. Whatever claims are made, Dr Johnson was never a true Hampstead type. But this is to jump ahead too far. Much more potent in the history of Hampstead than the disciplinary effects of any cucking pool was the small bottle containing four tears from the Blessed Virgin brought from Tours and scattered on these same manor grounds to create the chalybeate spring of later times.

Moreover, perhaps the real royal hero to whom we owe the proverbial happiness of Hampstead is not Ethelred but his much less controversial successor, Edward the Confessor. The eighty-odd-year interval between Ethelred's grant and Edward's death imposed, the good Mr Barratt assures us, 'no harassing strain upon the hundred or so inhabitants of Hampstead', and when Edward was magnificently entombed in Westminster Abbey, 'in the little chapel at Hampstead many candles would be burnt and many prayers said for the repose of his soul.'

And at this date, I would hope, we should all do the same for Ethelred, especially the organisers of the millennium, who should not take his name in vain.

However, let us ensure above all else in this millennial year that proper tribute is paid to the historians. Poets, painters, publicans, publicists, even politicians have all contributed to the glory of Hampstead, and each will receive a passing salute, but the historians of Hampstead are a breed all their own, from James Park to Ian Norrie.

Every favourite corner or grotto on Hampstead Heath offers a dozen different entrances and exits; and the Hampstead historians offer a similar criss-cross of pathways, leading inconsequentially to a multitude of new names and discoveries. John James Park was the first, and he learned his trade 'by desultory reading' in his father's library in Church Row. He produced, in 1814, before he was twenty years old, the first edition of his *Topography and Natural History of Hampstead*. Let us commend, for a start, his epigraph from Lord Bacon's *Advancement of Learning*: 'Out of monuments, names, wordes, proverbs, traditions, private records, and evidences, fragments of stories, passages of bookes, and the like, we do save and recover somewhat from the deluge of time.'

Francis Bacon did not pitch his claims for the historical art quite as high as some modern practitioners; he knew, like the greatest of the moderns, A. J. P. Taylor, how haphazard and unedifying but nonetheless enjoyable the whole pastime might be. Like Alan, he must have learned some of his wisdom walking across the Heath.

He died, as it happens, in nearby Highgate, having conducted – for he was also a scientist – an abortive experiment in the cooking of chickens. He should have stuck to writing essays. Hampstead has an even more extraordinary hold on Bacon's fame. Among the treasures beautifully preserved in Keats' House, Keats' Grove, is a well-thumbed copy of *The Advancement of Learning*. William Hazlitt thought it the best of Bacon's works; he scrawled many of his own comments on this particular copy, and he must have discussed it with the young John Keats, who attended so enthusiastically his lectures and went back to Hazlitt's home in York Street, Westminster, to continue the argument and his education. That must have been in 1818 or thereabouts.

It was not until more than a hundred years later, in 1947, that the story of the book, and this fresh proof of the Hazlitt–Keats intimacy, was established by an American scholar, Payson Gates. But back to James Park's first edition, before John Keats had ever been heard of. It is dedicated, with all the flowery embellishment of the time 'To the Right Honourable Thomas, Lord Erskine, Baron Erskine of Rostormel Castle in the Duchy of Cornwall etc. etc. etc.'

Thomas Erskine was once Lord Chancellor, but that is the least of his claims to our attention. He arranged for a wonderful monument to his wife to be placed in Hampstead Parish Church and there it still stands. He was also one of the first to campaign for a law to protect animals from cruelty; no doubt he learned that on the Heath too.

Most important of all, he resolved to defend Thomas Paine, charged with high treason for the publication of his *Rights of Man*. Erskine himself was accosted on Hampstead Heath by the Lord Chancellor of the day who threatened: 'Erskine, you must not take Paine's brief.' 'But I've been retained, and I will take it, by God.' And he went to the court and delivered a classic defence of a free press, worthy of any leading article in the *Ham and High:*

Let reason be opposed to reason, and argument to argument, and every good Government will be safe ... Opinions and understandings are not such wares as to be monopolised and traded in by tickets and statutes and standards. We must not think to make a staple commodity of all the knowledge in the land, to mark and licence it like our broad cloth and our wool packs ... The stage, my Lords, and the press, are two of our out-sentries; and if we remove them, if we hoodwink them, if we throw them in fetters, this enemy may surprise us.

Something in the Hampstead air turned even the lawyers, or at least the greatest of them, into champions of freedom. Erskine was not only ready to face his challengers on the Heath; they had a tunnel of some sort which ran through to Lord Mansfield's Kenwood. Lord Mansfield, as Lord Chief Justice, once had an old woman brought before him as a witch; she was charged, among other improbable things, with walking through the air. He attended coolly to the evidence and then dismissed the complaint: 'My opinion is that this good woman be suffered to return home, and whether she shall do this, walking on the ground or riding through the air, must be left entirely to her own pleasure, for there is nothing contrary to the laws of England in either!'

Never pass Kenwood House without a pause to recollect with what a wonderful English judicial flourish the original witch-hunters were sent packing. James Park had set the standard and style. William Howitt, with a touch of true excitement, included Hampstead in his *Northern Heights of London*. A Professor Hales ransacked again the old tales of Ethelred and his charters. F. E. Baines in 1890 presented a more substantial volume but it was still not the history which Hampstead deserved.

For that we had to wait until 1912 for the aforementioned Thomas Barratt to produce his masterpiece. And the truest successor of Thomas Barratt, an equal lover and servant of Hampstead, Ian Norrie of the High Hill Bookshop, once lamented the absence of such recognition and did much to remedy the deficiency in his own chapter, 'Walking the Barratt Way'.

Thomas Barratt and his successors have had the chance to recite the greatest Hampstead story; greater even than those other recitals of how Guy Fawkes's friends assembled one night on Traitors' Hill (Parliament Hill, if you like) to see the constitutional explosion which didn't happen, and how an earlier assembly lit the fires on Armada Heights (at Whitestone Pond, if you must have it that way) to help despatch the news of the would-be Spanish invasion.

Best of all, of course, is the oft told tale of how the big, bad, black-hearted Sir Thomas Maryon Wilson, unworthy holder of Ethelred's award, sought to sell off or deface the Heath in some free-market, Friedmanite orgy, and how the good Gurney Hoare and his backers, the ancestors, indeed the creators, of the Heath and Old Hampstead Society, upheld the cause of public ownership in the interests of the people, not that they found it necessary to use such provocative terms.

It is a tale retold again, and most necessarily by C.W. Ikin in 1971 in his *How the Heath Was Saved for the Public*, and reissued even more necessarily in 1985 when the old fight had to be renewed against much the same old enemies – blind, bovine, barbarian bureaucracy, disguised if at all in the latest Whitehall fashions.

Without the historians, without the *Ham and High*, without the free press which Hampstead had done so much to fortify, no battle for the Heath, defensive or offensive, could ever have been carried through to triumph.

Not everything the historians said, not even Thomas Barratt, could always be accepted as gospel. He half-suggested that in 1736, when all Hampstead and half London assembled once more on Traitors' Hill to 'see the end of the world', prophesied by some religious conspirators more credible than Guy Fawkes, that Jonathan Swift himself had been provoked to write a poem on the whole affair.

But it was not quite like that. Swift had said his sad farewell to London nearly ten years earlier and to Hampstead another ten years before that, and was by 1736 still banished to distant Dublin, and doubtless dreaming of the sorrel nag. A contemporary of Swift, a fellow pamphleteer and an even more diligent and trustworthy reporter, whom the *Ham and High* would have been happy to hire, had given his verdict too. Here is what Daniel Defoe wrote in his *Tour Through the Whole Island of Great Britain*:

Hampstead indeed is risen from a little country village, to a city, not upon the credit only of the water, though 'tis apparent, its growing greatness began there; but company increasing gradually, and the people liking both the place and the diversions together, it grew suddenly populous and the concourse of people was incredible.

This consequently raised the rate of lodgings, and that increased buildings, till the town grew up from a little village, to a magnitude equal to some cities; nor could the uneven surface, inconvenient for building, uncompact and unpleasant, check the humour of the town, for even on the very steep of the hill, where there's no walking twenty yards together, without tugging up a hill or straddling down a hill, yet it is all one, the buildings increased to that degree, that the town almost spreads the whole side of the hill.

On the top of the hill indeed, there is a very pleasant plain, called the Heath, which on the very summit is a plain of about a mile every way and in good weather 'tis pleasant airing upon it, and some of the streets are extended so far, as that they begin to build, even on the highest part of the hill.

But it must be confessed, 'tis so near heaven that I dare not say it can be a proper situation, for any but a race of mountaineers, whose lungs have been used to a rarefied air, nearer the second region, than any ground for thirty miles round it.

It is safer to descend from the heights, to turn aside even from the historians and the reporters, to leave the last word to the poets. If it were not for them, it would not be the same Hampstead and nothing like it.

A truly unforgettable encounter, or at least one never forgotten by one of the participants, occurred in Millfield Lane on a Sunday morning in April 1819. John Keats, twenty-three years old, bumped into the famous Samuel Taylor Coleridge on his way back to Highgate. According to Coleridge, this momentous meeting lasted for two minutes. Keats's memory was better:

I joined them, after enquiring by a look whether it would be agreeable. – I walked with him at his alderman-after-dinner pace for near two

miles, I suppose. In these two miles he broached a thousand things. –
let me see if I can give you a list. – Nightingales, Poetry – on Poetical
sensation – Metaphysics – Different genera and species of Dreams –
Nightmare – a dream accompanied by a sense of Touch – single and
double Touch – A dream related – First and Second Consciousness –
the difference explained between Will and Volition – so many meta-
physicians from a want of smoking the second Consciousness –
Monsters – the Kraken – Mermaids – Southey believes in them –
Southey's belief too much diluted – A Ghost Story – Good morning – I
heard his voice as he came towards me – I heard it as he moved away
– I heard it all the interval – if it may be called so. He was civil
enough to ask me to call on him at Highgate.

A few weeks later Keats, in his house in Keats' Grove, wrote his 'Ode
to a Nightingale'. A little while later again Keats's friend Leigh Hunt
lamented: 'Oh! It is too late now; and habit and self-love blinded me at
the time, and I did not know (much as I admired him) how great a poet
lived in that grove at Highgate.'

Keats and Shelley and Hunt and Hazlitt all came to appreciate and
honour the greatness of Coleridge and Wordsworth: they all became not
disciples but discriminatory admirers. Hazlitt in particular at Leigh
Hunt's fireside in the Vale of Health had done more than any one else to
extol the originality of their genius even while he still could not refrain
from denouncing their political apostasy.

Coleridge and Wordsworth, together or separately, could never muster
the magnanimity to repay the compliment: to acknowledge how much
they owed, how much English literature owed to the Cockney School,
poets and critics alike whose morn-elastic feet had trodden so often
across the Heath. The term, the Cockney School, was intended as an
insult but Hampstead transformed it into one of pride and glory; thus
offering further proof, if any were needed, how Hampstead Heath
belonged to all the people of London, the community at large. Even

Ethelred the Unready was prepared for the simple application of socialist principles, and it is high time Her Majesty's present assortment of Ministers caught up with him.

Postscript

This last invocation was of course addressed to the predecessors of the present administration. Some of them are catching up, guided by our excellent MP Glenda Jackson.

Wales to the world

Review of Dannie Abse (ed.), *Twentieth Century Anglo–Welsh Poetry,*
in the *Observer* 18 May 1997

Poets write the best prose. So my all-knowing, all-loving father used to
tell me. I dare say he had in mind some particular favourite of his own
– John Milton probably – but he also knew how poets have written the
best defences of their profession, with Shelley at their head. He would
gladly have hailed Dannie Abse, as I do now, as a wonderfully proficient
exponent of both arts. Abse writes in his brief but highly instructive
introduction how a special Welsh contribution to English literature must
be recognised: how there has been a recognisable Welsh pulse beat, how
there has been indeed in this short century a true renaissance of Welsh
writing. His whole anthology has been chosen with love and precision.

He starts with a worthy contribution from W. H. Davies, not usually
renowned for his wit, and Wilfred Owen, who was seldom acclaimed for
his Welshness. Owen was, however, the greatest of all Welsh war poets,
who was directing part of his fire against the greatest of all Welsh politi-

cians – since Owen Glyndwr at least – who happened at the time to be in charge of Number 10 Downing Street. Thereafter, Abse has sixty-eight separate contributors to his anthology and no fewer than forty-six of them are still alive and kicking. So Abse's own judgement is constantly at risk. And, talking of age, don't miss Jean Earle, born 1909 and still greeting May Days.

Is there not, however, an intrinsic difficulty in the fact that the Welsh have a wonderful language of their own and that the Welsh have suffered bitter defeats and humiliations at the hands of the English and that the resort to English is to acknowledge the language of the conquerors? The Welsh did suffer at the hands of the arrogant English hardly less than the Irish and the Scots. Modern Welsh historians and not merely the nationalist ones have proved that case to the hilt.

Indeed, the tyranny from Westminster was conducted on such a scale and the means of concealment were invoked in the Welsh case so shamelessly and successfully that the offence against the Welsh people was even more deep-seated. Apologies for crimes on such a scale seem now to be in order. Tony Blair has offered his to the Irish and Mr William Hague seems to be a most appropriate English politician to offer his Tory apologies to the Welsh. How the Tory machine in London dealt with the Chartist upheaval or the Rebecca riots may be included in the reasons that the Tories in Wales were wiped off the political map altogether in May 1997.

Some Welsh writers did write, as Abse says, as if they were a defeated race. But several more, with the great Idris Davies at their head, describe not merely the pitiless terms of subjection, but the magnificent defiance which can settle the outcome. Abse has not much time for the poetry of the platform patriots. Indeed, it almost always falters and fails to do the allotted job. Orwell said that almost the only truly good patriotic poem was Byron's *Isles of Greece*, and that was for the Greeks. Witness the latest modern fiasco in Hong Kong, the singing of 'Rule Britannia' when the only visible water over which Britons still ruled was Chris

Patten's tears. And how soon can we English secure a tolerable national anthem? Could not New Labour put through the often-mooted change over to Blake's 'Jerusalem?' (Don't tell Tony it's a hymn to free love.)

The Welsh are more subtle. Having already a matchlessly splendid national anthem, they don't have to go looking for another. They will never be persuaded to desert the land of their fathers; the rhythms are part of their life, more than that of any other peoples. If they ever did want something new it wouldn't be the much too martial 'Men of Harlech'. Much more likely something to suit their special taste. Hear the Slaves' Chorus from *Nabucca* sung by the Beaufort Male Voice Choir or 'Cwm Rhondda' by the Tredegar Town Band, and any touch of defeatism is quickly dispelled. These victims defend themselves: they are the Chartists marching on Newport.

Abse's Wales speaks to the world, and he recruits the strongest voices for the purpose. Dylan, the most famous of the Thomases, returned to his beloved coastline, but the Campaign for Nuclear Disarmament happily appropriated his rage against the dying of the light and carried it across every continent. Two of his contemporaries would acknowledge how much they owed to their discovery of Heinrich Heine. Henceforth, Idris Davies's Rhymney was touched by the same mordant immortality, and Vernon Watkins, valiant comrade of them both, offered an unforgettable English, or rather Welsh, epitaph: 'Your love forgiving every fault / Could not forgive the grave.'

A Welsh renaissance indeed, in whatever word may be preferred to describe it. Not that Abse's judgements will be universally adopted. He may be thought too austere in his rejection of all flag-waving, flag-burning exercises. One critic, Tony Conran, has produced for the University of Wales a richly informative *Frontiers in Anglo-Welsh Poetry*. Conran takes his own place in Abse's book but generally strikes a more militant chord. Others besides the Welsh have discovered that the language of the conquerors has a potency derived from the fact that the English themselves nurtured the first rebels, and designed both a poetry and a prose to serve the same high revolutionary purpose. Like my father, they did not bother to draw too sharp a distinction between the two. The first great practitioner in the double art was Jonathan Swift. He wanted everyone to understand who and what was the enemy and how they must be fought. No printer in Ireland, north or south, would dare to print today his 'Excellent New Ballad' – or the 'True English Dean to be Hanged for a Rape'. 'This Protestant zealot, this English divine / in church and in state was of principles sound.' But no more: the Reverend Ian Paisley will be reaching for his writ, and even the all-discerning, ever-tolerant Mo Mowlam may be reaching for hers.

Jonathan Swift would certainly be proud of his Welsh pupils, as paraded by Abse three centuries later: the Wilfred Owen who would accept no excuse for the horrors of war or the Idris Davies who searched out the Sacred Road:

They walked this road in seasons past
When all the skies were overcast,
They breathed defiance as they went
Along these troubled roads of Gwent
They talked of justice as they strode
Along this crooked mountain road
And dared the little lords of Hell,
So that the future should be well
Because they did not count the cost
But battled on when all seemed lost
This empty ragged road shall be
Always a sacred road to me.

There is nothing religious, of course, about Idris's sacred road. It is the Welsh way of describing how victory may be drawn from defeat, in language worthy of Heine or Swift or even John Milton himself.

Dubrovnik

Serving my country

Unpublished review of Hrvoje Kacic, *Serving My Country*, 2003

Two women's voices became for me – and I'm sure even more so for Jill, who had the discriminating ear of an expert film director in all such matters – the symbol of Dubrovnik's resistance to tyranny, a name softly resonant all on its own, but a name also to rank in modern times with reverberations, say, from the siege of Troy. A scandalous, persistent effort has been made, as we shall see, to rob Dubrovnik of its true glory. Kathy Wilkes always spoke with the voice of authority, with a faint Scottish accent also derived more from the hero she truly worshipped, David Hume. Vesna Gamulin could adapt any language she chose to the infamies done to her native city and her own beauty suited best the place in all its moods; a toss of that head could best assign Serbian war criminals to their fate. My own Jill seemed to hate all photographs of herself: the one she tolerated at least was the last taken high up among the mountains above the city she had come to love best.

Kathy Wilkes' voice was heard first in unforgettable circumstances on the telephone in my House of Commons, room one early October morning in the year 1991. We had never met before, but the place from which she was speaking I knew well enough. It was the studio of Duro Pulitico, the Dubrovnik painter, in which Jill and I had had many happy meetings, but which, since the siege of Dubrovnik had started a few weeks before, had been converted into an emergency press office. Of course, Kathy spoke not only for herself; at her side were the leaders of the city who had resolved never to accept the demands of the assailants. But how long and how effectively could the resistance be sustained? Kathy Wilkes wanted to arouse the world, but sometimes it seemed as if official London was deaf to all such appeals. Dubrovnik could be left to stew in its own juice – like the faraway country of which pre-war England knew nothing.

Just a few months before, in mid-September 1991, Jill and I were completing our annual holiday in Dubrovnik. Rumours of war had been heard in Belgrade: indeed some professors at their university had been preaching a doctrine which sounded more like Hitler's fascism than any natural product of Yugoslavia. Serbia must have the right to rule wherever the Serbs lived: the first time I heard the phrase 'ethnic cleansing'. But even as late as September in that fateful year, the general scene was not clear. We had to make our way home via Montenegro and Belgrade itself instead of the direct flight.

The new book on the subject which Kathy Wilkes introduces has an authenticity all its own. No previous writer on the subject has had the same combined experience of the subject as Hrvoje Kacic. His knowledge of the old Dubrovnik and the new Croatia, the country he has sought to serve, according to his title, is one with the deepest roots but with a quite modern flowering. Croatia was not supposed to exist at all; according to the most wretched Serbian gibe, it was just a German invention. And in the chancelleries of Europe where such nonsense was accepted, why should not old Dubrovnik be wiped off the map altogether? Fortunately for us, all the men, women and children of

Dubrovnik had a different idea. Kacic has a special insight into that story and a special obligation to tell it.

Little Slovenia had given bullying Belgrade a bloody nose on the actual battlefield which should have taught the military chieftains in Belgrade a lesson. Instead they drew the opposite moral. They would act more fiercely, more viciously. Who was giving the military orders in Belgrade? It was not easy to tell. Slobodan Milosevic was the recently elected President. Sometimes he would give orders. Sometimes it looked like an army off the leash. Both the political and the military leaders might be looking for a chance to repair the ignominy of the Slovenian defeat.

Kathy Wilkes singles out as the greatest disaster to befall Croatia the appalling siege and eventual fall of Vukovar. This new book calls it the crucifixion of Vukovar. Vukovar was a Croatian town roughly the same size as Dubrovnik at the very top of the Eastern-most frontier of the new Croatia, nearest to the Serbian border, just as Dubrovnik was at the furthest point to the east. But the people of Dubrovnik felt the lash of Vukovar across their own backs. Indeed, their would-be assailants from the nearby mountain posts threatened them with the same fate. So the massacre of the Croatian men, women and children of Vukovar maybe had a military purpose after all. It was a return to the special kind of savagery which Yugoslavia had experienced when Hitler's cronies had invaded the country in 1940, and all the different races – Serbs, Croats, Slovenes – had combined together to defeat the fascist enemy.

It was a terrible insult when the assailants of Dubrovnik sought to brand the defenders as fascists or Ustase, the friends of the fascists. It was worse still when they sought to use the example of Vukovar to intimidate the defenders of Dubrovnik. Worse still again, they started to apply the same methods in the villages round Dubrovnik or when allied forces from Montenegro seized the neighbourhood township of Cavtat. All these threats and incursions could have produced the surrender which the people in charge in Belgrade certainly expected. But there was no wavering inside old Dubrovnik, as Kathy Wilkes was so eager to tell the world. And there had also been a properly directed military defence. Higher up on one mountain above those seized by the JNA, a handful of defenders were there to ensure that if the victors of Vukovar sought to repeat their final tactics in Dubrovnik, they would pay a terrible price for it. Month after month, the defenders of Dubrovnik – men, women and children, as Kacic emphasises – held their own.

All this evidence was available when Jill and I returned to Dubrovnik, just about Christmas time, to make a film about the siege. Croatia was now involved in the larger war next door when the military authorities in Belgrade resolved that the people of Bosnia must be denied the right to vote for their independence, just as Croatia had been denied the same right two years before. How could such monstrous demands and proscriptions be allowed to continue in our civilised Europe without effective protest? Could they not hear the appeals from Kathy Wilkes and Vesna Gamulin in Dubrovnik? Theirs was the true voice of civilised Europe.

What was truly happening in that part of world was faithfully reported by some of the great reporters of the age: Maggie O'Kane of the *Guardian*, Ed Vulliamy of the *Observer*, Emma Daly of the *Independent*, Mark Thompson of *Tribune*. But what Kacic adds to the indictment, as Kathy Wilkes emphasises, is the series of individual diplomatic initiatives he sought to undertake on behalf of his newly created Croatian state and the dusty answers he received from various authorities who should have known better, most notably Lord Carrington, whose official position throughout the period was that of Secretary General of the NATO Alliance. He was speaking too, I am sorry to say, for the British Government of the time. If their policies had prevailed, the defenders of Dubrovnik would have surrendered and the monstrous regime in Belgrade would have triumphed.

Hrvoje Kacic sings the praises of his beloved native Dubrovnik in a modern accent. Some others during the horror of the Milosevic dictatorship in Belgrade sought refuge there to speak the political truths which they had learned at their mothers' knees but which they were no longer allowed to express in their native Serbia. One of these was Stevan Dedijer. His brother, Vladimir Dedijer, had risked his own life to defend the case of Milovan Djilas when Marshal Tito's Yugoslavia started to use Stalinist methods against them. Each of these had a voice of his own and a determination to express it which all the censors of various breeds could not suppress. Milovan Djilas's account of the operations of the new class, both in Soviet Russia and in Tito's Yugoslavia, is the best in Communist literature. Vlado Dedijer, while never yielding to his particular pressures, wrote a classic, *The Road to Sarajevo*, in which the competing horrors of pre-1914 are exposed and the people of Bosnia and the rest of the Balkan territories are allowed to speak for themselves.

Stevan Dedijer has no such magnum opus to warn the world of the perils it risks running, but he has also used his own special knowledge as an intelligence officer to understand Dubrovnik afresh. For several centuries, from the harbour of Dubrovnik – it was called Ragusa then – the sailors sailed out as confidently as Vesna's husband does today. Once brave Ragusa was derided as Venice's monkey. She was not afraid of the comparison with the place where truly men and often women also were beginning to display their finery and demand their rights. She too was a modern city learning more of the real world. Soon also she inscribed the word 'Libertas' on her flag. In all the wars that followed and not least the most terrible ones of our century, Dubrovnik held its head high, however infamous the assault from any quarter.

A paper house

Review of Mark Thompson, *A Paper House: the ending of Yugoslavia*, in *Tribune*, 15 May 1992

My first introduction to Yugoslavia was a book or, rather, the beautiful woman who incited me to read a book. Stoyan Pribichevich's *Living*

Space was published at just about the time when the Nazi conquerors of
the 1930s had fixed their covetous ambitions on the Balkans. Stoyan
described what stubborn enemies tyrants, old and new, had found there;
he showed how deeply civilised so many of those communities were,
how they were often inspired by a primitive, peasant democracy, long
before that word had become fashionable.

I would like to quote page after page of Pribichevich; he had the same
kind of random taste for forgotten wisdom which Mark Thompson also
displays in his book, *A Paper House: the ending of Yugoslavia*. Maybe it
is a Balkan literary taste. 'Whoever does not recognise a brother as
brother will acknowledge a stranger as master' – that was a Balkan
warning five hundred years ago.

The beautiful woman, by the way, was a Jewish Slovene, proud of her
Jewishness and proud of Slovenia too. Born and bred there and
protected by Slovene decency from anti-semitic persecution, she knew,
even before Pribichevich recorded the facts, how 'this tiny people,
numbering little over a million, maintained itself through eleven
centuries.' Thompson is especially good on the Slovenes and their
latest accomplishment; it sets the flavour of his whole book. However,
I must first be permitted one relevant diversion on the beautiful
Jewess. Thompson's book, like all the best ones, is full of diversions,
relevant and irrelevant.

She and her family had had some experience of fascist methods
before Hitler appeared on the scene. She was told what Gabriele
D'Annunzio and his gang had done when they seized Fiume; she told
me how that outrage would have to be avenged too, along with the
infamies in Abyssinia and Spain. However, for her and her people,
everything else paled before the Nazi horror. And then gradually,
month by month, came the news that all the various peoples of
Yugoslavia, Slovenes, Croats, Serbs and the rest, were fighting back
against the fascist assailants, German and Italian, under an inspired
guerrilla leader, Josip Broz Tito.

I shared her exultation, as did decent people everywhere: probably those victories were more hardly won on Yugoslav soil than anywhere else on our tortured planet, and that did give some substance to the strange, awkward composite, Yugoslavia.

What Tito and his fellow partisan leaders achieved was of world-historical importance; without it, we might all have been enslaved. What Tito and his fellow political leaders achieved in their break with Stalin and the Soviet Union a few years later was also of great significance far beyond the borders of Yugoslavia. But, tragically too for the world at large, Tito failed to learn the lesson.

One brave man, just about the bravest of the century, tried to tell him. Milovan Djilas risked his life, heaven knows how often, to fight the pre-war dictatorship and the Nazi invasion, to oppose the Stalinist dictatorship and then to warn against the indecencies and infamies which would be perpetrated by the New Class.

Thompson seeks to analyse, as he was surely required to do, how much the failures of the Communist regime, inherent or acquired, have contributed to the present tragedy. His portrait of Marshal Tito in his Brioni palaces, amid all his impotent grandeur, is deadly and indelible. It is indeed a pitiful tale, all the more so since some of the achievements of the regime were genuine and important. But may I digress again so that every intelligent reader should be encouraged to go back and read Djilas's own books? His *The New Class* was published in 1957; *Conversations with Stalin* in 1962; *The Imperfect Society* in 1970, and *Tito* in 1981.

All are classics, and the other autobiographical works sustain the same high standard. All were reviewed in *Tribune*, I'm proud to say; all were part of our education. And Thompson includes in his volume the report of his interview with Milovan Djilas. Some of his stabs are as sharp as ever but the profile should not be taken for the whole man.

No other Communist or ex-Communist state had so persistent and knowledgeable and brave a critic as Milovan Djilas; no other critic similarly placed foresaw the democratic reawakening. He did not foresee the scale of the present disintegration, but that is barely a criticism.

A later experience, a later vision, was needed to set these terrible events in a proper narrative, and the best recommendation of Thompson's book is that it deserves to rank with these other classical studies. The pace of the tragedy was moving so fast that he might have been tempted to pause afresh. But we are the gainers. Nothing so good on the subject has been written anywhere so far as I know.

The real achievement of his book – miracle might be a better word – is that he combines past and present, today's headlines and the myths of the past centuries, into a work of literature. He most reminded me of the other undisputed classic by a journalist–traveller in the same country, Rebecca West's *Black Lamb and Grey Falcon*. What would she say, I wonder, about the performance of her beloved Serbs – the inexcusable, unspeakable campaign of the Federal Army which has cut such a gulf across the land and across history?

Thompson puts the whole terrible affair in its proper perspective. 'Along with the rest of the outside world,' he says, 'I watched Serbia destroy Yugoslavia, in the name of Yugoslavia, while storing up disaster for itself in the name of its own future.'

Page after page undermines the moral with wisdom and wit. The insistent claim is pasted across so many walls: 'THIS IS SERBIA'. The best answer, says Thompson, can be read on Sarajevo's main post office. Below this crass slogan, a Bosnian sage has replied, 'WRONG, DIMWIT, IT'S A POST OFFICE'. And maybe in the last few days that essay in sanity has been wiped off the map by so-called Federal guns.

At some moments it is impossible not to yield to despair, yet something new and true would often sprout from such a rich soil. I recall a comparison which Pribichevich would cite to comfort his generation of Slavs betrayed by their neighbours. 'Edward Gibbon,' he wrote, 'presented the Balkan Slavs as a mixture of low-caste invaders who destroyed the splendid old Roman civilisation. Gibbon wrote those lines at the very time when the Balkanite, Roger Boskovitch, was perfecting the mathematical and astronomical studies which made him and his city of Dubrovnik famous in the scientific world and the basis of modern physics.'

And our Dubrovnik of 1992 is the place which refused to bow to the Serbian military bombardment and to the threat from Colonel Koprivica (recorded by Thompson's unfailing eye) which was even more obscene than the bombardment itself. 'We are going to force the Ustase to surrender because that is the only way to protect the city.'

Maybe that resistance against the combined military and moral threat saved the whole cause of Balkan freedom. Maybe also the name of Yugoslavia is apposite no more but the people who live in those parts, including Serbs and Croats who long lived there peaceably too, have qualities all their own and Thompson is their latest herald and champion – which reminds me to mention that the only criticism I have about this book is the title. It is not good enough for such a great book: the author should have asked Djilas or considered Rebecca West's example.

The paper house was torn to fragments by insensate hates and national ambitions but the people inside, headed by such rare men as Milovan Djilas, comprised heroes and heroines of several very rare breeds. Among other qualities they had this peculiar love for their own homes which proved stronger than any other instinct. Without that, fascist Germany would still be in control of the Balkans as the Turks were for centuries, and every house in Dubrovnik would now be the possession of some Serbian stormtrooper.

A new statue for Trafalgar Square

Review of Geoffrey Robertson, *Crimes Against Humanity: the struggle for global justice*, in the *Observer*, 18 May 1997

A book to stop another Holocaust or whatever fiendish horrors the twenty-first century may devise to outdo our own, with nuclear knobs on. A combination of the highest qualities of the heart and mind each raised to the highest pitch and never one without the other is needed for the task.

Kosovo naturally figures prominently in Geoffrey Robertson's pages. He offers overwhelming proof to show how justified was the NATO action, and how hopeless it would have been to make any further propositions or speeches about protecting human rights if the Kosovars had once more been left to the mercy of their masters in Belgrade. Indeed, Robertson explains more intractably how the failure of the international community to act in Bosnia and Croatia led inexorably to the later tragedy. How pitiful were the excuses that nothing could be done to prevent the recurrence of such horrors as happened at Vukovar or

Srebrenica. One excuse was that it was too difficult to detect the difference between the aggressor and his victim. Thus was the reputation of the United Nations undermined. Orders were given to UN operators on the spot to abide by these rules. Belgrade bowed to the decree, sometimes supported even in statements from Milosevic himself.

The British variation of this doctrine, at least in the early years, was that the Serbs were going to win anyhow; so it would suit our *realpolitik* role if our policies favoured that outcome. Occasionally, this neutral position seemed so offensive to common decency that officials in charge felt compelled to hand in their resignations. A few such cases occured in the American State Department, but none from the British Foreign Office. It was left to the British journalists to report the facts and save our country's honour.

The men in charge of the foreign policies in Washington and London had their own particular reasons for avoiding the supreme commitment of the UN Charter to resist aggression. Sometimes it was just a disreputable surrender to the worst elements of isolationism. More often it was a craven or purblind acceptance of lesser evils. Since at some stages in the proceedings chronic anti-Americanism became the excuse for British inaction, Robertson's catalogue of American delinquencies has a flavour all its own. One such was the voice from the Pentagon, brayed most loudly by Senator Jesse Helms, who in 1998 threatened to block United States ratification of any international criminal court if it had power to indict a single American soldier. Our author has a special eye for such moments: 'There was also the futility of the soft-shoe shuffle, as Vance and Owen solemnly worked out together how the aggressive factions should be rewarded, only to produce a plan that failed to presage their greed.'

Thus several of the lesser performers receive their deserts, but of course the larger figures must be given pride of place: Milosevic, who bears a 'guilt of Goeringesque proportions'; General Pinochet, guilty of directing crimes against humanity, especially torture, which his defenders would argue could not be tackled because it would involve an invasion of the rights of the nation.

With a splendid irony which only Robertson would have the knowledge to observe, the ruling against Pinochet came on the same day NATO started its campaign to come to the rescue of Kosovo: 'It was as if the world community had finally decided to obliterate its memory of appeasing Hitler by evolving international law to the position where it could no longer accept that the way individual states treat their own citizens is purely an internal matter.' Such a conclusion may be slightly premature. But Robertson's general prospect for the coming century should win support across the whole planet.

Parisians have a happy habit of renaming some of their most famous streets, often ensuring that military leaders are displaced by revolutionary writers. Geoffrey Robertson deserves honour on every count. He derives his humanist creed from the purest sources: Michel de Montaigne, Thomas Paine, and H. G. Wells, each of whom makes a notable contribution in these pages. No proper memorial for any of these three exists in this country, Geoffrey once reminded me. I suggested changing Trafalgar to Thomas Paine Square, a nice gesture to both our French and American friends. Paine was the best defender ever of their independence. Leading off the new square, I suggest that instead of the nonsensical Northumberland Avenue or monarchist Malls, we should have an H. G. Wells Court. But why not a Geoffrey Robertson triumphal arch? Millions will be reading his book in the century to come if we are serious in our intention to stop those massacres.

Postscript

I know our Mayor of London has a different suggestion: a new Nelson Mandela, with his eye fixed on the old South Africa House. All us Thomas Paineites would happily make way for him.

Footnote: Cats, dogs and Ursula

Hampstead and Highgate Express, 30 August 1996

My old dog Dizzy learns new tricks so fast that I cannot understand how the proverbial libel against the breed ever gained currency. The more decrepit my own pace becomes, the more he looks for new diversions of his own with a mixed glance of scorn and insolence. His latest escapade is a sudden turn of speed down Parliament Hill, which famous mount fringes the Heath itself, with no less than three subsequent glances backwards to ensure that I am properly limping along the same alley.

Once Guy Fawkes' friends watched from those same vantage points; if they had shown an ingenuity comparable to Dizzy's they would never have been caught. However, dogs are seldom given credit for their wisdom, inherited or acquired. There seems to a feline conspiracy to deny it to them, whereas cats are constantly accorded a whole range of subtle virtues.

H. N. Brailsford wrote magnificently not only about the Levellers and the Thomas Paineite revolutionaries, but also about his appreciation of cats. He was not content at all to extol their haughty independence. 'The smuggest of suburban hearth-rugs is a crossroads between Delphi and Thebes, and the homeliest of tabbies a sphinx who defies you, as she purrs, to answer the simple question – whether a cat has ever purred alone.'

But all good dogs, with Dizzy at their head, have a virtue for which they are seldom given credit and to which no cats of any breed have ever aspired. It is their sudden gift for forgiveness, their readiness to forget what must seem to them interminable periods of absence, their over-whelming magnanimity. It is the most glorious of human qualities but one which dogs seem to acquire and display much more naturally.

It is second nature for them; they can restore high spirits with a simple yelp or a single lick. Where did they learn the effects of an endearing demeanour to be unloosed at the most significant moments? If the human race had acquired such a gift for discounting offences, how the history of mankind and womankind might have been bettered – say since the Trojan Wars. But wait. We dog lovers may suppose that the mere mention of Troy may clinch our case, but somehow my mind is jogged in the opposite direction.

The Trojan war was one thing: Odysseus's voyage was another, and now I recall how the wittiest and most wondrous of our modern poets, one who writes in an idiom all her own, one who can herself touch the heights of Alexander Pope or Andrew Marvell, has written on this theme. She puts a leash on the dogs, glorifies the cats and exposes the *Odyssey* all in the same piece.

The author is U. A. Fanthorpe: her latest book of poems is called *Safe as Houses,* published by Peterloo Poets. Nothing is safe in her hands: not even my Dizzy, who listened in rapt but discriminating adoration at Dartington Hall, when she recited her poem. Her poetry is one of the delights of the age. Her 'Odysseus's Cat' is only one of her perfectly executed pieces of impertinence.

A note on the typographer: Stanley Morison

This book is set in 11/16½ -point Times New Roman, the typeface originally designed in the early 1930s under the supervision of the great typographer Stanley Morison. Michael Foot's review of *Stanley Morison* by Nicolas Barker appeared in the *Evening Standard* on 16 April 1972.

Stanley Morison was a name which, for several decades on end, was darkly whispered in the corridors and caverns where Fleet Street assembled to discuss its professional secrets. He was the most reticent of grey eminences, and yet his power was surely immense. He had a passion for anonymity but anyone in the know could discern his imprint on almost every leading newspaper in the land. Meeting him face to face, this impression might be dissipated at once. His charm would embrace the whole company around him and what someone called his 'black look, black suit and blue jaw' would give place to schoolboy grins, even guffaws, and a quite unheralded surrender to gaiety.

But still the mystery remained: he exuded an air of inner conviction and certainty not necessarily deriving from the light of his Roman Catholic faith. So it was not surprising to read that Nicolas Barker, charged with the task of writing the official life, had the idea of treating the subject as a new Quest for Corvo, but the temptation had to be resisted. His Stanley Morison, has the appearance of an orthodox, elaborate, expensive biography. But there is more besides.

First, however, let it be clearly stated that pride of place in this volume is properly given to Morison's achievements as a typographer. By prodigious individual labour he made himself the master of twentieth century methods of printing; partly he did it by distilling the wisdom of the past. He was, in his own field, that most rare of combinations, an antiquary-cum-revolutionary, an historian-cum-man-of-action. Having defined so firmly his own principles ('The body is more than raiment, it is not the business of the printer to costume his text') he brilliantly and surreptitiously imposed them on others.

While he sat in Printing House Square redesigning the whole anatomy and wardrobe of *The Times*, a messenger carried across to the offices of the Communist *Daily Worker* the Gill Sans Bold title block which helped that penurious journal to put its capitalist rivals typographically to shame.

Similarly ambivalent features seemed to characterise every aspect of his life, but no one ever dreamed of calling him a humbug or a hypocrite. He went to prison in the First World War for his near-pacifist allegiance, learned part of his political creed from Pentonville and Karl Marx , and yet lived to help devise the notorious 'Top People' advertising campaign and to instruct his respectable proprietors how to provide a paper for the British governing class instead of 'two *Telegraphs* struggling for the same lower-middle class patronage'.

For a confirmed Catholic convert snugly settled into the Establishment, he assembled – and never disowned – a curious array of heroes: Thomas Paine, inherited from his militantly agnostic mother; Thomas Barnes, the famous but not very devout first editor of *The Times* ('not a gentleman, a complete professional', was Morison's accolade): the disciple Doubting Thomas who insisted that he must see before he believed; or a gallery of power-interested, worldly-wise, not-too-reputable churchmen.

The catalogue may suggest just another young rebel and idealist who drifted expediently rightwards. But not a bit of it; the word profit never ceased to stink in Morison's nostrils, as his friend Eric Gill said it should in the nostrils of any decent man.

Mere cleverness was something he also despised: 'there is no more disgusting word in the language.' During the Spanish Civil War he cut himself off from many of his Catholic friends with his view that 'the church militant' allying itself with the 'creditor class' was 'the worst scandal of the day.'

Although the convivial recluse would select the best drink with almost the same care he lavished on his type books – 'He does not make the mistake of pouring old wine into new bottles,' said his friend Beaverbrook. 'If the wine is old and really good, he has another use for it' – he could still expound, literally on his deathbed, the same rationalist ideas he drank in with his beloved mother's milk.

The full revelation remains infuriatingly elusive, despite Nicolas Barker's scruple and research. For example, there is the story of the wife whom he had happily married and then, as he believed, bitterly wronged, and the discovery in his old age that perhaps the lifelong sense of guilt was misplaced. When they married, he was twenty-six and she was thirty-three, or so she said. In fact, she was forty-three. She never told and he never realised, and the strangest retrospective light is thus cast upon his long years of loneliness and courage.

Even in these five hundred beautifully produced pages, nothing like the last word has been spoken in the Quest for Morison. For one thing, as Mr Barker hints, he would certainly have made a better Pope than Corvo. What a Pope indeed! The patron of art, scholarship, good printing and good living; the sworn enemy of usury, big business and all other forms of vulgarity; a Voltaire in the Vatican; a sceptical St Thomas taking over St Peter's; the modest, faithful guardian of a religion too secret to be revealed.